TERENCE: THE   BROTHERS

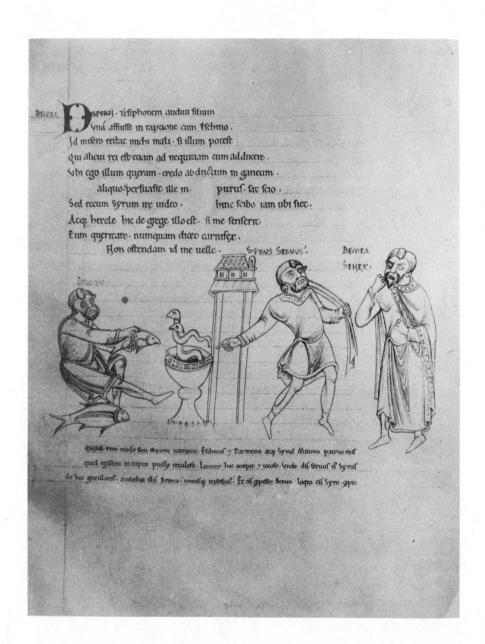

Frontispiece: Codex Oxoniensis (O) lines 355-64 with the sequel, see pp. 128-31.

TERENCE
THE BROTHERS

Edited with translation and notes by

A. S. Gratwick

For Edward and Henry

 British Library Cataloguing in Publication Data

Terence
    The Brothers. — (Classical texts).
    I. Title   II. Gratwick, A.S.
    III. Adelphoe. *English*   IV. Series
    872'.01   PA6756.A5 *C7 1987*
                     57, 673

ISBN 0 85668 315 9 *cloth*
ISBN 0 85668 316 7 *limp*

Printed and published in England by ARIS & PHILLIPS Ltd,
Teddington House, Church Street, Warminster, Wiltshire, England.

CONTENTS

INTRODUCTION

Terence's *Adelphoe* in Latin verse with a prose
translation, '*The Brothers*', and, behind both, the ghost
of Menander's lost Greek original. The TRANSLATION aims
to represent Terence's script in any given speech or
exchange. That is not simply a matter of rendering word
for word; English and Latin idiom are too different to
allow that approach to communicate enough of Terence's
grace and timing in what is meant to be an actable version
of his script. On the other hand, the translator has
tried to deal in a more or less self-consistent way with
the same exclamations, phrases, idioms, and evaluative
terms when they recur.

But converting Terence into prose from verse (however
direct and colloquial) radically changes his dramatic
form, and by eliminating contrasts large and small that
depend on the verse-form, one accidentally makes him
sound more like Menander than he really was. For
Menander's Greek form and style suffer conversion into
English prose with less overall distortion.

'We cannot step into the same river twice', said
Heraclitus; and it is the same with plays. No two live
performances of the same play, let alone two different
productions, are ever quite the same, and even how and
with whom we watch a film affects its meaning. Our
business is, in fact, with three different but related
plays - this new imitation of Terence, Terence's much
freer handling of Menander, and Menander's Greek original.
Further to complicate things, what a script *says* is only
one aspect of what it *means* - that depends on the
collaboration of a producer, of players, and of us, an
audience in experiencing it.

To do justice to Terence and Menander as dramatists,
it is important to keep clearly separate in our minds the
translation as a play in its own right, intended to follow
Terence's closely but inevitably differing from it, and
in turn to keep Menander's distinct from Terence's.
Fortunately less here depends upon a knowledge of Greek
or Latin than one might suppose, and more on tuning our
sense of what works in the theatre and on our *humanitas*.

What that word means is a minor theme of this play,
and in the INTRODUCTION and NOTES TO THE TRANSLATION the
editor has kept as far as possible to matters which can
be profitably discussed without his assuming a knowledge
of either ancient language in the reader. These are not
few or unimportant: the *milieux* of the two plays, the
genres, the dramatic content, the characterization,
ironies, production.

Our knowledge of Menander has greatly increased in the
last quarter-century, and important advances have been made
in our overall appreciation of Terence's place in the comic
tradition. The editor's main aim in exegesis is to make
available to a wider public the interesting problems of
interpretation which have made *Brothers* a particularly
controversial and puzzling play ever since the Enlightenment.
The notes as such are meant to complement and certainly not
to supplant the long tradition of grammatical exegesis which
goes back to Aelius Donatus in the fourth c. A.D. and is
represented in English by the commentaries of Martin (1976),
Ashmore (1908), and Sloman (1884). Those studying the play
in Latin, and those teaching it, will, it is hoped, find
this edition a useful adjunct. But Terence best explains
Terence, and they will want to consult not only those
commentaries but also the greatest contribution to Terentian
studies since Bentley's edition (1726), the *Lexicon
Terentianum* by P McGlynn (1963/7).

As for the transmitted TEXT, the editor has taken a
more sceptical view of its quality than recent editors;
see Appendix I. In accordance with the scope and scale of
this edition, textual discussion has been kept to a bare
minimum, and fuller treatment is reserved for a more
appropriate place. Fragments of the Greek play are given
in Appendix II.

To appreciate Terence's best and most original qualities,
the subtle variety of his verse-rhythms, the reader must
first *hear* his Latin as a living language, and, next, become
confident about his SCANSION. There is, alas, no royal
road leading thither and traditional Anglo-German axioms
about ictus and accent seem unsatisfactory. See Appendix
III. The dots under the lines, the short-marks, and the
layout of the text are meant to help the reader's eye *and*
ear, whichever of two ways he interprets the dots; see
Appendixes III and IV. Complete beginners and the tone-
deaf may just ignore all that, read Terence as prose, and
thereby sustain a long-standing tradition of ignorance;
but the true student of Latin and the just critic of Terence
will not.

The editor's particular thanks are due for the care of
Professor M M Willcock, who read and criticized various
drafts in detail, and to Professor H M Hine; both have
prevented many slips. Special mention must be made of
J N Grant's Ph.D thesis (1971 a); and of R H Martin's
apparatus criticus (1976) for the way the Calliopian Mss.
are cited here. Warm thanks are also due to Miss J H Lambie
who typed the camera-ready copy.

St Andrews: May 1987   A. S.   G R A T W I C K

INTRODUCTION

1. Terence and Menander

1. 1. 1. *Terence's Life.* PUBLIUS TERENTIUS AFER was
supposed to have been a Carthaginian slave, freed 'on'
account of his brains and his good looks' by his Roman
master; hence his Roman name and citizenship. But which
representative of the Terentian clan had been his master
and when Terence was born were disputed. Some said
before the end of the Second Punic War (201 B.C.), others
rather later (194 B.C.), others later still (184 B.C.).
The last was the prevalent view; it tidily put Terence's
birth in the year that the comedian PLAUTUS is supposed
to have died, and close to the birth of P. CORNELIUS
SCIPIO AEMILIANUS (b. 185 B.C.), the noble with whom
some evidence and much rumour later associated the playwright and whom some even claimed as the real author of
the plays [1]. He and his brother lavishly funded the
occasion at which *Brothers* was produced (160 B.C.),
apparently as a special commission, and there was gossip
which Terence does not deny that 'prominent Romans kept
helping Terence and closely collaborated with him in
writing' (*Brothers* 15 ff.). This certainly left room
for Roman scholars to speculate, but we shall never know
whether Aemilianus really did have any 'helpful'
suggestions. What is certain is that *Brothers* is a
brilliant play - Terence's masterpiece according to some
modern critics - blemished by heavy-handed writing at the
beginning and end of the *finale* (855 ff., 985 ff.) and
here and there elsewhere (333 f., 592 ff.). Problematic
as this is, it is not inconsistent with what we can
discern of Terence's artistic personality in general.

1. 1. 2. As to his real identity, however, even the ideas
that Terence was a slave and from Carthage may merely be
unjustified inferences from the form of his name. For an
ex-slave from across the water might indeed be called
'Publius of the Terentian clan, the North African', but
it is not the case that anyone so named needs to have been
either African or an ex-slave. We simply do not know.

1. 1. 3. These traditions for what they are worth were
recorded by SUETONIUS in his *Life of Terence* (early 2nd
c. A.D.). This comes to us incorporated in DONATUS'
commentary on Terence (mid 4th c. in origin; drastically
cut and added to in the late antique and early mediaeval
transmission). But the earlier sources used by Suetonius
seem themselves to have little more to go on than what
comes down in the production-notes and the argumentative
prologues with which each of the six scripts begins.
Terence disappears after *Brothers*; he is said to have
died in 159 or 158 B.C. while visiting Greece (accounts
differed), and to have left a modest estate and a
daughter who married in the second rank of Roman society.

1. 2. 1. *Terence's genre*. The Roman 'Comedy in Greek
Dress' (*fabula palliata*) outwardly offered the storylines
and *dramatis personae* of the latest flowering of the
Athenian theatre, the so-called New Comedy, which
focussed on family life and romantic love; it was in
verse, about five-sixths spoken and the rest 'chanted';
at its best it was notable for conviction and directness
of characterization, as well as irony and fun. It
flourished at Athens from c. 330 to c. 270 B.C., and from
about 290 B.C. its most famous exponents MENANDER,
DIPHILUS, and PHILEMON (by then all dead) became central
to the repertoire of the travelling Artists of Dionysus
(as the Greek acting profession was known) in an
expanding 'circuit' of theatrical festivals throughout
the Hellenistic world, including Sicily and South Italy
[2].

1. 2. 2. At the same time MENANDER was acquiring a
permanent place alongside Homer in an emerging 'syllabus'
of Greek authors read in Hellenistic schools. Thus New
Comedy and especially Menander as the 'mirror of life'
were doubly important in the 3rd c. B.C. and subsequently
in broadcasting and encapsulating what was Greek about
Greeks; and he held that Shakespearian status for the next
eight centuries, only losing it in the time of JUSTINIAN
(6th c. A.D.),more because his Attic Greek was not
reliably pure as a model than because his humanistic ethos
and his themes of love were now out of tune with the
times.

1. 2. 3. The earliest known *fabula palliata* was put on at
Rome in 240 B.C. by LIVIUS ANDRONICUS, a native Greek
himself; then were NAEVIUS (active c. 235-201 B.C.),
PLAUTUS (c. 210 (perhaps)-184 B.C.), and CAECILIUS STATIUS
(c. 190-168 B.C.); of whom only PLAUTUS is well known.
But the image of life which he offers is anything but
realistic, and it is clear that behind his (and Naevius')
work there lie Italian traditions of popular entertainment
other than the New Comedy in which music and extempore
development of a *scenario* were important. We only hear
of the so-called Atellane Farce and know but little about
it: but we should not suppose that this kind of thing had
disappeared from Latium before Terence's time, the 160's.

1. 2. 4. CAECILIUS' place in the development of the genre
is important but unclear. He later counted as its 'best'
(i.e., most vigorous?) representative, but not as a writer
one trusted for 'good Latin'. He *may* have been more
faithful to the content of his models than Naevius and
Plautus, who had no compunctions about cutting and adding

and generally transmogrifying; but his fragments show that
he made extensive use of polymetric songs and wrote in the
same extravagant style as Plautus, a medium more suited to
caricature than to the subtle characterization associated
with Menander [3].

1. 2. 5. CAECILIUS died in 168 B.C.; Terence's first play
was produced in 166 B.C. Here he appears fully 'himself',
rejecting and adjusting features of the *genre* to sound
more authentically Menandrian. The overall shape of the
play matters; there is no more hanky-panky with the
dramatic illusion; the style is pruned and realistic; song
is less prominent; the rhythms of the spoken verse are
more various and expressive; and his opening scenes never
even aim at raising a laugh sooner than engaging our
interest in apparently 'real' people and their situation.

1. 2. 6. Long stretches in each of the plays really are
sophisticated literary translation - the world's first -
faithful to the pacing, tone, and substance of their
models and potentially to their characterization in
production. But at the same time Terence reserved the
right to part company with Menander without telling us or
wanting us to know; as if he were Menander re-incarnated
revising old scripts. But when he does make changes,
Terence reveals himself not as a dramatist who really
thought like Menander, but as a native Italian writer of
palliatae; in particular, he shares with his Roman
audience a cavalier indifference to perspective in the
background to the action, and an attitude to dramatic
characterization that depends upon simple oppositions
and categories. His changes go much further than was
necessarily imposed by the conversion of five-act
originals five-sixths in spoken verse into a continuou~
dramatic form in which the alternation of speech and
'recitative' was the main articulation; much further, in
fact, than is stated in the prologues in response to
criticisms made by the 'malevolent old playwright'
LUSCIUS LANUVINUS, Terence's enemy.

1. 2. 7. It is not clear whether these prologues are
actually from Terence's pen or from that of his artistic
'director', business patron, and principal actor
AMBIVIUS TURPIO; there is a good case for the latter, but
anyway, we should be naive to suppose that the prologues
deal exhaustively or even fairly with the views of
Luscius [4].

1. 2. 8. Apart from accusing Terence of being an upstart
who depended not on his own talent but that of his
'friends' (*Self-Tormentor* 23 ff., repeated more specifically

at *Brothers* 15 ff.), Luscius found fault with Terence's
style as 'thin and light' (*Phormio* 5). He further made
what are meant to sound niggling objections to Terence's
adding material to his Greek models and so 'spoiling' or
'vandalizing' them (*contaminare*, Luscius' word): in *Woman
of Andros*, material from another play of Menander, in *The
Eunuch*, characters allegedly filched from an identifiable
Latin source, Plautus' and Naevius' version of Menander's
Kolax, '*The Toady*'; in *Brothers* the scene incorporated from
a play of Diphilus. Terence is at pains to refute the
charge of plagiarism from Latin sources, but has no
apologies to make for his additions as such, simply
claiming the same latitude as that taken by Naevius,
Plautus, and Ennius in their *palliatae*.

1. 2. 9. Luscius seems to have been taking the line that
a play presented to the public as *Adelphoe* under its Greek
title ought to present the same material as its model, a
fair point if that is what he and Caecilius and most
recent writers did; and his refusal to see merit in
Terence's reformation of the stage-language suggests that
he too wrote in the older extravagant style. But then
Terence could justly claim that he really was being more
genuinely faithful than anyone so far for large stretches
of his plays (a little more than half in *Brothers*, in
fact) and much more debatably assert that his departures
were artistically justified by his Menandrian style. One
should like to know what Luscius thought of the ending
of *Brothers*.

1. 2. 10. This involves *reductio ad absurdum* of the very
premises upon which the *genre* had depended for eighty
years, and *Brothers* is not only Terence's last play but
also the latest surviving of its *genre*. For while others
continued to write *palliatae* in the old, broad manner for
some time, the 'Comedy in Roman Dress' (*comoedia togata*)
was now heir to the comic stage at Rome. Its chief
exponent AFRANIUS evidently admired Terence, but his
fragments clearly show that this did not extend to
imitation of the dramatic form and style so ingeniously
cultivated by Terence, who was first and last of his own
in the Roman theatre [5].

1. 3. 1. *Terence's plays*. The usually accepted order is:

> ANDRIA (*An.*) 'The Woman from Andros', 166 B.C.
> HECYRA (*H.*) 'The Mother-in-Law', 165 B.C.
> H(E)AUTON TIMORUMENOS (*HT*) 'The Self-Tormentor', 163 B.C.
> EUNUCHUS (*E.*) 'The Eunuch', 161 B.C.
> PHORMIO (*Ph.*) 'Phormio the Parasite', 161 B.C.
> ADELPHOE (*Ad.*) 'The Brothers', 160 B.C.

1. 3. 2. Four of these are from Menander (*An.*, *HT*, *E.*, *Ad.*) and two from Menander's disciple APOLLODORUS OF CARYSTUS (*H.*, *Ph.*). Terence keeps the Greek titles except in the case of *Ph.*, originally *Epidikazomenos* 'The claimant to her hand'. These ways of entitling plays agree with the practice of Caecilius rather than with that of Plautus or Naevius, who might have preferred to call an Ἀδελφοί e.g. *Gongralia*, 'The Eel-Comedy' on the basis of lines 376 ff. Maybe Terence simply meant to label his plays as *palliatae* and not *togatae* by not even going so far as to translate the Greek title and give us *Fratres* 'Brothers'; but the implications of keeping the Greek title were and are specially ambiguous in Terence's case.

1. 3. 3. Most of the plays were produced first at the annual Festival of the Great Mother (*ludi Megalenses*) held in Spring by the curule aediles (holders of a junior magistracy of great importance in the career of a young noble). There was now a well-established local 'circuit' of public Games at Rome; the theatrical profession attended the public at these; and plays, light and heavy, were only some of the 'events' offered. We hear of tight-rope-walkers, gladiators, and boxing-matches too (*H.* prol.). The business-side was in the hands of actor-*impresari* like Ambivius Turpio, a more important personage it seems than the mere script-writer. Such tycoons would negotiate terms with the magistrates in charge, and they owned the wooden stages, gear, masks, and props; there was no permanent stone theatre at Rome until 55 B.C. Plays would also feature at privately financed spectacles put on by prominent families and such was the occasion for *Brothers* (see p.23, p.73). In general the circumstances in which the *Palliata* had thrived and developed could hardly be more different from those in which the Artists of Dionysus worked [*C*].

1. 3. 4. *Mother-in-Law* stands furthest from the main tradition of the Roman *Palliata* in the quietness of its action, subtlety, and fidelity to its model; it failed in 165 B.C. and again when presented on the same occasion as *Brothers* in 160 B.C.; it was eventually a success at a third showing later that year. The broad public was not interested in what Terence was best at doing; with them, *Eunuch* was the great success; someone was willing to pay what was regarded as an extraordinary fee to repeat the play. Here Terence made extensive changes intended to make it appeal to a wide audience, at the same time rendering extensive parts very faithfully; his tactics in *Brothers* were similar, but how the play went down we do not know.

1. 3. 5. There is confusion in the production-notice
(pp. 72-3) of *Brothers* over the principal actors, and in
his introduction Donatus records without espousing a view
that *Brothers* was Terence's second not sixth *opus*. There
is also some evidence that different recensions of the
play were in circulation in Imperial times (cf. Donatus on
511 ff., quoted in the app. crit.). This cannot be
unscrambled; it is, however, generally accepted that
Brothers is in fact Terence's latest work and that the
extant prologue refers to a first performance in 160 B.C.,
not some earlier trial.

1. 4. 1. *Terence's subsequent reputation.* Terence soon
became required reading alongside ENNIUS' new epic, the
Annales, in a crude Latin imitation of the well established
elementary rhetorical syllabus of Greek education in which
Homer and Menander held vital places (see p. 2). Whether
Terence had a reading audience in mind as well as a
theatrical cannot be determined but is not unlikely. His
language was that of contemporary upper-class Roman
society and was held to be 'better' in detail than that
of Caecilius as a model and standard. At a time when
Latin was becoming an international language and when many
dialects were still current, some written standard for
what counted as *le bon usage* at Rome itself was desirable
and Terence, treated as that standard, contributed to the
establishment of the Classical Latin of the 1st c. B.C.
Even the young Cicero may have had to un-learn things
which sounded all right in his native Arpinum but not in
the circles to which he aspired. The rumours associating
Terence with the nobility can only have lent him prestige
in this connection. LUCILIUS, CICERO, CAESAR, and VARRO
allude to Terence as someone we have all read, and when
VIRGIL ousted Ennius in the classroom, Terence held his
position. Little awareness however of his metres or
verse-style is apparent after the time of QUINTILIAN
(late first c. A.D.). Read then and later virtually as a
prose-author, and fortified by DONATUS' commentary, which
replaced earlier equivalents, Terence and Donatus were
still there in late antiquity as rhetorical fodder; and
they survived relatively strongly alongside Virgil and
his commentator SERVIUS into the Middle Ages at the heart
of Latin schooling - that is, of any humanist schooling
in the West. He has thus enjoyed a 'run' longer and more
continuous than any other Latin writer, but for reasons
that have little enough to do with his being playwright
as such or a *poeta* at all, the maker of subtly-tuned verse.
In the Renaissance and later, Terence influenced all the
emerging national Dramas of Europe [7] and counted for
critics as the model of theatrical correctness and the

true representative of Menander, to whom, however, he is
in fact at once a most accurate and most misleading
witness.

1. 4. 2. His fortune in the live Roman theatre was much
more equivocal. About 100 B.C. he figures sixth in a list
of the ten 'best' (i.e., funniest?) representatives of the
genre, by then evidently a closed book [8]; in the 1st c.
B.C. Varro praises his characterization in general and
says he prefers Terence's version of the beginning of
Brothers to the original [9]. Caesar and Cicero refer
respectfully to his pure style, but Caesar qualifies this
by referring to him as 'Menander halved' (*o dimidiate
Menander*) and found him generally wanting in 'drive' (*uis*)
and 'comic excellence' (*comica uirtus*), i.e., 'Menandrian
quality'. In the 1st c. A.D., Quintilian in his survey
of Roman achievement versus Greek in the then long-
established genres of literature dismisses the *palliata*
as represented by Plautus and Caecilius as a disaster-
area compared with Menander's New Comedy. But
'nevertheless Terence's plays are the most discriminating
(*elegantes*) in that genre and would have had still more
grace if they had kept to trimeters', i.e., spoken senarii
rather than recitative [10]. Such evidence as there is
from this whole period for actual theatrical performances
of Terence is at best ambiguous [11], and from Horace's
time (late 1st c. B.C.) ignorance of Terence's metres and
of his dramatic structure is such as to cast doubt on the
continuing existence of a real acting tradition to
compare with that of the Greek Artists of Dionysus who
were still keeping Menander very much alive in the theatre.

1. 5. 1. *Menander's fate and resurrection*. Menander
failed to survive the bottleneck of direct transmission
through the Byzantine period (cf. p. 2), and this is less
remarkable than that any of the great Athenian dramatists
did survive - AESCHYLUS, SOPHOCLES, EURIPIDES in Tragedy,
ARISTOPHANES representing Old Comedy. For in each case
the survival of a single copy over a lengthy period
appears to have been crucial. It is only in the last
century and more particularly the last quarter-century that
Menander has been emerging in tattered guise from papyri
preserved in the Egyptian desert. Some eighteen plays out
of more than a hundred are now known in stretches of
varying length. Of these only *Dyskolos* 'The Bad-tempered
Man' is virtually complete; but we have more than half of
six, of which *Samia* 'The Woman of Samos' is particularly
relevant to *Brothers*. Of the others, some scenes of *Dis
Exapaton* 'The Double Deceiver' are important as preserving
passages of the model used by Plautus in his *Bacchides*
'The Bacchis Sisters', and one in *Sikyonioi* 'The Men of

Sicyon' as the probable model of an alien insertion made
by Plautus in his *Poenulus* 'The Carthaginian' [12]. These
with passages quoted by GELLIUS from Menander's *Plokion*
'The Necklace' along with Caecilius' Latin versions are
the only extensive examples of the way that earlier writers
of *palliatae* 'translated' Menander [13]. As yet, nothing
in Greek of any length can be quoted from the originals
of any of Terence's plays; but a good deal of Terence stands
to be positively identified as pretty pure Menander.

1. 5. 3. Ancient criticism rated Menander very highly [14].
ARISTOPHANES OF BYZANTIUM (c. 257-180 B.C.) originated
the tag 'O Menander and Life, which of you imitated the
other?', and reckoned him second only to Homer [15]; this
is clearly related to Menander's place in the Hellenistic
school syllabus (p. 2), and that syllabus was probably
being used at Rome by Greek schoolmasters already before
the end of the Second Punic War. Cicero later defined
Comedy as 'the imitation of life, the mirror of behaviour,
the image of truth' [16]; the theory of drama implicit in
this was possibly already current in Menander's own time
(see on line 428), and was adopted in the Renaissance
from Latin sources; it is most memorably stated by Hamlet
in his well-known Advice to the Players (Shakespeare,
Hamlet iii 2). The point of the 'mirror' theory of Comedy
was to give it status as something 'serious'; it was a
particular application of an older conception of poetry
in general as mimetic (so PLATO), therefore potentially
didactic, therefore worthwhile, and putting Comedy on a
par with Tragedy as literature: if the comic poet portrays
us with conviction, he may make us think in ways that the
caricaturist will not.

1. 5. 6. In the Roman world QUINTILIAN went so far as to
say that Menander 'even by himself would, if carefully
read, be sufficient to bring about everything that one
seeks to impart in a rhetorical education; so well has he
imprinted the image of life, such is his fertility of
ideas and facility of language, so accurately tuned is he
to every subject, personality, and emotion' [17]. What
disappointed GELLIUS in comparing Caecilius with Menander
[18] was the Roman writer's positive disregard for the
very best things in Menander - his 'simplicity, truth,
and charm' (*simplex et uerum et delectabile*). Both
writers are referring to what we should call characterization
and they are right. Though farce and theatricality are
by no means absent from Menander, and though his *dramatis
personae* can be categorized externally by class, type,
even name, he presents real individuals and rarely if ever
merely relies on our *a priori* expectation of sentiment

and behaviour. His stagecraft is superbly economical, and one technical manoeuvre in the plot will unobtrusively achieve several aims at once, like a good move in a game of chess [19]. This is important as a means of identifying in Terence the Menandrian and the Terentian in dramaturgy; for Terence's standards in dramaturgy are really those of the older *palliata*, looser and more tolerant of implausibility, awkwardness, and redundancy than Menander's [20].

2. The Action of Terence's *Brothers*

2. 1. 1. The act-divisions given more or less prominence
in printed editions are an inept imposition on Terence
made in antiquity in the light of Horace's precept that
plays ought to have five acts [21]. In what follows the
ends of these 'acts' are noted in Roman numbers in
brackets. The real articulation of Terence was metrical;
it is enough here to distinguish spoken verse (SV), i.e.,
iambic senarii, and recitative (R), i.e., the longer
iambic and trochaic measures which were somehow accompanied
by the musician. There is also one 'aria' (A) not in
iambo-trochaic verse [22].

2. 1. 2. Menander's play was in five acts (the Greeks
simply said 'parts') separated by *entr'actes* for the
chorus; the decline of the dramatic role of the chorus is
seen already in the late works of Aristophanes, and in New
Comedy its 'numbers' were unscripted and were integral
only in that they might cover the passage of dramatic time.
Further, some appropriate god or abstraction interrupted
the first act to give us the background in a set speech;
the technique is well known in Menander (e.g. *Aspis*
'The Shield', *Synaristosai* 'The Ladies at Elevenses').
Roman scholars started to go wrong by labelling the break
for Menander's prologue as their 'Act I'. In Menander,
probably only about a sixth was not in spoken iambic
trimeters; in Terence the balance of spoken and chanted
verse is about even.

2. 2. 1. *Terence's play*. 26-154 (SV): It is dawn. Micio
enters from his house alarmed at the all-night absence of
his son Aeschinus and the escort sent to fetch him home
last night. Any loving father makes himself a unique
prey to anxiety: has there been some dreadful accident...?
How illogical (but human) to choose and cherish something
more dear than one's own life! Besides, Aeschinus is not
Micio's natural son but an adopted nephew, son of Micio's
brother Demea,

* (40) a man of very different outlook from Micio, who
  has gone for a life of urbane ease as a bachelor;
* Demea has gone for a life of thrift and hard work as a
  farmer, doing his duty and marrying; Micio has adopted
* the elder of his two sons (47).

Micio has brought the young man up from babyhood and all
his happiness lies in his love for Aeschinus; he aims to
make him reciprocate that love by liberality and avoiding
prying and training his son to be frank with him in ways
that conventional strictness fails to achieve (58).
Demea does not approve but he is too strict himself (64);

* and in general the key to maintaining authority (not
* just paternal) is not vigilant repression but
  openhandedness which will inspire children to give as
* good as they get (77).

Demea arrives from his farm with news that Aeschinus has
abducted a slave-girl; it is the talk of the town; Micio
is to blame; Demea's younger son Ctesipho is a paragon by
contrast (97). Micio avoids the issue by attacking Demea's
outlook and interference and threatens to return Aeschinus
to Demea's jurisdiction if he goes on. Demea backs down
and leaves for town (140). Micio explains that the news
does alarm him, but that there was no point in inflaming
the volatile Demea by agreeing with him; the only way to
deal with his passions is to treat him like a fierce dog.
Micio had been hoping that Aeschinus was nearly past the
adolescent phase; the other day, he mentioned marrying
and settling down. Micio leaves for town to look for
Aeschinus (154). ('I')

* (Menander's prologue followed here)

* 155-287 (R): Aeschinus and his retinue bring the
  slavegirl home to the protests of her master Sannio,
* a procurer. She and the other 'extras' are sent in
  to Micio's (175). Aeschinus outfaces Sannio's bluster
* and proposes to offer him what he himself paid for the
  girl as compensation or face prosecution for depriving
* a freeborn girl of her status; he leaves (196).
  Sannio reflects on his chances of getting any money at
* all (208),

and Syrus, the senior servant in Micio's household, enters
assuring those within that he will have Sannio eating out
of his hand. Posing as a neutral party he criticizes
Sannio's tactics and reveals that he knows Sannio is in
a hurry to be off to Cyprus (227).

228-53 (SV): This revelation undermines Sannio, who ends
begging Syrus to take his part.

* 254-87 (R): Ctesipho arrives, overjoyed at hearing what
  Aeschinus has done; for it is Ctesipho, not Aeschinus,
* who loves the girl; Aeschinus is covering for his
  brother by taking the blame (264). Aeschinus joins
* the other three; Ctesipho had been thinking of leaving
  Athens, Aeschinus had found out 'almost too late' (272)
* Ctesipho is despatched indoors; the others go to town
  to find Micio and settle (287) ('II').

* (Here was the end of Menander's first act)

* 288-354 (R): Sostrata, a widow, and Canthara, an old
  nurse, enter from next door. Sostrata's daughter
* Pamphila is about to have a baby; Aeschinus is the
  father; he has been their mainstay these recent months
* (298). Geta, an old servant, arrives with the news
  about Aeschinus: he has evidently abandoned them all
* for someone else without a thought for the poor girl
  he had raped (308); he is outraged (319). Sostrata
* is cast down: Aeschinus had sworn to approach his
  father for permission to marry after the child was
* born (!) (334). Geta argues for keeping quiet (341);
  Sostrata rejects that (350); Geta is to fetch the
* daughter's only male relative Hegio and tell him
  everything; maybe he will help them to prosecute.
* Canthara is to fetch a midwife from town. *Exeunt
  severally* (354).

355-516 (SV): Demea returns, disturbed to hear that
Ctesipho had some active part in last night's affray. In
comes Syrus, laden with 'the goodies' for a celebration
at Micio's. He explains that they had found Micio,
told him about Ctesipho and the girl, and that Micio was
very pleased; he settled with Sannio in the spot and gave
extra for the celebration (371).

Demea reveals his presence; Syrus coolly goes on dealing
with his purchases while making out that he disapproves
of Micio's eccentric ways. Flattering Demea for his
sagacity, Syrus tells him that Micio intends to let
Aeschinus keep the girl at home (390). Demea 'casually'
mentions Ctesipho; Syrus determines to get rid of Demea.
Ctesipho, he says, is at the farm: he had earlier put
him on the road there himself (402). He unexpectedly
turned up at the moment of the settlement in town and
roundly denounced Aeschinus' profligacy (410). This
relieves and pleases Demea and prompts him to describe
his 'system' of education - precept and observation 'as
if in a mirror' of what draws praise and blame in others'
behaviour. Syrus ironically endorses all this with his
own below-stairs parallels and goes in (432) confident
that Demea is leaving for the farm. But as Demea makes
to leave he sees Geta bringing his old friend Hegio
from the country (446) and he stays to speak to him.
On greeting Hegio Demea is shocked by the grave charges
of rape and abandonment now laid against Aeschinus, and
the baby arrives on cue in Sostrata's house (486).
Hegio champions the women's cause and reminds Demea of
the responsibilities of rich men like him and Micio.
Demea indicates that he means to find Micio in town and
tell him; Hegio and Geta go into Sostrata's; Demea leaves
for town (511; *the end of Menander's second act*). Hegio
returns from Sostrata's and also leaves for town to look
for Micio (516) ('III').

517-609 (R): Syrus complacently reassures a nervous
Ctesipho that Demea has gone home, but suddenly (537) he
turns up from town complaining that he cannot find Micio
and that he has heard Ctesipho is not at home (542).
Syrus with comic difficulty disposes of Ctesipho and
pretends he has been beaten by him for being behind the
purchase of the slavegirl. This again wins Demea's
pleasure and approval (564). He wants to know where Micio
is; Syrus sends him on a wild-goose-chase to the far side
of Athens (586). Sure this time that Demea has gone,
Syrus goes home to have a little drop (591).
* Micio and Hegio return from town, where Micio has
    corrected Hegio's wrong opinion of Aeschinus and
* learnt from Hegio of the rape, pregnancy, and
    arrangement with Sostrata. He promises to do the
* proper thing and they go in to Sostrata's.

* 610-37 (A, R): Aeschinus, shocked at the suspicion
    he has incurred and learnt about from Canthara (616),
gradually brings himself under control, reviewing his
position, and blaming himself for not telling his father
(630); he resolves to be more positive, and, screwing
up his courage to approach Sostrata, is faced with his
father as he leaves her house (637).

638-78 (SV): Micio pretends that he has been supporting
the claim of a 'friend from Miletus' to the hand of
Pamphila; he is the closest kin and as such has the option
to marry her; but the women claim there is 'someone else',
the alleged father of an alleged baby - all nonsense of
course, says Micio. Aeschinus is dismayed (678).

679-712 (R): Micio reveals that he knows the whole story,
lectures Aeschinus, and gives permission for his
marriage (696). He is delighted; Micio goes home (706);
* Aeschinus follows him after expressing appreciation
    of Micio not as a wise and humane individual but as
* a bizarre but convenient inversion of what one
    expects of a father-figure; in future he will be very
* anxious not to hurt his feelings.

* (Here was the end of Menander's third act)

713-854 (SV): Frustrated and exhausted Demea returns and
at last finds Micio at home (720). He is aghast to find
that Micio seems content to house both a poor wife and
a mistress for Aeschinus (747). Micio goes to see
Sostrata, leaving Demea alone to comment on the lunacy of
Micio's household (762) ('IV', edd.). He is joined by
Syrus, now tipsy. Demea is further outraged that they can
be carousing under the circumstances (775) ('IV', Donatus).

A slave calls out that Ctesipho wants Syrus' company.
Syrus cannot prevent Demea's irruption; he follows; Micio
returns from Sostrata's; commotion from within; eruption
of Demea (789). Demea reminds Micio of their agreement
not to interfere with each other's charge and Micio
counters by proposing that henceforth they should pool
their resources for the benefit of both boys: 'friends
say not mine and thine but ours' (804). He argues that
Demea had reckoned that by hard work he could create
enough wealth to leave a good inheritance for both his
sons, and has succeeded; Micio's own fortune was an
unexpected windfall; let them use that up, and inherit
from Demea (819). As to their characters, there are
signs in people which allow one to say that X can get
away with that, but Y would be harmed; it is the doer as
well as the deed that must be assessed. What signs does
Micio see in the boys that makes him confident they will
turn out as the fathers wish? Discrimination,
appropriate respect, mutual affection; one can tell
mettle and spirit; they will respond to the whistle
whenever one wishes them to (830). Thirdly, their
extravagance is a symptom of their age; in due course
they will tend towards the opposite error (835). Lastly,
Micio asks Demea to be cheery just for today for the
wedding. Demea reluctantly agrees, and without explicit
prompting from Micio proposes to keep the slave-girl on
the farm where she is to earn her keep the hard way.
Micio goes in, inviting Demea to follow (854).

(*Here was the end of Menander's fourth act*)

* 855-81 (R): Alone, Demea reflects that one is never too
  old to learn; henceforth he is going to change his ways;
* why? Anyone can see from him and his brother that
  easy-going mildness is 'better'. (861). Micio's life
* has been one of Epicurean sociability, avoiding all
  offence; result, universal popularity. (865). Demea
* has played the part of the thrifty, formidable peasant-
  farmer, marrying and having sons; result, they hate
* him; Micio has unscrupulously diverted their affection
  (876). Since Micio challenges him to it, Demea
* proposes to try affability and mildness; he too wants
  to be appreciated by his own; if that means
* fawning and largesse, he will not play second fiddle.
  Ruin? So what? He is eldest; *après lui le déluge*
* (881).

* 882-933 (SV): After rehearsing affability first on
  Syrus (888), then Geta (898), Demea wins instant favour

* with Aeschinus by proposing that Syrus should breach
the garden wall so that the bride may cross over
* that way (911). Demea takes malicious pleasure in
thinking what Micio will make of that (915) and sends
* Syrus in. Geta thanks Demea and goes back to Sostrata.
Micio comes out in surprise (924). He agrees that
* they must do all possible to unite the households; the
logic of that, says Demea, is that Micio should marry
* Sostrata (933).

* 934-55 (R): Micio objects to this strongly; but he
gives way to the combined pressure of Demea and
* Aeschinus (945), who shows himself utterly 'unimproved'
by his education; Micio is shown to be a fraud. Demea
* further extracts financial help for Hegio from an
unwilling Micio,
*
956-7 (SV) who reluctantly concedes because Aeschinus
* wants it.

* 958-997 (R): Syrus reports that the wall is breached;
Demea proposes that he be freed for his good services;
* Micio grumpily accedes because Aeschinus wants it
(970); Demea offers to pay for the freedom of a female
* slave of Micio's to be Syrus' bride (977); and Syrus
is to be given financial help by Micio (983). Asked
* why he has become so generous, Demea replies that it
was to teach us a lesson: Micio's easy-going, jolly
* ways are not the expression of a true philosophy of
life but of fawning, laxness, and extravagance. He
* ends by proposing himself, take him or leave him, as
a true and wise father-figure for the boys. Aeschinus
* submits to his authority for himself and Ctesipho, who,
Demea rules, is to be allowed to keep his girl, but
* she is to be his first and last (997).

2. 2. 2. In the above account, the passages asterisked
are those where there is reason to think that Terence has
departed more or less substantially from Menander; or, to
put it another way, those set to the margin are the
stretches where Terence appears to be following Menander
more or less closely. The evidence for this diagnosis
is set out on pp. 31-57 and in the Notes to the
translation, and a Scenario for Menander's play is
sketched on pp. 58-64. But our first business is to do
as we are bidden in the prologue (24) and try to become
fairminded Roman spectators in 160 B.C.

3. The Roman Context of *Brothers*

3. 1. 1. *The irrelevance of the Greek original*. Terence
neither invited nor expected his broad audience to make
comparisons: since the original is lost (all but the
flotsam on pp. 263-7) we easily qualify on that count.
But it is not so easy for the alien visitor to Terence's
city-state to attune his values and attitudes appropriately.
The social fabric of the Hellenistic city-state was very
different from that of any modern society; as Hellenistic
city-states Menander's Athens and Terence's Rome differed;
and in Terence's time, Roman life itself was changing
under Greek influence in ways which are imperfectly
documented and of which Terence's plays are themselves
one complex symptom. We should not expect this approach
to be straightforward, but we must at least try it.

3. 2. 1. *The theme*. A perennial topic: the means chosen
by parents (so we would say; but then it was father's
business more than mother's) in dealing with teenagers to
make them responsible adults and good citizens, and the
effectiveness of the means. Should fathers be strict and
old-fashioned, or permissive and modern?

3. 2. 2. One cause of confusion among modern critics may
be disposed of at once. Neither Greeks nor Romans believed
in either Original Sin or in Primal Innocence. Terence to
be sure starts by making Micio expound a general theory of
education behind which there lies an optimist's view of
human nature: anyone will respond well to liberality (65-
77). In context, this is certainly meant to convince and win
applause (65-77). But it appears to be Terentian
simplification and expansion, for it is not strictly
compatible with Micio's views as expressed in 820 ff.;
Micio's axiom there is that there are good and bad natural
dispositions and that it is certainly wrong to allow bad
dispositions free rein. This apparently more subtle
position in fact corresponds better with popular Roman and
Athenian belief about human nature. In the good old days,
everyone was virtuous; but this is the degenerate Age of
Iron; the quality of men has been constantly declining and
will probably get worse, until, perhaps, a new Golden Age
comes. What is 'born in' a person (his *in-genium*) is a
matter of breeding, or, as we might say, his genes.
Naturally good *ingenia* are nowadays rare (e.g. Hegio,
440 ff.); so moral education is more important now than
ever it was - *if*, that is, virtue is teachable - because
there are so many bad influences about. In this play both
fathers tacitly agree that the boys have the right raw
material, but may go wrong if handled wrongly. Their

views differ on the content and aim of moral education and the proper nature of a father-son relationship. The play deals with the specific cases of two boys with good *ingenia* at a certain stage of development; but Terence (not necessarily Menander) wants to draw simple, broad conclusions. Consciously or unconsciously giving Micio views of human nature which are strictly inconsistent, Terence ends with a clear decision for Demea and a very definite 'message'.

3. 2. 3. 'Virtue is teachable, and it is Father's solemn duty to teach it by precept, example, and vigilant control, even at the price of unpopularity. Nor can there be a time when Father's job can be said to be done. Sons should always listen with respectful awe to the accumulated and accumulating wisdom of their *paterfamilias* [23], even after they have married and set up for themselves. Any idea that father and son might be friends on an equal footing like brothers, though superficially attractive, is really the topsyturvy stuff of comedy; a fraud in the end, subversive of the sacred ideas of authority (*auctoritas*) and respect (*pudor*) at home, and, it follows, in Society. You will take the medicine, my lads, because it is good for you and I know best'.

3. 2. 4. This paternalistic message comes as a surprise at the end. As far as line 854, the lenient Micio has been winning hands down both in the play and in gaining our approval as a man and father [24]. Demea, though well meaning, honest, and constant, has been the butt, and no model *guru*. He completely lacks *auctoritas* in comparison with Micio. But he suddenly acquires standing and pathos in his soliloquy at 855 ff., and Micio too is redefined as a kind of parasite. After the excellent Saturnalian farce leading to the liberation of Syrus, that model Educator, we are told that the worse cause had only been made to seem the better. The view that there is a 'British compromise' and that each brother is supposed to have learnt something from the other is a misreading of the script [25].

3. 2. 5. This is certainly not how Menander ended his play; how he did, what Terence's changes amount to, and whether in Menander Micio was shown to be 'wrong' (which is one thing) and Demea 'right' (which is another) are the central problems of the play. But we, as members of Terence's audience, will be unaware that Menander said anything different and will assume that what Terence vindicates in Demea, namely respect for what happen to be very Roman ideas about fatherhood and what he condemns in Micio, that is a denial of those ideas and parasitism, were both likewise dealt with by Menander.

3. 3. 1. *The character of the action*.   But one must not
get this out of proportion. *Brothers* is an entertainment,
a play for acting, not a social treatise. Its qualities
as theatre lie in the variety and pacing of a basically
simple plot dominated by two strongly drawn characters and
an excellent part for 'Figaro' in the person of Syrus.
Dramatic tensions arising from the main theme are
skilfully developed to engage our commitment; these are
released in comic sequels in which farce, irony, parody,
surprise, and visual humour make us laugh without losing
the thread and from 882 to 982 we are rocking in our seats,
not moralizing. The rhythm and timing of this repeating
pattern are excellent, and Caesar's reservation about a
want of 'verve' in Terence scarcely seems fair in this
play (cf. p. 7).

3. 3. 2. Credit for this robust layout is Menander's in
the first place and Terence's in that his alterations of
presentation and substance, which are very extensive, have
not in general spoilt the pacing (except perhaps at 196 ff.,
510/1, 591 ff., 855 ff.). Deception and misapprehension
permeate the play and will carry in the theatre in any
time or place without glossing. Both young men are
deceiving their fathers; Syrus outwits Sannio (209 ff.)
and then Demea thrice (375 ff., 401 ff., 553 ff.); Demea
tries to outwit Syrus (364 ff.) and thinks he succeeds;
he does so without realising it at 537 ff., and catches
him out by accident (776 ff.). Micio misleads Demea
twice (141 ff., 745 ff.), and Demea finally outmanoeuvres
Micio – but only after being the subject of two
misapprehensions about Aeschinus (82 ff., 462 ff.) and
the victim of half a dozen deceptions. For good measure,
Terence fools us too: for a quarter of the play we are
under the false impression that Aeschinus loves the girl
abducted from Sannio and we know nothing about Pamphila;
and then there is the sting in the tail of the play.

3. 4. 1. *The setting*. This 'Athens' is a secular world
in which the divine does not control or affect our
behaviour; Terence even eliminates the 'divine prologue'
common in New Comedy [*26*]. This concentration on the
human assists the play to survive translation into the
modern world, but there remain many features more or less
strange to us which Terence could take for granted.

3. 4. 2. His play takes place 'now' in a deracinated
Athens. Certain things here are explicitly un-Roman –
the costumes, what makes a good *menu* (376 ff.), the rules
about who should marry whom (751 f.), even the suggestion

(quite misleading) that in 'Athens' there is no formal
equivalent to Roman 'guardianship of women'. But the
inhabitants do not speak with funny foreign accents
(this had never been a feature of the *palliata*) and at
a deeper level everything is really Roman and
contemporary. This is better disguised than in Plautus,
but it is only disguised and one regrets the lack of
local colour and specificness (see on 228 ff., 318,
692); in the translation, we have made bold to refer
to 'Athens' and 'Athenians' in an un-Terentian way.
All that we have are two side-entrances for 'Town' and
'Country' and two doors for the houses, the simplest
and most universal of sets.

3. 4. 3. Terence and Menander take slavery as a fact
of life; on the one hand, slaves are outsiders to
society; their evidence can only be taken in court if
extracted under torture (482 ff.). On the other, they
count as members of the family in proportion to their
devotion to its interests. The family is a self-
sustaining 'business' run by a male head, the father
or father-figure. He is the only person relatively
free to be himself; but his freedom to do as he likes
is limited by his role, his wealth, and his respect
for what other people think, never mind by the law.
His powers are matched by responsibilities. It is up
to him to arrange the marriages of boys as well as
girls; they have no business taking their own initiatives
over this.

Marriage is a secular contract available only to
citizens of *this* city, not to slaves or aliens. A
bride should have an appropriate dowry (345, 729) and
be a maiden at the time of her first marriage. The
chastity of freeborn girls matters not because sexual
relations outside marriage are sinful as such but
because marriage is for breeding and for the descent
of patrimonies. All women are properly subject to some
man's authority - father, husband, guardian - and only
have access to the law through that person. There is
no police-force as we understand it. Violating a girl
is a serious offence against her kin as much as against
her. The proper place for unmarried girls is at home
and opportunities for boy to meet girl unchaperoned
are very limited. The bachelor can get himself an
heir by adoption, thus avoiding the risks, friction,
and worry of raising a family; but the man who does
take all that on is doing his duty as a citizen and
deserves respect. A father or guardian should find a
husband for an unmarried girl in his charge. Women

cannot choose for themselves whether to marry or stay single
as at least some men can, and, having lost their menfolk,
women are to be pitied; a lonely mother and daughter without
a husband are scarcely a family. As for non-citizen women,
anything goes; keeping one as a mistress is all right (but
not alongside a wife, 747); and a man who runs a brothel
is in a sleazy but legally tolerated trade, for pimping and
prostitution are not against the law as long as the girls
are slaves or aliens.

3. 4. 4. These things were taken for granted by Terence as
by Menander. There were, however, important differences
of emphasis. In *Brothers*, the most important are that at
Athens a woman's guardian had more powers and duties than
he had at Rome, where women without a *paterfamilias* were
legal persons in their own right and could own property,
and that at Rome the concept of *patria potestas* 'fatherly
authority' was far stronger and more institutionalized than
at Athens or indeed in any known patriarchal society; see
pp. 25, 37.

3. 5. 1. *The Political Background to 'Brothers'*. The play
was produced at the Funeral Games for L. AEMILIUS PAULLUS
MACEDONICUS in 160 B.C. In later times, he was remembered
as blending traditional Roman virtues with Greek
enlightenment and for his liberality. As a soldier, his
greatest achievement had been the decisive victory at Pydna
in 168 B.C. over Perses the last successor of Alexander
the Great as king of Macedon, and as a citizen, his
censorship in 164 B.C. [*27*].

3. 5. 2. In his lifetime Rome had survived her second war
against Carthage only to become immediately engaged in wars
of pacification and settlement against the Celtic tribes
of North Italy and of Spain, the latter newly inherited
from Carthage, and in the diplomacy and wars of the kingdoms
and leagues of Greece and Asia Minor. In these Rome posed
as the champion of Greek liberty where it was threatened
by regal tyranny. Spectacular successes were won by land
and sea; much wealth and booty were taken. But Rome
avoided imposing imperial rule on defeated Greek states.
The policy was rather to promote the interests of friendly
classes or parties, and to leave them to get on with their
own affairs.

3. 5. 3. The relationship was not to be that of master and
slave but of patron and client, based on mutual trust and
services freely rendered. Rome became the focus of the
inhabited world without yet controlling it directly. The
trouble was that too few Greek states seemed to understand
the terms. Aemilius had been one of these enlightened

paternalists. Another fourteen years were to pass before
Carthage and Corinth were sacked and destroyed, the former
by Aemilius' adoptive son Scipio Aemilianus; our play,
then, dates from after Rome's decisive emergence as the
strongest of the great powers of the Mediterranean, but
from before the time when there was a Roman Empire as we
usually think of it.

3. 6. 1. *The Cultural Background*

In the eyes of a Greek contemporary, the historian POLYBIUS,
the battle of Pydna marked the end of the most remarkable
period in history - the fifty-three years during which
Rome had risen from provincial obscurity to world power.
He himself was one of a 1,000 prominent citizens of Achaea
held hostage at Rome as a consequence of Pydna, and came
to admire the victors. Terence's audience of 160 B.C. will
have included some who had seen it all; the champion of
the 'ways of our Roman ancestors' CATO THE ELDER, censor
in 184 B.C., now seventy-four years old but still vigorous,
might have been there if he was one to bother with Greek
plays; his elder son Cato Licinianus had married a daughter
of the deceased some time in the last few years. [28].

3. 6. 2. Rome had long been open to the mainly Dorian Greek
influence of Southern Italy and Sicily; Greek was the
accepted language of international life. Its usefulness
was obvious to any Roman ambitious for his sons in the
great world, and that had meant Greek tutors and their
books at least since the middle of the third century B.C.
But it was in the generation of Aemilius that 'captive
Greece captured her fierce conqueror and introduced system
and style (*artes*) to rustic Latium' [29], the more
intensely after Pydna, which marks a watershed.

3. 6. 3. ENNIUS had died in 169 B.C., leaving the Romans
their first 'proper' Epic, the *Annales*, Roman in substance
and language but Greek in form, ambition, and execution
[30]. On the eve of the battle of Pydna, a Roman had been
able to offer the Roman troops a rational explanation of
an eclipse of the moon which terrified the superstitious
Macedonians [31]. In the sequel, Aemilius claimed no
personal booty except the contents of the Royal Library
at Pella. Then, about the time that Polybius must have
come to Rome, we hear of CRATES OF MALLOS lecturing on
rhetoric at Rome [32]; he was an exponent of the mannered
antithetical style that we hear in the prologues to
Terence *passim* and occasionally in his plays, notably
Demea's two last speeches (855 ff., 985 ff.). But such an
elaborate 'science' of persuasion was going to appear
suspect to men like Cato, whose only rule of rhetoric is
well known: 'stick to the point, and the words will
follow' [33].

3. 6. 4. But Terence was not particularly successful with
the conservative public; and in 161 B.C. the Senate had
exiled Greek rhetoricians and philosophers from Rome [*34*].
That in itself shows that Greek philosophies and systems
were of controversial interest in Terence's Rome: potted
Epicureanism and Stoicism will certainly have been familiar.
After 160 B.C. Scipio Aemilianus came under the influence
of PANAETIUS' brand of Stoicism, which emphasized the
humanitarian duty of the wise ruler [*35*]. But captive
Greece was only gradually capturing her fierce conqueror.
In 155 B.C. the heads of the three leading Athenian schools
of philosophy visiting Rome on a diplomatic mission were
sent packing when one of them, the Sceptic CARNEADES had
drawn crowds to hear him argue persuasively like the
Athenian sophists of the fifth century on both sides of
ethical questions as a demonstration of the inadequacy of
'common sense' as a criterion of right and wrong. Cato's
own views on the dangers of an indiscriminate willingness
on the part of Romans to accept all Greek gifts are well
known, and making the worse cause seem the better was
definitely not something to be encouraged [*36*].

3. 6. 5. In the first scene, Micio introduces himself and
his brother as having had different values (*studia*) ever
since they were young men (*ab adulescentia*) - not different
personalities ever since the cradle. They have 'gone for'
(*sequi* is the verb) opposite ways of life (*uitae*). *Abeunt
studia in mores*, it is true: our values pass into our
characters; but we start by choosing our *studia*, like a suit
of clothes. Terence is implying a contrast not of basic
personality (*ingenium*) but of sects of philosophy which
affect one's personality. He is inviting us to see a
straightforward Epicurean in Micio. He opts for the Quiet
Life, he is sociable, avoids offending anyone, his
happiness lies in his training of Aeschinus, and 'that
happiness is the only thing that matters to him' (42 f.,
49, cf. 861-5). One does not need to know much about
Epicurus to get the point: *senex lepidus* = an Epicurean
[*37*].

3. 6. 6. If Micio is a 'cavalier', then Demea will be a
'roundhead': in the popular mind austerity goes with the
philosophical outlook that one might broadly call Cynic
and Stoic. The contrasts of town and country, work and
idleness, hedonistic bachelorhood and dutiful family
commitment are emblematic. Demea's badges are those
issued long before by Hesiod in his *Works and Days*, but
by Terence's time that strand in Greek thinking which
emphasized the Simple Life as the foundation of private
virtue and social stability had entwined itself very
acceptably with Roman ideas about good citizenship [*38*].

Cato was writing his *De agri cultura* about the time *Brothers*
was put on, and he begins it by praising the life of a
Demea in just these terms. In the play, it is hinted, we
are likely to see the embodiments of two 'faiths' or
'persuasions', and the possibility opens that there may
be a 'conversion' or a vindication of one of them; scarcely
a compromise though, because the stereotypes are too
clear-cut. One would like to know when Pacuvius translated
Euripides' *Antiopa*: that play had contrasted the Theoretical
and the Practical Life in the persons of the twins Amphion
and Zethus and was cited as such by Plato when the things
controversial at Rome c. 160 B.C. had been controversial
at Athens too [*39*].

3. 6. 7. To be sure, this 'philosophical' aspect of Demea
is left on the shelf in the main body of the play. Here
Demea is anything but the sage who by living the Simple
Life has arrived at that calm self-sufficiency of spirit
and harmony with Nature which marks the Wise Man like the
old gardener in Virgil's fourth *Georgic* [*40*]. But the hint
that Demea *has* a philosophy of life on a par with Micio's in
its systematic character makes room for what happens at
the end of Terence's play. Demea respects the axioms
underlying that most Roman of all Roman ancestral ways,
patria potestas, 'fatherly authority', Micio does not.
The morality of rhetoric, the role of the philosopher,
the ends and means of education were specially controversial
around 160 B.C. at Rome in ways they no longer were at
Athens when Menander wrote.

3. 7. 1. *Education in Terence's Rome.* Aemilius' funeral
games were organized by P. Cornelius Scipio Aemilianus
and his brother Q. Fabius Maximus Aemilianus, the
surviving sons of Aemilius. They had been given in
adoption into other noble houses probably about 169 B.C. -
hence the form of their names - for his other two sons
died at the moment of his triumph in 168 B.C. Aemilianus,
now twenty-five, the inheritor of two great names and
destined to be a leading figure in the politics, wars
and cultural life of Rome over the next forty years, had
found a third father-figure in Polybius, who describes
in a famous passage how the shy and serious seventeen-
year-old Scipio had approached the Wise Man from abroad
as a disciple seeking a master [*41*].

3. 7. 2. Before this Aemilius is said to have seen personally
to the education of his sons,

> 'not only in the traditional Roman manner in
> which he had been brought up himself, but also
> and more systematically in the Greek manner.

For Greek grammarians, philosophers, and
rhetoricians surrounded the boys, as well as
sculptors, artists, riding-experts, and
huntsmen; and the father, unless prevented by
some public business, would always take part
in their activities as the fondest father then
alive at Rome' [42].

3. 7. 4 The son of Cato referred to above (p. 21), a lawyer
of note in adult life, had been born about 191 B.C., and

'when he came to the age of reason' - i.e.,
c. 184 B.C., the year of Cato's famous censorship
- 'Cato himself undertook teaching him his
letters. Though Cato owned an accomplished
Greek slave, one Chilon, an elementary teacher
of Greek who attracted large numbers of (paying)
pupils, Cato did not think it right that, as he
says, 'the boy should have his ear tweaked or
be bawled at by some slave for being slow at
his lessons, or that he should be indebted at
all to a slave for something as important as
his education'. Instead Cato himself became
his instructor in letters, the law, and physical
training. He taught him not only how to handle
the sword and the spear and how to ride but
also fist-fighting, endurance of extreme
temperatures, and survival-swimming in dangerous
waters. He mentions that he set down stories
in his own hand in big letters so that the boy
should have his own private store of material
for learning Roman history and custom' [43].

3. 7. 5 The differences of approach between these two most
'professional' of Roman fathers is less than might appear
at first sight. Both reckon education the prime duty of
a father, to be undertaken in person and not merely
delegated to the expert; it is physical as much as
intellectual, and even Aemilius seems to have drawn the
line at having his boys learn music and dancing too [44].

3. 7. 6 There are curious partial parallels between themes
and relationships arising in *Brothers* and the real
circumstances and experiences of Aemilius, Cato, and their
sons. The reader will note these for himself and decide
what to make of them, if anything: the editor at any rate
is stuck. For the similarities between Cato and Demea
seem remarkably close and Terence has made a special point
of preserving not only the substance of Demea's role in
Menander but also its metrical presentation in 26-854,

modifying it in the sequel 855-997 so as to render Demea's
revenge successful and to vindicate his values. It is as
if Terence were at pains to avoid the accusation that he
personally rather than Menander were in any way responsible
for the systematic disrespect shown towards *durus senex*,
i.e., Cato, in 26-854 and felt it right, or politic, to
change the ending in his favour. But there are similarities
between Micio and Paullus too: their names mean the same
(cf. p. 228), both are notable for enlightened paternalism,
fondness as fathers, and openhandedness. But we can hardly
be meant to press *that* equation, for how could a play in
pious memory of Paullus end with such forthright
condemnation of his values? The problem unfortunately will
not go away by our ignoring it [45].

3. 7. 7 What seems certain, however, is that to be a good
Roman father in a changing world full of Greek experts in
this or that ready to take money for doing Father's job
was a question of lively concern in the real Rome of 160 B.C.
Other features of the play which will strike the modern
reader as remarkable or offensive - its sexism, its
assumptions about class and status (p. 19-20) - will have
bothered no-one, Greek or Roman, and are not under
examination.

3. 8. 1 *Roman patria potestas* [46]. In Athenian as in
most patriarchal societies, it went without saying that
when a young man married, he became 'his own master',
inheriting responsibilities, of course, towards his aging
parents, but no longer subject to his father's legal
authority: he has 'grown up', father's role *qua* father
has ended. So in Menander, Aeschinus' marriage to Pamphila
was supposed to mark a definite end and a beginning: Micio's
'job' has been done, for good or ill. But in Terence this
is far less clear-cut. A young Roman on marrying inherited
responsibilities towards his aging parents, but remained
in the legal control of his father as long as the old man
lived. For the head of a Roman family was by definition
its senior living ascendant in the male line; he was
paterfamilias and ruler of his own roost, whether a young
bachelor or an aged great-grandfather. The powers of a
paterfamilias over his own were much stronger than those
of an Athenian father, e.g. in his freedom to dispose of
his property by will; and his responsibilities were felt
by Romans to be correspondingly the greater. Thus he
continued to rule and be responsible for those of 'his own'
who were married, as well as their children if any. The
strangest consequence of this was that women on marriage
either passed wholly into the *potestas* of the *paterfamilias*

of the husband's family, who would be the husband himself
only if he had lost all his own male ascendants in the
male line, or she would remain fully under the control of
her own original *paterfamilias*, only her children belonging
fully to her husband's family.

3. 8. 2 In Roman eyes, Micio has lifelong power over and
responsibility towards Aeschinus and his baby son. These
are not changed or ended by the fact of his getting married
as such, and it makes no difference that Aeschinus is an
adopted son. Micio does not merely fail to exercize the
control allowed by 'the letter of a father's legal rights'
(52), he does not accept the lifelong and unchanging
character of fatherly authority anyway. That Aeschinus
at the end of the play (995) 'disowns' Micio and returns
to Demea is of course legally absurd, but it points up
Micio's humiliation and failure as *paterfamilias* and the
thoroughly Roman idea that no-one can possibly become
'his own master' as long as his *paterfamilias* lives.

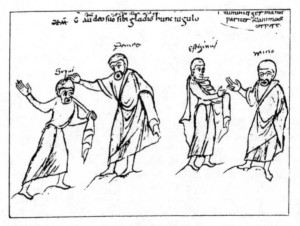

F: fol. 74 ᵛ

4. Character and Stereotype in Terence

4. 1. 1. Terence's approach. Traditionally, roles in the
Roman *Palliata* had been based on simple oppositions: old
and young, rich and poor, good and bad, etc. Each broadly
drawn type had its own checklist of traits and acquired
an existence outside any given play, rather like Harlequin,
Columbine, Pierrot in the tradition of the Italian
Commedia dell'arte [47]. Like the masks and the costume,
the type's behaviour was hanging there in the wardrobe
waiting for the scriptwriter and the player.

4. 1. 2. No doubt the same was true in the worst and most
tired of the Greek New Comedy. But we should perhaps be
less dismissive than Terence, Horace, or Quintilian about
Plautus, Naevius, and Caecilius. They assumed that the
old writers were simply inept at 'mirroring life' – but
that is not what they were trying to do. They *tell* us
that we are going to see a New Comedy; in fact the
entertainment is a carefully rehearsed imitation not of
Life, but of a traditional extempore performance. In
Farce like that, the representers are only pretending to
be the represented; the representers are not simply the
actors, but The Types themselves, permanent residents of
Plautopolis, a theatrical place where theatrical behaviour
is normal. It is a charade in which the performers too
are characters, doing apparently spontaneously what they
think we think they think they ought to do in that
situation.

4. 1. 3. Terence entirely rejects this complex 'play'
between audience, representers, and represented. He thus
boldly denies us a whole essential aspect of the
entertainment we expect. But we spectators nevertheless
bring with us a litany of expectations about the proper
behaviour of the Young Lover, the Sensible Maiden, the
Filthy Villain, the Jolly Old Man, and all the rest.
Willy nilly Terence has to satisfy these if his play is
to work as a *palliata* at all. But the more he actively
exploits them – and he does – the less faithful is he to
the best qualities of Menander.

4. 1. 4. There are in fact two Terences. There is the
one, admired by Quintilian [48], preoccupied with adapting
form and style to render Menander more accurately than his
predecessors and succeeding, so that beyond and above the
basic typology and as a function of the style adopted,
Menander's characterization 'carries'. But there is also
the ambitious writer of a new kind of *palliata*. He thinks

that he can use his new style and form to write independently
of Menander but in the same spirit, developing character
more or differently, and integrating the fresh material in
a satisfying way. But this Terence is not quite up to it:
he simply reaches for what is in that wardrobe, and expects
it to pass as convincing.

4. 1. 5. We meet the first Terence mainly in his spoken
verse and sometimes in his chanted trochaic septenarii,
rarely elsewhere; the other may appear anywhere. Since
about five-sixths of Menander was in spoken verse but only
about half of Terence is in the equivalent form, one
important facet of characterization in Terence is the
metrical presentation of a role. As a rule of thumb, the
more a character 'sings' in the long metres, the more
impressionistic his presentation as a simple type; the more
he 'speaks', the more genuinely individual. In *Brothers*
there are highly significant differences between the different
characters in this matter of presentation; see Appendix III.
Here it should be emphasized that a prose translation of
Terence is bound to give a false impression of homogeneity
by sacrificing the variety of presentation overall and the
varying musical character of the roles in particular.

4. 2. 1. *Micio and Demea in Terence*. Micio's opening speech
quickly identifies him as 'Jolly Old Man', *senex lepidus* and
Demea as *senex durus*, 'Grumpy', and that is all there is to
it. We do not have to derive the reasons for their attitudes
from what we are told about the past, or even from particularly
close attention to what they say. The typological contrast
is strong, simple, and, for Terence's audience, needs no
exposition or further perspective.

4. 2. 2. Periplectomenus in Plautus' *Miles gloriosus* ('The
Boastful Soldier') was the most memorable incarnation of
senex lepidus in the *Palliata*, a sort of Falstaff-figure:
a bachelor on principle, he lives for himself, but helps
young lovers like a friend of their own age; love is *facere
sapienter*, 'good sense' to him; he is rich, urbane, gregarious,
adaptable, and he will even dance (*M.G.* 618-764). In short
he is an utterly un-Roman *boulevardier*. *Senex durus*, a
role apparently favoured in Caecilius, is simply the opposite
of all that.

4. 2. 3. In real life we Romans respect the old-fashioned
gravity of the strict father-figure. But at the theatre
we are not watching 'real life'; it is a holiday, we leave
that behind. We are 'for' *senex lepidus* and it will be
thanks to him that young love triumphs in spite of old
Grumpy. Or so we think for more than four-fifths of *Brothers*.

4. 2. 4. Micio and Demea play out these roles as far as
854. Everything seems settled, including Demea's
agreement to let Ctesipho keep his girl. Demea then puts
on Micio's cap, beats him at his own game, and is given
the last word. *Senex lepidus* is really a shallow fool,
true wisdom and right belong with *senex durus*. A bold
twist, quite against expectation. Farce here overturns
Farce, and bids us not to be silly. We have been
deceived into taking the wrong side throughout the play.
This is a dramatic ploy which could scarcely be repeated,
for it amounts to the rejection of the Saturnalian
premisses of the genre itself. See further pp. 49 ff.

4. 3. 1. *Aeschinus and Ctesipho in Terence.* Ctesipho is
simply the 'Young Lover' whose dominant trait is a lack
of a sense of proportion (*immodestia*). For in Comedy love
is not so much divine madness as amiable lunacy, which
causes the victim to over-react to everything and time
everything badly. His role is wholly musical. The
background to his affair *needs* no explanation, and we get
virtually none. As the conventional lover and deceiver
of *pater durus*, Ctesipho does not need sharper definition
and the question of the rightness or efficacy of Demea's
policy towards him is not examined. As a bijou Calidorus
(the lover in Plautus' *Pseudolus*) Ctesipho is merely a
source of good fun in himself and in the ironic contrasts
between what he is and what Demea wants to believe he is.

4. 3. 2. The Roman audience would have more difficulty
in pigeonholing Aeschinus. His presence is continuous in
that even when not on stage, he is the object of concern
in others. There are four phases to his presentation.

4. 3. 3. (i) For the first quarter of the play the questions
are, is this young man really going to be frank with Micio
about his escapade, and how is it compatible with the quality
implied by his name (αἰσχος, *pudor* 'consideration', 'respect')?
We assume with the cast that he has seized Sannio's girl
for himself; that shows daring and decisiveness unusual in
the lover, but is he a rake? Then (252 ff.) we learn that
he has been acting for Ctesipho, and that they are going to
confide in Micio in the certainty of his sympathetic aid.
That answers both questions, and illustrates the sort of
affection and commitment that ought to exist between brothers.
At the end of this sequence, we are to be thinking highly
of Aeschinus and Micio, and simple black and white are the
only pigments Terence has been using.

4. 3. 4. But then (288 ff.) (ii) Terence introduces the
theme of Pamphila and her baby, and that complicates things.
Aeschinus has violated her: that is bad. He has sworn to

stand by her: that is good. But he has been putting off
telling his father: that is bad but understandable and
arises from shame. So he is not what he seemed at all,
and even the idea of the raid is ascribed to Syrus (315,
368).

4. 3. 5. Micio too is wrong about Aeschinus' frankness.
But he is not as wrong as Demea is about Ctesipho, for he
did not start with the assumption that Aeschinus is an old
head on young shoulders. This is all getting complicated.

4. 3. 6. (iii) Aeschinus' second main appearance is very
unlike his first. Now he too is *adulescens amator*
displaying *immodestia* (610 ff.), but he is able to reason
himself out of consternation to a right decision,
acknowledging his own faults. In his ensuing encounter
with his father he displays shame, naiveté, strong feeling,
respect, remorse, joy, and extravagant admiration for
Micio's qualities as a man. Micio for his part does not
fail to give his son the sort of lecture that one does
not actually expect of *senex lepidus* (679-96). This is all
brilliantly portrayed as a real human relationship without
recourse to stereotype. But it is only after Micio has
departed that Terence gives editorial comment, and here
(707-12) he suddenly does fall back on stereotype, making
space available for what is to happen at the end of the
play. See the note *ad loc*.

4. 3. 7. For there (iv), Aeschinus is simply Spoilt Brat.
There is variety and surprise in all this, but scarcely
the consistently observed subject of an educational
experiment, or, except in 610-706, a convincing individual.

4. 4. 1. *Other roles*. For Sannio, see on 161, 197-208,
252-64; for Syrus, on 209-52; for Geta, on 299-326; for
Sostrata and Canthara, pp. 46-7.

5. The Exposition in Terence and Menander

5. 1. 1. *The Relevance of the Greek Original.* So far we
have attempted to make ourselves members of Terence's
audience ('The Roman Context of *Brothers*', pp. 16-26) and
to look at it from their point of view ('Character and
Stereotype in Terence', pp. 27-30) without reference to
the Greek original. But with limited success. It is not
so easy to think ourselves into a society in which the
principle of *patria potestas* affects personal life so
fundamentally and in which last year a ban was imposed on
the public teaching of rhetoric and philosophy, not to
mention again any of the other perplexities and difficulties.
Then there is the problem of the 'two Terences'; the highly
original artist who offends the conservative and pleases
others with his striking modifications of form and style
in his genre, and the writer of *palliatae* who not only
expects but shares with his audience very simple
categorical ideas about dramatic characterization.
Audience, play, and author remain out of focus. We turn
now to the original; determination of what Terence has
changed and (equally significant) what he has kept will
help us to understand all three better, and to say which
springs and cogwheels in Menander's clock have been
tampered with and how it worked (cf. 'The Action of Terence's
Brothers', pp. 10-15, and 'Menander's Scenario', pp. 58-64).
It is convenient as shorthand in this and the following
sections to refer to Menander's play simply by the line-
numbers of the corresponding passage of Terence and to its
characters by Terence's names, none of which except
possibly Aeschinus is likely to come from the original;
see p. 224 'Dramatis personae' and on 84 f.

5. 2. 1. *Exposition of the past in Terence.* 'And next,
the background to the play? No; it's the old fellows who
come on first who will partly expound...' (22 ff.): evidently
a formula (cf. Plautus *Trinummus* 16 f., *Vidularia* 10 f.),
itself implying that there *was* a narrative prologue in the
original; for proof of that, see below, p. 34. Terence
thinks that the only background of any significance is some
of what affects *senex lepidus* and *senex durus*, and has in
fact only made token compensation (40-7) for dropping the
narrative prologue of the original. This drastically affects
the way that even the faithfully translated parts of the
play come across, and for the worse. This is what we learn
as the play progresses:

26-39 Micio's son Aeschinus and his escort have been out
all night. The father, a rich man, is alarmed.

40–7 Micio is *senex lepidus*, his brother Demea *senex durus*.
Micio is a bachelor, Demea a widower (or divorced). Micio
has adopted Demea's elder son Aeschinus as a baby and

48–57 brought him up under an unconventionally liberal régime
with a view to winning the boy's affection and respect on
the basis of a frank relationship.

59–65 Demea does not approve of the method or its application:
Aeschinus is extravagant.

88–96 Demea reports that Aeschinus has shamefully abducted
a girl with whom he has been having an affair. Demea's
younger son Ctesipho is a paragon by contrast, mature and
hard-working.

103–5 Micio and Demea were poor when young and had no
opportunity to 'have a fling'.

149–53 Aeschinus has been drawing heavily on Micio's
uninquisitive generosity, apparently for a string of girls.
But recently this seemed to have stopped and Aeschinus had
brought up the subject of his marrying and settling down.
This had pleased Micio as a sign of approaching maturity;
evidently he was wrong.

194 The girl whom Aeschinus apparently loves is said by
him to be freeborn.

224 Her master has been meaning to leave for Cyprus very
soon, taking her and his *ménage* there with a view to
nefarious profit.

252 f. It is Ctesipho, not Aeschinus who loves the girl.

262 f. Aeschinus has been creating the impression that he
loves the girl to divert suspicion from his brother. For
how long is obscure, cf. 88–96, 149–53.

274 f. The crisis, whatever it was, caused Ctesipho to
contemplate leaving Athens (*in Menander, suicide; cf.
p. 263*). Aeschinus and Syrus found out almost too late.

287–98 Aeschinus has got the widow Sostrata's daughter
Pamphila pregnant; there is no man of the house; Aeschinus
has been a constant visitor and their only support. We
infer that Micio knows nothing about this (cf. 149–53, 629,
640, 684–95) and that his confidence in the frankness of
his relationship with Aeschinus is mistaken. We are given
no time to reflect on this second (cf. 252 ff.) correction
of our opinion of Micio's handling of Aeschinus.

307 It was a rape, as already hinted at 296.

315 Syrus instigated the abduction and apparent betrayal
(cf. 368, 967 f.).

329 Geta witnessed the abduction.

332-4 Aeschinus had approached Sostrata swearing that he
would commit suicide unless she would permit him to see
Pamphila, and that he would 'lay the baby on his father's
lap as he begged his blessing on his marriage to
Pamphila' (!).

347-50 Sostrata produces a ring which Aeschinus had 'lost'
(*not 'sent'; see on 347 and p. 36 f.*), i.e., when he
violated Pamphila: this will prove paternity in court if
necessary.

351 Pamphila has one distant male relative, Hegio, a
kinsman of her deceased father Simulus. (*In Menander Hegio
was Sostrata's brother, cf. p. 263*).

355 f. People are saying that Ctesipho was directly involved
in last night's *fracas* and this distresses Demea who puts
it down to Aeschinus' bad influence.

402 Demea is satisfied with Syrus' claim that he had earlier
set Ctesipho on the road home to the farm; this and 355 f.
show that in Menander Demea must have known that Ctesipho
was not at home 'last night' and that Ctesipho had given
him some worthy excuse for staying in town at his uncle's.

413 ff. Demea's method of educating Ctesipho - precept and
pattern.

438 ff. Hegio is the salt of the earth, a fellow-parishioner
of Demea, a lifelong friend.

455 ff. Simulus on his deathbed entrusted his wife and
daughter to Hegio's care and protection.

469-75 Aeschinus raped Pamphila, a stranger, at night when
drunk. When he 'found out what had happened' (!) (471)
he approached Sostrata on his own initiative and emotionally
begged her pardon, swearing he would marry Pamphila; Sostrata
gave him her forgiveness, consent, and trust, and agreed
to keep the pregnancy a secret. In Terence, we are to
understand that Hegio knew none of this until 'today'.

502 Hegio regards Demea and Micio collectively as prominent
and rich and as social superiors.

523 f. It is not far to Demea's farm.

529 Demea is not a recluse – he has quite a wide circle, including dependants and business-associates in town.

629 Aeschinus has not told his father the truth.

649 Sostrata and Pamphila have only moved next door recently.

809 Demea was prepared to take on the raising of two sons in the belief that by hard work and thrift he would be able to create an honourable patrimony for the two, and he has succeeded.

815 Micio's great wealth, on the other hand, was an unexpected windfall.

826 ff. Both Aeschinus and Ctesipho have good inborn dispositions.

867 Demea's marriage was a trial.

881 Demea is older than Micio.

931 Sostrata is well past having any more children.

938 Micio is sixty-four.

5. 3. 1. *The background to Aeschinus' affair.* This is communicated so haphazardly that no spectator could make clear sense of it, and it is incomplete. The inconsequential sequence of allusions (151, 287–98, 307, 332–4, 347–50, 469–75, 629, 649) would, however, be perfectly comprehensible as the complement to a prior narrative explaining:

(a) Aeschinus' drunken assault on Pamphila, a stranger, at a night-festival (the only occasion when a respectable young lady could be plausibly represented as out on her own), and her wresting a ring from him;

(b) her resulting pregnancy and how she and Aeschinus were brought into contact, the ring furnishing mutually satisfactory proof of identity and paternity;

(c) Aeschinus' confession to Sostrata;

(d) her agreement to keep things quiet for the sake of her daughter's reputation and to let Aeschinus broach his father;

(e) Aeschinus' subsequent good attention to Sostrata
and Pamphila, securing them accommodation next door, but

(f) his failure through guilt and shame to approach
his father except once recently when he raised the topic
of marriage in a general way.

5. 3. 2. It follows from this alone that there was an
expository prologue in Menander and that the above was one
coherent section of it (cf. p. 58 f.); also, that it
cannot have come as a surprise in Menander that it is
Ctesipho who loves the slave-girl (252 ff.).

5. 3. 3. As it is, Terence postpones our knowing anything
about Pamphila too long: this deprives the allusion at
151 to Aeschinus' interest in getting married of its proper
point, and entails two gratuitous switches in our view of
Micio's policy (252 ff., 287 ff.). The theme of rape is
insinuated most awkwardly (296, 307) and is only faced when
at last Hegio makes his accusations (467-77). Here
Terence glosses over how Aeschinus 'found out' (471), but
clearly the lost ring (347) is involved: it has the same
function as in *Hecyra* (574, 811 ff.) and in Menander's
Epitrepontes (455 ff.). Aeschinus is in exactly the same
position as Moschion at the beginning of Menander's *Samia*:
brought up by a kind and generous father, he cannot bring
himself to confess a base act.

5. 3. 4. Terence, observing that most of the story was
alluded to somewhere or other in Menander's script, and
evidently judging like a Plautus that the audience would
be satisfied with a very impressionistic treatment of the
background anyway, has simply dropped the prologue-account
without making any compensatory adjustments regarding
Pamphila. He overlooks the point that would occur to a
really Menandrian talent, that if a story is to be gradually
built up, the order in which its parts are revealed is of
paramount importance. What Terence offers is really only
the outward appearance of attention to dramatic perspective.
He is really being just as cavalier as Plautus, relying on
the comic typology itself to serve as a character's
introduction, and without the excuse that in Plautine farce
it does not matter if the plot does not 'hang together'.
This is incompatible with Terence's pretensions to Menandrian
qualities in other respects and is one fundamental flaw
in his whole approach; for throughout his career he had
made a point of dropping expository prologues without
adequately compensating [49].

5. 3. 5. His indifference is such that at first (332-4)
the arrangement with Sostrata is supposed to involve
Aeschinus' approaching Micio only *after* the birth of the

baby, if you please. Terence here evokes a sentimental
image of the Roman *paterfamilias*, son, and grandson, but
the more one thinks about it, the more tasteless it will
appear.

5. 3. 6. In the Greek play and later in Terence's (473, 629,
690 ff.) it is obvious that Aeschinus was meant to approach
his father as soon as possible, but has failed through guilt
and shame, though he has tried (151).

5. 3. 7. The discreditable and disturbing theme of rape was
more frankly prominent in Menander. Terence puts it out of
focus, but cannot simply dispense with it; it is essential
to the plot in the middle reaches of the play and by the
conventions of the *genre* no respectable young lady still
living with her mother could possibly be depicted as
willingly losing her chastity. So Terence greatly restricts
the domain of a leading idea in Menander's play - Aeschinus'
overwhelming shame that he has let his father down as a
person and his consequent deception of all those nearest him,
except perhaps Ctesipho. For the deception in Menander
included Sostrata and Pamphila, who have assumed that
obtaining Micio's consent presents no problem; also Hegio,
who, in the Greek play, was a necessary partner to the
arrangement in the first place, as will now be shown.

5. 4. 1. *Aeschinus, Sostrata, and Hegio.* Terence makes out
that there is no-one other than his own father that
Aeschinus should or could consult about Pamphila. Mother
and daughter are bereft of agnate relatives, and Hegio is
cognatus to Simulus and to his daughter (351, 494); by this
Terence means that the blood-tie only arises through some
female given in marriage and that Hegio does *not* descend
from the same source of *patria potestas* as Simulus and his
daughter. In Roman eyes, that kind of blood-relationship
is next to none; 'clan' is defined by the descent and
multiplication of *patria potestas* through male lines.
Again, Sostrata, Pamphila, and Hegio are each *sui iuris*,
'of his/her own right' (for what that is worth in their
straitened circumstances), for none of them has a
paterfamilias; and they are each *ultima/us suorum* 'last of
their line', the ends of three distinct 'clans' which
instead of thriving and multiplying through brothers
inheriting *patria potestas* have withered and shrunk. Among
the many odd effects of the Roman conception of *patria
potestas*, there is the paradox that a mother and daughter
in the position of Sostrata and Pamphila do not constitute
a family at all strictly speaking and personify the
extinction of two separate families.

5. 4. 2. This is all very pathetic and Terence is emphasizing
Sostrata's isolation and unfairly imposed responsibilities.

Hegio has no legal obligations to help either her or her
daughter: if he does, it will be for friendship and humanity
(350 ff., 459, 493 ff.). In particular, Terence has it
that Hegio has had no contact with them since Simulus died
and that the story of rape, pregnancy, and arrangement is
unpalatable news only learnt 'today' from Geta (447 ff.,
469 ff.). Sostrata acted on her own initiative in dealing
with Aeschinus.

5. 4. 3. But in real life Roman widows and fatherless girls
had to have a guardian (*tutor*) [50]; and Terence as good
as says that Hegio should be that person when he makes
Geta appeal to him so emotionally at 455 ff. But we are
not to think of him as such, for if we do, he must appear
negligent and Sostrata at fault for not involving him in
the arrangement. In Terence's 'Athens' women's
guardianship has as it were been repealed in the interests
of sentiment. This does not protrude as a difficulty,
because in Roman law there was a sharp distinction between
the powers of a *paterfamilias*, which were positive and
absolute, and those of his nominee, the guardian, which
were negative and relative. He was the indispensable
representative of a woman in litigation; but she was a
legal person in her own right, and he could not *tell* her
to do anything, only having powers of veto in certain areas.
The relative freedom of the Roman woman who was *sui iuris*
enables Terence to depict Sostrata taking the initiative,
and to divert attention from Hegio's strict legal
position to his moral goodness, thus appealing to Roman
sentiment.

5. 4. 4. But at Athens, a widow or fatherless girl was
subject to a 'master' (for such is the meaning of κύριος,
not 'guardian'). He would normally be the nearest male
kin of the deceased husband, or, failing that, of the
widow [51]. He had exactly the same positive authority
over his ward as a father or husband and a woman could
never be 'of her own right' as at Rome. Further, there
were no taboos at Athens on the marriage of kin as close
as half-brother and half-sister, but the Roman conception
of an incestuous union was much stricter. 'Master' at
Athens if a bachelor had the option to marry a
fatherless daughter himself, and the duty in any case to
arrange her marriage as her father would have done.
Menander criticizes this in *Aspis* [52], it is at the
heart of the plot in *Phormio*, and is the right which
Micio's imaginary 'friend from Miletus' proposes to
exercize at *Brothers* 650 ff. Romans will have regarded
Athenian ways here as shockingly incestuous and restrictive
of the right of a *paterfamilias* to dispose of his own just
as he chose by will.

5. 4. 6. In Menander, Hegio was Sostrata's brother (p. 263);
clearly therefore 'master' to both women and in line to
marry Pamphila if he chose (cf. on 652). Given the nature
of Athenian 'mastership', it is out of the question that
in Menander Hegio should appear *not* to have been involved
in the arrangement arrived at with Aeschinus; see on 471-7.
Thus item (d) (p. 34) in Menander's prologue must have
included mention of Hegio as guardian and a good man.

5. 5. 1. *Ctesipho's affair* is even more obscure; see p. 29.
Sannio's proposed trip to Cyprus (224, itself an 'unfair'
surprise to us) has precipitated a crisis demanding
selfless action from Aeschinus (274 f.) to prevent the
flight (in Menander, suicide) [53] of Ctesipho; the idea
is attributed to Syrus (315, 368, 967 f.); Ctesipho appears
as it were from nowhere (252), for at first he is supposed
not to have taken part himself and like the public at large
only to have heard this morning's 'talk of the town'. But
it is clear from 355 f. and 402 that in Menander both
brothers have raided Sannio's, and that Demea knew that
Ctesipho was not at home 'last night' and was supposed
to be safely tucked up in bed at Micio's.

5. 5. 2. One is left wondering about the duration of
Ctesipho's affair, how he has been able to hide it from
Demea, and where the money has been coming from. How
Menander dealt with the background to Ctesipho's affair
must remain a mystery, because Terence has undertaken major
surgery in the section where it was the principal theme
(155-287). Two pure guesses may be permitted. If in
Menander the brothers were identical twins whose mother
died in childbirth, this would help to explain the odd
circumstance unexplained in Terence, that Demea allows
Micio to adopt his *elder* son as a baby (47); it would add
point to the educational 'experiment'; and clothes-
swapping would be a useful way of hiding things from
Demea if the affair is supposed to have lasted any length
of time. Secondly, one misses in Terence any sign that
Ctesipho knows about his brother's predicament or has done
anything to help him- for his allusion to Aeschinus' having
neglected 'everything from his angle' (262) conveys nothing.
Yet something positive seems wanted to justify Micio's
assessment of the quality of the boys' *mutual* affection
and support (828). Perhaps Ctesipho was supposed somehow
to have been instrumental in identifying Pamphila to
Aeschinus? But in any case, Menander must have said
something about Ctesipho, and in clearer detail than is
suggested on p. 59 *faute de mieux*.

5. 6. 1. The Earlier Lives of Micio and Demea. In Terence,
the detail that Micio and Demea were once poor (103-5)
raises the question, how has Micio become so rich? There
is no answer to this except that it was not the result
of hard graft (815). And while Terence begins by allowing
us to think that if Micio is rich, then Demea must be poor,
it turns out that is wrong; Hegio reckons both brothers
socially above himself (500), Demea has dependants (529),
he employs labour (541), and he has made enough by his
honest efforts to provide amply for both his sons (809).

5. 6. 2. Terence takes it for granted that no *senex lepidus*
willingly marries, and confirms that axiom for us in his
version of the end of the play. But we know from Donatus
that in Menander Micio 'did not object'; on the significance
of this, see p. 56. But earlier in the play too Micio is
not quite the conventional bachelor on principle. At 28 ff.
he quotes conventional opinion about wives, but then
distances himself from the equally conventional estimate
of bachelorhood (43) and he did the same in Menander (p. 263
and note on 40-7); marriage seems the right thing for
Aeschinus (151); and the younger Demea did not see his
brother as set against marriage (811). Menander seems to
have been presenting us with a rich old bachelor who was
not positively averse to marriage: the rich old bachelor
Megadorus in Plautus' *Aulularia* (probably also from
Menander) is similar in his view of marriage.

5. 6. 3. In each case, Menander is characteristically
taking a conventional type and modifying it in one particular:
Demea, the *well-off* grumpy farmer; Micio, the rich old
bachelor who does not mind marrying the right person and
has 'socialist' views about the intermarriage of rich and
poor. It is easier to guess some of what Menander will
have said about the two in his prologue than in Ctesipho's
case (see p. 58), but the most peculiar *desideratum* in
Terence's treatment of the remote background is an
explanation of why and under what circumstances Demea ever
let Micio adopt a son of his, the elder son at that, when
still a small child. See the note on 40-7 and above,
p. 38.

5. 7. 1. The Place and Speaker of the Prologue. Expository
prologues in Menander come at the start (e.g. *Dyskolos*) or
after an initial scene engaging interest (e.g. *Aspis*). In
favour of the earlier place there is the point that having
heard the prologue we shall know that both fathers are
wrong and that will be ironical [*54*]. But against that
the quarrel-scene is constructed to engage and intrigue
us; we may well suspect that both fathers are wrong -

after all this is a comedy, and in Comedy fathers are
usually wrong. But we are not to be certain. Menander
meant us to share the doubts and puzzlement of Micio in
his important speech *'What he says is neither spot-on...'*
(141 ff.). In particular, the allusion at 151 to Aeschinus'
recent interest in marriage is clearly a cue for the
prologue-speaker to pick up ('You heard what he just said
about his wanting to get married? There's more to that
than our rich friend suspects...').

5. 7. 3. The opening lines of the play are masterly as an
opening gambit, unpreceded by anything, and have a truly
Menandrian economy and originality; compare the opening
of *Misoumenos*. Among other things, the reference to the
missing escort-staff cleverly foreshadows the return of
Aeschinus and these servants by the town side-entrance in
due course, so the essential arrangement in Menander was
like what we have in Terence: Aeschinus will have returned
with the 'minders' and the girl at 155 ff., accompanied
however not by Sannio as in Terence but his brother
Ctesipho as explained above.

5. 7. 4. The decisive point is that there must therefore
have been a break in the action at 154/5, for otherwise
Micio departing would meet Aeschinus arriving (the staging
in Terence is a problem: see on 155-96). That break,
however, cannot have been the first of the four 'for the
chorus', because these are already accounted for.
Consequently the break at 154/5 in Menander *must* have
accommodated a postponed prologue in iambic trimeters
about fifty lines long and dealing with the three topics
indicated on p. 58-9.

5. 7. 5. The only character in the play who *might* know
enough to deal with those three topics is Syrus. But it
is much more likely that Menander enlisted some relevant
god or abstraction (such as Φιλαδελφία, 'Brotherly Love',
Νοῦς 'Sense'; cf. p. 265), for the prologue-speaker has
to appear to have been an eavesdropper like ourselves,
able to comment on and explain what we have heard, and
only a spirit could do that.

5. 8. 1. *Act-divisions and Continuity in Menander*. We
are told that *Brothers* in Greek 'had like the others of
its genre a five-act structure with four intervals for
the chorus, and that for the sake of keeping their
unsophisticated audiences, Roman comedians avoided
distinguishing these lest the inattentive spectator should
take the end of an act as a hint and excuse to go home' (!)
[55]. 'Nevertheless', Donatus goes on, 'these act-divisions

have been marked in Terence by the Roman scholars of olden
time', and he then states where they come. This
corresponds to the act-division found in part of the Mss.
tradition and followed by printed editions except for
equally inept differences in the placing of the end of
'Act IV'. This Roman act-division combines ignorance with
pedantry and immediately goes wrong by identifying 154/5
as the end of 'Act I'; see p. 10.

5. 8. 2. The *entr'actes* in Menander were organic in that
they could conveniently represent the passage of time
where necessary, that they gave each act a certain
aesthetic unity of theme and arrangement, and that they greatly
assisted a dramatist in his deployment of a troupe of three
actors whose task it was to wear the masks and costumes
of perhaps a dozen characters.

5. 8. 3. Though the stage is momentarily empty also at
354/5, 516/7, 591/2, 609/10, 786/7 (as happens commonly
enough in Menander) there is no just doubt about the 'parts'
of Menander's play:

> Part 1: Exposition with embedded prologue (26-287)

> Part 2: Complication (Pamphila's baby) (288-510)

> Part 3: Deception, error, enlightenment (511-712)

> Part 4: Resolution (713-854)

> Part 5: Demea's 'revenge', double wedding (855-997)

5. 8. 4. If Terence's play is to be played literally
continuously difficulties of staging arise at 154/5, 510/1,
and 854/5. These are of kinds well known *passim* in Roman
Comedy [56]: A departing fails to notice B coming by the
same route, too little time is left for an off-stage
conversation, the script seems to indicate the same
character leaving and then immediately returning. But
Donatus' assertion quoted above should not be taken too
literally: there are definite examples of musical and
other interludes positively indicated in Plautus' scripts,
e.g. at *Pseudolus* 573 *a*, and we do not know that these
could not be intended elsewhere too.

5. 8. 5. The primary articulation of the *Palliata* was in
any case musical as indicated in the summary (pp. 10-15).
As for the English translation, ways around the
difficulties at 154/5 and at 854/5 are suggested in the
stage-directions, but the only thing to do at 510/1 is
to have a definite interval, making a two-acter of the
whole.

5. 8. 6. No problem of continuity arises in Terence at 287/8, because what Geta subsequently claims to have witnessed is the actual abduction of the girl from her master (328 f.). But that must be Terentian rhetoric; what was Geta doing wandering around Athens in the middle of the night? In Menander, it seems that what Geta was supposed actually to have seen was the *sale* of the girl involving Sannio, Micio, Aeschinus, and Syrus in the market. Thus what in Terence is strictly inference by Geta and Sostrata, that Micio has no intention of letting Aeschinus marry Pamphila, will have appeared in Menander as an evident fact from his presence and approval at the sale itself. It is the sale which is subsequently emphasized throughout (369 f., 406, 477, 628, 742 ff., 800, 967). This, however, requires the sale to be located specifically in the interval at 287/8; so in Menander all the act-breaks except the one at 712/3 marked the necessary passage of time.

5. 8. 7. It is instructive to consider the very different ways in which Terence has tackled each of the five Menandrian acts in terms of fidelity and of metrical presentation. This is left to the reader; cf. the summary (pp. 10-15) and the Scenario (pp. 58-62).

5. 9. 1. *Number of Actors*. Scenes involving four, five, or even six full actors (not just 'extras') are not exceptional in the *Palliata* (e.g. Plautus *Poenulus* and *Casina* in their latter scenes) so that while 'doubling' of roles by the same actor may have been practised as convenient, it will scarcely have been necessary to have two actors splitting a role between them. There was obviously no rule limiting the size of troupes, and the native Roman tradition, dependent on the Atellane farce [57] and like entertainments, was evidently like our own or the Italian *Commedia* in its principle 'one part, one player'; but, as in Elizabethan drama, there were no female players.

5. 9. 2. In New Comedy, on the other hand, playwrights do seem to have been limited to the services of three full actors (all male) and 'extras' who could say the odd line on (786) or off (486). This was the convention in Tragedy; Old Comedy had been freer. The weaker evidence for the three-actor rule in Menander is that all the extant Menander *could* be staged by a company of three if we assume that roles were sometimes 'split'. Odd and alien as this seems, it was certainly resorted to in Tragedy. The stronger evidence is, firstly, that the victory-lists of the troupes playing Menander and others in the 3rd c. B.C. at dramatic festivals regularly name just three actors and a musician as if it went without saying that all New

Comedy could be put on this way [58]; secondly, that the
scenes in Roman Comedy where four or more actors are
required are generally suspect of being adjustments of
the Greek model for some other contingent reasons. This
affects three of the roles in *Brothers*; for Syrus' part
in the last act, see p. 240, for the continuity at 354/5
and Canthara's role, see p. 46 f.; the third is Sannio's
role, to which we now turn.

5. 10. 1. *The Scene from Diphilus (155-96)* [59] Among
Terence's alterations of Menander's *Brothers*, the best
known is his use of a scene from Diphilus' *Partners in
Death*, because it is the only one he admits to (6-14).
This is in fact not the most important, and is intimately
connected with his omission of the prologue and cannot
be appreciated in isolation from that; the invitation to
the audience to evaluate what he has done (4-5, 12-14) is
of course mere flattery.

5. 10. 2. The issue as presented is one of specific
sources, and Terence's real concern is to avoid a
repetition of the controversy of the previous year
involving charges of plagiarism from older Latin sources
(see p. 4). But what he or Ambivius Turpio on his behalf
chooses to say is both misleading and irrelevant to the
question what difference the Diphilus-material makes to
Menander's original. The scene in question (155-96) is
elaborate Roman recitative mainly in iambic octonarii,
a medium which Terence never uses elsewhere for
'rendering word for word' (11) in the way that he does
in senarii or trochaic septenarii, so even that must
be taken *cum grano salis*. Nor is the scene an addition;
it replaces Menandrian material and involves consequent
adjustments of dramaturgy in the sequel, of which one
sign is the need for four actors in the last part of
the sequence (265 ff.).

5. 10. 3. It is clear how the sequence *began* in
Menander: after the prologue, Aeschinus has to come back
by the town entrance along with various extras representing
his escort as foreshadowed in Menander in the opening lines
of the play (26 f.). Terence would have done better to
keep the same name for the 'minder in chief' in both places,
26 and 168, either Storax or Parmeno. He also has to have
the girl with him, probably a non-speaking part as in
Terence; and he is accompanied by or immediately followed
by his brother Ctesipho, who in Menander took part in the
escapade (355 f., 402; p. 38). That probably rules out
Sannio at this stage: the brothers were represented as
escaping with their prize, confident that they would find

Micio at home, and that he would harbour them and pay
Sannio off when all is explained (cf. 364 ff.). Whether
instigator or not, Menander's Syrus cannot have been one
of those returning; he has to be at home to explain to
Aeschinus that Micio has gone out looking for him and he
has to appear to Sannio as one who definitely had no hand
in the raid and whom Sannio thinks he can perhaps make his
ally. Clearly in Menander the thing to do was to get the
raiders indoors as quickly as possible. Only then should
an angry Sannio turn up ('Ah, here's the place...' and
after a monologue different in substance from 196-208,
which is Terence's handiwork, be confronted by Syrus much
as he is in Terence (209 ff.).

5. 10. 4. It is also clear that the whole sequence has to
end as it does in Terence at 287 with the departure
together of Aeschinus, Sannio, and Syrus on their way to
find Micio in town and settle (cf. 364 ff.). That rules
out the presence of Ctesipho in the latter part of the
sequence: that would require four actors.

5. 10. 5. Menander's *dramaturgic* plan is therefore clear
enough; what must remain obscure is the *dramatic content*
of the conversation at the start between the two brothers
and of Sannio's entrance monologue.

5. 10. 6. The main difference in Terence is the postponement
of Ctesipho's entrance and the anticipation of Sannio's;
and rendering the whole as lively recitative, Terence is
clearly aiming at variety, spectacle, and a strong contrast
with the content and.presentation of the quarrel-scene.
The main effects of his changes are:

(i) to increase the length but scarcely to improve
the quality of the villain's role, see on 161, 197-208,
228-35, 252-64;

(ii) to introduce a 'number' popular in the older
palliata, 'Nasty Villain Tries It On', cf. Plautus *Rudens*
706 ff. (also from Diphilus); there was no violence in
Menander;

(iii) to draw as strong as possible a contrast between
an active and masterful Aeschinus and a more juvenile
Ctesipho; but first

(iv) to mislead us into thinking that Aeschinus is
the lover and to postpone the Pamphila-theme;

(v) to put Ctesipho's affair out of focus, as of no
interest in itself; and

(vi) to introduce as climax to the Diphilus-insertion an ultimatum involving the status of the girl, who is said to be free for this purpose; see on 193. This probably 'hangs over' from Diphilus, and is certainly irrelevant to Menander.

6. The Middle of the Play: Menander, Acts II-IV

6. 1. 1. *Fidelity*. Terence's extensive alterations of
Menander's exposition and dramatic form at the beginning
of the play naturally have effects pervasively in the
sequel, some major (the presentation of Aeschinus and
Ctesipho), some middling (the status of Hegio), some minor
(what Geta has seen); he now becomes steadily more faithful
to the substance of Menander, and renders the whole of his
fourth act (713-854) with close adherence not only to its
substance but also to its uniform metre (iambic senarii
throughout for trimeters); therefore, to its pacing and
characterization as well. There are, however, other
changes of substance and form in what precedes.

6. 2. 1. *Menander Act II* (288-510). Terence's aim in the
Sostrata-scene (288-354) is to set off the consciously
Plautine extravagance and humour of his running slave
'number' (see on 299-326), which is excellent, against a
sentimentalizing presentation of the good and lonely lady
in reduced circumstances which is less appealing. The
stereotype to which he here turns is not the traditional
matrona of Plautine and Caecilian comedy (cf. his *Plocium*)
[*60*] - that is evoked later when Micio is forced into
marriage, 939 - but the tragic heroine as portrayed by
Ennius and Pacuvius; hence her command of rhetoric (330-4,
341-50). The type is best represented for us by Plautus'
presentation of Alcumena in his 'tragicomedy' *Amphitruo*.

6. 2. 2. Tragic heroines have faithful retainers; and
Terence appears to have given her two by inventing the
role of the nurse Canthara, rendering in dialogue what
were probably two deliberative speeches in Menander
(288-97, 330-50) in which we heard Sostrata bring herself
from emotional alarm to rational self-control and decision
in the same way as Micio in 26 ff. and Aeschinus at 610 ff.
In Menander, Sostrata was to be a good match for Micio;
it was to be a marriage of true minds, not a farcical
punishment.

6. 2. 3. Canthara's mission to fetch a midwife (353) is
odd. She fails to return, there is no midwife, the baby
is safely delivered by Sostrata (486), and both older
women have been introduced at 288 f. as capable anyway.
What is first offered as a reason why Canthara cannot go
to fetch a midwife, the absence of Geta, turns out to be
no reason, for Geta too is despatched, to fetch Hegio (350).

6. 2. 4. Canthara has no real *raison d'être* in the
Sostrata-scene except as a partner to the dialogue and as
a visual foil to Geta. In Terence, that is justification
enough, but scarcely in Menander, for she has too much to
say to count as a mere 'extra'; and if she figured as a
speaking role in Menander, a fourth actor will be required
to play Demea in 355 ff., for there was no act-break at
354/5 (see p. 40 f.). It follows that Terence has created
her role; cf. the cases of Sosia in *Woman of Andros*, and
(probably) of Antipho and Dorias in *The Eunuch*.

6. 2. 5. But Canthara has a vital function in the sequel:
according to Terence, it is through her that Aeschinus
learns that Sostrata has misinterpreted his behaviour and
no longer trusts him (616 ff.).

6. 2. 6. There is slight awkwardness there too: Terence
makes Aeschinus begin his account 'For when she had been
sent off to the midwife...' in words that suggest that
he already knew or could somehow tell by looking what she
was up to; it would certainly have been better to say,
e.g., 'when I saw her looking agitated outside the
midwife's...' or the like [61].

6. 2. 7. It has been plausibly suggested that in Menander
Sostrata sent Geta both to fetch Hegio and to get the
midwife. This is attractively economical, but a difficulty
is that the midwife-theme requires the messenger to be
located in the market, while Hegio lives in the country -
as a fellow-parishioner of Demea (439) he naturally has
to enter from there (435-46).

6. 2. 8. The less of that midwife the better; and a way
of accounting for Geta's leaving one way for town at 353
and returning by the other from the country at 447 is
suggested in the Scenario (p. 60) in the form of the
instructions given to Geta by Sostrata at the end of the
scene. This would locate his encounter with Aeschinus
during the scene between Demea and Syrus (355-434), an
encounter he has comically anticipated (318).

6. 2. 9. In the brilliant scenes in senarii which follow
(355-510) Terence is for the first time since 154 closely
following Menander. For though the Roman audience
understands that Hegio has been told the whole 'sordid
story' for the first time at 447 ff. and Terence has
adjusted his kinship and legal position regarding the
women, that scarcely affects the wording of the text.

6. 3. 1. *Menander Act III* (511-712). Terence is at his
most various in his metrical treatment of the central
section of Menander's play, but this does not entail mere
expansion: he has preserved the pacing, tone, and substance
most admirably. A change of detail at 616 ff. has been
noted above (p. 47), and there is a probable shift of
emphasis at the very end (see p. 30 and the note on 707-12).
There is only one real blemish in the handling of this act.
In contrast with the high quality of invention and
execution elsewhere, the scene in which Micio and Hegio
return from town and enter Sostrata's house is weak in its
substance, the balance of its emphases, and its ethical
focus; see the note on 592-609. The passage is in iambic
octonarii, a metre reserved elsewhere by Terence for places
where he is substantively departing from Menander; and in
the Scenario it is suggested that here Terence has cut the
dialogue. For the theme of Micio's discovering from Hegio
that he is mistaken about Aeschinus' frankness is not made
explicit; and if Micio is to marry Sostrata willingly,
this is the place for him to ask her guardian's formal
permission, as Leo seems to have observed [*62*]. See pp.
57, 61.

6. 4. 1. *Menander Act IV* (713-854); Terence's fidelity and
execution here is like that in the quarrel-scene and both
scenes between Syrus and Demea; Terence and Menander both
at their best. This is the approach which Quintilian
admired in Terence and wishes he had practised all the time
(cf. p. 7). The only points of obscurity arise at 809 ff.,
where the allusions to the remoter past lack focus without
the backing of Menander's prologue; and if the suggestion
that Micio has already in Act III broached the subject of
marrying Sostrata is correct, there is additional irony
in Micio's encounters with first Aeschinus (Act III) and
then Demea (Act IV).

7. Micio, Demea, and the Ends of the Two Plays

7. 1. 1. *Micio and Demea in Menander*, 26-854. We have
briefly considered the fathers as types of the traditional
Palliata, p. 28 f.; and observed that Terence has made a
special point of rendering Demea's part in 26-854 very
faithfully, even to the preservation of his metrical
presentation in spoken verse and trochaic recitative
(p. 24); Micio's too, except for 40-7, 68-77 (p. 22 f.
and notes *ad loc.*), 592 ff. (p. 48 and note *ad loc.*),
and the form of the verdict passed on him at 707-12
(p. 30 and note *ad loc.*); this fidelity extends to a
significant detail of linguistic characterization (see
on 683). But by deleting the prologue and only making
token compensation for this (40-7) Terence has put the
brothers' earlier lives out of perspective and is content
to rest on a schematic opposition of types, in the first
place as *senex lepidus* and *durus*, with, at the start,
the hint that there is a philosophical dimension to the
contrast as well: cf. p. 16 f., 22 f., and the note on
26-40.

7. 1. 2. Thus Micio 'stands for' the Quiet Life, Demea
the Active; Micio has a general theory of education and
so by implication has Demea; and general theories of
education imply definite views about human nature. But
these 'philosophical' dimensions to the characters have
been given prominence in the first scene by Terence,
not Menander; the quarrel in the play is about particular
cases, and the conflict in 26-854 is not in fact between,
so to speak, a pair of walking ideas, as it might be in
Shaw or Brecht, but between basically different
temperaments.

7. 1. 3. In the opening scenes we see Micio display
anxiety controlled by reason; detachment; foresight;
self-knowledge; caution, and the capacity to dissemble;
that is, the qualities which distinguish men from animals
- *humanitas*, intelligence at work. From a Greek point
of view, he is the representative not of any particular
'ism' but of the thinking man, the philosophical type.
Demea comes off badly by contrast: prejudiced, naive,
mean, the victim rather than the master of his passions.
We are not even sure that he loves Ctesipho, and it is
left open how bad the relationship is (107 ff.).

7. 1. 4. In our subsequent encounters with Micio in
28-854 this impression of humane intelligence is
consistently maintained (though see p. 51 for another
view). It turns out that he too is wrong about his
son's frankness, but he is less wrong than Demea, for he

starts with a less false and not uncritical estimate of
his son's character; and Micio's reaction to learning the
truth about Aeschinus is more impressive than the emotional
Demea's to learning about Ctesipho. In his encounter with
Aeschinus Micio displays forbearance, tact, intelligence,
and firmness (680 ff.), and real communication takes place,
though Terence, having let this happen by following Menander
exactly in 635 ff., subsequently implies that it has not
(707 ff.).

7. 1. 6. But Demea is consistently depicted as lacking the
essentially intellectual qualities which constitute
humanitas and it is a leading theme that we are always a
step ahead of him (81 ff., cf. 60 ff.; 548). He may be
a fool, but Menander modifies the first impression that
he may also be a villain. He evidently really does care
about Ctesipho (355 ff., 379 ff., 395 ff., 411 ff., 435 ff.,
533 f., 553 ff.) and the boy does not in fact hate him
(519); he is, however, excessively afraid of him. Demea
is transparently honest and pertinacious and he has
successfully made his own way by his own hard graft and
by taking on the commitments that conventional opinion
approves. He is no misanthrope (529), and he has his own
mirror and example to look into in the person of Hegio.
But, ironically, success has lifted him out of the class
he admires and whose 'image' he cultivates. For if he
was a peasant once, he is no longer, having dependants
(529), employing labour (541) and having made a substantial
fortune (809 ff.); his friend regards him not as a peasant
at all, but a rich and powerful person (500 ff.). He is
like a fervent Marxist – whose mortgage is paid off; you
know the type. He is neurotic, constantly worrying about   ·
things that he cannot control. He means well, but his
values are unorganized, and he depends heavily on what
other people are going to say as his criterion for right
and wrong (91 ff., 412 ff., 734 ff.). Thus his theory of
education turns out to be no theory at all (see on 414),
and when Demea is right, it is by accident, because his
life is unexamined: doing the right things 'by number'
is not to understand why they are right. He is not very
intelligent: it is a nice touch that on both occasions
that Syrus fools him, the deception begins with his
accepting something Syrus says which is in fact illogical
(see on 406, 561).

7. 1. 7. Such is the real character invented by Menander
and preserved as a function of faithful translation in
Terence. A worse Greek dramatist might have just given
us a villain. But in watching Terence a large part of the

audience is not going to notice the subtleties; they will
simply see him as *senex durus*, and interpret him
schematically. After all, the 'other Terence' (p. 31) is
giving them plenty of encouragement to take that line.
A real character like Menander's might be portrayed as
deciding to change his life-style; but he cannot change
what God has given him by way of brains, any more than
he can change his height.

7. 1. 8. In Terence's last act, Demea is vindicated and
Micio humiliated. Supposing for the sake of the argument
that the same happened in Menander, one can see that there
is enough 'good' in the Demea of 26-854 to make that
plausible in principle. But is there the intelligence?
The Demea of 26-854 simply lacks the qualities of
judgement and objectivity essential for the true and wise
guru. Yet Terence suddenly lends him authority and wisdom
at the beginning of the last act (855-60, 985 ff.). In
Menandrian terms, there is a severe problem of psychological
continuity in this. But in the *Palliata*, psychological
continuity is at no premium.

7. 1. 9. In Micio's case, Terence makes out that he is a.
humbug; Donatus, seeing the problem in this, finds moral
fault in Micio at 803 (see *ad loc.*). Several recent
critics of the play have gone much further in moralistic
criticism of Micio in 26-854, failing to distinguish
adequately between the aesthetics appropriate to New
Comedy and to the *Palliata*. Their aim is to find 'faults'
in Micio which would correspond to the 'good points' in
Demea and thus prepare ground for the reversal of favour
at the end. In this way they try to show that Terence's
alterations at the end need not be seen as very extensive
or regrettable. This is in reaction to the view of Rieth
(1964) who argued that in Menander Micio and Demea
respectively embodied the virtues of the Mean and vices
of Excess and Defect as seen by the school of Aristotle;
a view which obviously implies that Terence has radically
changed the ending of Menander's play, though Rieth could
not suggest how it actually did end. Specious support for
the idea that there was some sort of vindication of Demea
and mockery of Micio in the *finale* has been found in the
'conversion' which the misanthropic Knemon undergoes in
Menander's *Dyskolos* and the farcical ending of that play;
where, however, it must be pointed out that it is the
character of the comedy that changes, not the ethos and
continuity of Knemon's intellect and personality [*63*].

7. 1. 10. Micio has accordingly been accused of long-
windedness, of being dogmatic and arrogant, of having a
'cruel streak' which shows in his tricking Aeschinus

and later Demea (719 ff.), of failing to tell Demea the
truth about Ctesipho at the first opportunity (723 ff.)
and especially (so already Donatus) for agreeing to harbour
Ctesipho and pay Sannio after their agreement not to
interfere with each other's responsibility, and of evasion
and flippancy when faced with this. It is only necessary
to read the script to determine how plausible this is [64].

7. 2. 1. *Micio's views in Menander*. Terence has modified
Micio in 26-854; in an early and memorable passage, he
appears the advocate of liberality towards *all* children,
and not just children (see on 68-77; pp. 16-18), a view
which is not strictly compatible with what he says later
on (820 ff.). Further Terence only has Aeschinus praise
Micio at 707 ff. as a conveniently Periplectomenoid father-
figure of a paradoxical but convenient kind (cf. p. 30).
What views did Micio hold in Menander?

7. 2. 2. First, the aim of life is pleasure and the
minimizing of care. The wise man will avoid unnecessary
commitments. He will value wealth as a means, not an end.
But man is a social creature and the highest pleasure is
in friendship. The logic of this is that the wise man will
avoid being a father or educator. The best children are
a hostage to fortune and a worry. If one needs an heir
one can always adopt a young man of good health whose
upbringing has been someone else's worry [65].

7. 2. 3. Micio has taken the apparently illogical step of
adopting Aeschinus as a baby and bringing him up himself.
This is worth the worry and expense because Micio sees a
favourable disposition in the child and calculates that
if he succeeds in making the boy his friend he will get
more pleasure in the long run; i.e., he should aim at
making himself redundant *qua* father-figure. For a family
should be a 'society of friends', a microcosm of the
ideal community in which 'friends say not mine and thine
but ours'. Thus Micio will end his days in the enjoyment
of a true and equal friendship with a loving son; Demea
risks frustration and isolation. So much from the
'selfish' point of view.

7. 2. 4. Second, as to how much and what an educator can
do. There are good and bad dispositions, genetically
determined. The child with a good natural disposition
arrives with a certain potential for discrimination and
will incline to affection, respect, generosity, and the
other virtues. This is essential if one is to grow up to
be truly 'human', but it is not given to all, and one
cannot make a silk purse out of a sow's ear: *pudor doceri
non potest, nasci potest*, 'consideration for others is
born, not taught' [66]

7. 2. 5. There are also bad dispositions. The father or
educator has to estimate what he is dealing with from
'signs', like a stockbreeder dealing with foals or puppies.
Not everyone is adept at reading the signs. The educator
himself must be fully 'human', and recognize that his role
is limited. He cannot create virtue in a vicious
disposition, and the best he can do for a good disposition
is to work with nature rather than against it by providing
the best conditions for growth and development. Even so,
being human, the educator can make mistakes as well as the
pupil and he is in for a lot of worry.

7. 2. 6. On a homoeopathic principle, the good disposition
will respond to affection, respect, and liberality, and
that is best, because it will foster a frankness in the
child's relationship that is desirable in all its
relationships, and because, being naturally resilient, the
good disposition should be exposed to as wide a range of
experience as possible rather than be protectively closeted.
For, like any young animal of mettle, the child is eager
for experience and experiment, and will learn from them.
It will be worrying and expensive and mistakes are likely,
but they will be useful mistakes. Therefore Micio's self-
interest and the best kind of education from a social point
of view coincide in his treating Aeschinus with liberality.

7. 2. 7. A child with a good disposition may turn out well
in spite of accidental limitations such as poverty or lack
of understanding, but there is a risk that it may be
perverted and become bad: the educator cannot create a
good disposition, but he can destroy it.

7. 2. 8. The naturally bad child cannot be reformed. For,
lacking the capacity to respond to kindness, it will simply
take advantage when it is offered. Because of its inherent
weaknesses, the very experiences which will be profitable
to the robuster good disposition are likely to confirm the
propensities of the bad. The only thing to do with children
like that is to restrict their scope to do harm to themselves
and others and to treat them with a tiresomely constant
vigilance and the threat of punishment; no fun for anyone,
and ineffective anyway, as soon as you turn your back. But
that is not the case with Aeschinus or Ctesipho.

7. 2. 9. Third, we should distinguish the signs of a
naturally good disposition, which are as it were constants,
e.g., Aeschinus' blush (643), from the interpretations which
we put upon behaviour; age is a variable here. We are all
subject to different faults of excess or defect at different

ages, and there is a definite pattern in this. The young
are in general too careless about money and the old too
stingy. The young seek sexual adventure and attempt to
hide this from their parents, who for their part have said
goodbye to all that and never expect *their* sons to deceive
them. The good disposition will come with time to see that
there is a mean to be observed. It is no good preaching at
them, and the educator must have self-knowledge. He must
remember what it was like to be young, and make allowance
for faults of perspective associated with his own age.
It is difficult to get the balance right, but especially
for the young.

7. 2. 10. In Micio's view, Demea is wrong in failing to
make these allowances, in thinking that all children should
be dealt with in the way that some have to be *faute de
mieux*, and in supposing that virtue can be taught at all
by direct precept or exemplification. It is a tender
plant that can be stimulated to grow from its own natural
root and fathers have less positive control over this than
they commonly think; they should give it room to grow, and
when it has reached maturity, they should stop being its
proprietor, and not imagine that they created it anyway.

7. 2. 11. This is a coherent view of human nature and
education which is in some respects critical of Athenian
family life in Menander's day. It favours a conception
of the family as a microcosm of the ideal state, which is
not a tyranny, oligarchy, or a democracy but a 'society of
friends'. Menander will scarcely have offended a
sophisticated Athenian public with ideas like these. But
at Rome in 160 B.C. they would appear frankly Epicurean,
and, worse, at odds with Roman axioms about the nature and
duration of fatherly authority. A Roman is either a
paterfamilias himself or subject to one; this has nothing
in principle to do with reaching a certain age or marrying
or having children of one's own and depends on the accident
of deaths. To become a *paterfamilias* confers status and
powers on a man ready or not, and corresponding
responsibilities which last for life. So in Roman minds
the very idea of individual freedom and maturity within
the family structure as advocated by Micio will have been
inextricably tangled with reverential ideas about
paternalistic authority and responsibility. The true
Roman father will be anxious to see that 'his own' are
ready and able to inherit and multiply his status when he
dies, but a father's job is never done, and he should not
demean it by trying to break out of the role. That is the
way things are. If fathers were really like Micio, it

would undermine all respect and order in society. This
is really why Micio has to be condemned in Terence.
Senex lepidus can say all that as a Greekling, but it is
not to be endorsed as true; it is *senex durus* who takes
his job seriously that we should approve.

7. 3. 1. *The End of the Play in Terence.* At 855 ff. we
are suddenly bidden rather than persuaded to change our
conception of both characters. In 26-854 Demea has been
the Fool; now he is suddenly the Wise Man invested with
philosophical *grauitas* (855-60). Micio, the man who
seemed wise, is in fact a malignant parasite (861-76).
Very well, Demea will give up his harsh life (859-60) in
a bid to win back the boys' alienated affections by
fighting Micio with his own weapons (877-81). *Senex
durus* is going to become *senex lepidus*.

7. 3. 2. This is offered as a long-term strategy (859-60,
881), and Terence complicates things with a typically
heavy irony (cf. 197-208): when Demea says his lesson
learnt today is that 'nothing is better for a person than
affability and mildness' (861), he does not mean in
themselves or for the good of the boys, but for courting
selfish popularity. There is a sombre nihilism in this
and a sentimental, Chaplinesque appeal to the emotions:
'Forget your principles, nothing matters more than winning
the boys' affection': the end justifies the means. This
scarcely belongs to the domain of Farce at all, let alone
New Comedy. We are simply being told that the worse cause
has only seemed the better.

7. 3. 3. Equilibrium is quickly restored after this uncertain
wobble: in the sequel (882-985) Demea is the Wise Man as
redefined pretending to be the Fool as redefined finally
revealing himself again as Wise Man in the final speech
(985-997). His ploy has three results: he wins back his
sons' affection, he takes vengeance of Micio, and vindicates
his own outlook on life as the right one. Corresponding
to the results there are three ill-assorted motives. The
first is pathetic: he changes *strategy* to compete on a
long-term basis for his sons' affection. In fact there is
no contest (911). The last is didactic: he has changed to
teach us a lesson. In between, Demea is taking malicious
pleasure at Micio's discomfiture (915, 958); and that
corresponds to a third motive - spite. Two of these
motives are incompatible, while the other, much the simplest
and best, is kept in the background as unworthy of the Wise
Man; but it is clearly there.

7. 3. 4. A man can change his opinions, like Knemon in
Menander's *Dyskolos*, or change his opinions *and* his
behaviour, like Scrooge in *A Christmas Carol*. Nor is there
difficulty in a man *pretending* to change his mind for an
ulterior purpose or even several, as Demea does in 855 ff.
But the reasons in Terence are too many and seem incompatible.
The real problem of continuity here in *Brothers* is not the
awkwardness internal to 855-997, but the premiss leading
to the whole sequence, that Demea has suddenly become wise
and that Micio is the fool. This only works, if it works,
as a deliberate surprise, exploiting our conceptions of
senex lepidus and *durus* in the traditional *Palliata*, and
involves Terence in twice stepping outside the proper limits
of his genre to initiate and then terminate an episode of
Saturnalian farce excellent in itself but aimed at showing
that we have all been hoodwinked by what went before.
This is unique in the *Palliata* and worlds away from the
New Comedy of Menander.

7. 4. 1. *The End of the Play in Menander*. Ignoring the
incompatible sentimental and didactic motives ascribed to
Demea in Terence, we are left with spite; and that is
excellent and sufficient for Demea 'the Fool'. Demea's
plan involves uniting Micio's and Sostrata's dwellings,
getting him to marry Sostrata, and giving financial help
to Hegio. These go together as a malicious application
to Micio of his own proposal that henceforth the brothers
should share and share alike: 'friends say not mine and
thine but ours'. By *reductio ad absurdum*, this is a licence
for Demea to give away what Demea thinks Micio holds most
precious – his independence as a bachelor.

7. 4. 2. Syrus' presence in the *finale* must be ascribed to
Terence; his presence (882 ff., 958 ff.) entails four
actors, cf. p. 42 f. For Menander's dramaturgy, see the
Scenario, p. 62 and the notes on 882-8, 911-5. Terence
has evidently transferred the theme of deserved manumission
from Geta to Syrus. This gives rise to excellent topsyturvy farce, but farce which crucially depends on Micio's
unwillingness to cooperate, and that theme is entirely
Terence's. It incidentally leaves Demea's promise to 'see
Geta right' unfulfilled (896), though of course it is Geta
who has really impressed Demea.

7. 4. 3. Now we know that in Menander Micio 'did not complain'
at the suggestion that he should marry Sostrata (Donatus
on 938, see p. 264 and on 934-46). The full implications
of this are important:

(i) **If** Micio did not complain, he **must** *at least*
have said 'Not a bad idea!' or (better) 'Yes, I'd thought
of that already!

(ii) Similarly with the suggestion about help for
Hegio.

(iii) Either way, there is no room for the portrayal
of a rift between Aeschinus and Micio, and without that,
there is no scope for a humiliation of Micio, or a
vindication of Demea.

(iv) Either way Demea's ploy falls flat; its point
is to make Micio do things he is really unwilling to do,
whatever his motives.

7. 4. 4. This means that in Menander Aeschinus will have
heard Demea make three apparently kindly suggestions
affecting his bride (906-10), her mother (932), and her
brother (948 f.), all readily accepted at least and two
of them probably *anticipated* by Micio as suggested in
the Scenario, p. 62. The young man must be delighted by
Micio's plans, news to him as to Demea, but equally pleased
by what seems a most welcome liberalization in Demea.
Both his fathers think alike! They are the best and
kindest men in the world! His contributions to Menander's
dialogue must be to applaud a brave new Demea at least
as much as a well-known Micio.

7. 4. 5. The irony in Menander would be superb: it is only
with these expressions of appreciation from Aeschinus that
Demea realises that his suggestions, made out of spite,
are incidentally winning him favour with the boys. Cultivating
this, Demea proposes to free Geta at his own cost. Micio,
fully aware as ever of what is going on, keeps silent; and
Demea locks himself into a new pattern from which he will
not be able to escape 'tomorrow' without loss of face and
respect. Demea is hoist with his own petard, but with
precious and unanticipated compensations. And so Menander's
play would end on a note of humane reconciliation and with
irony rather than with the crude evaluations and didactic
moralizing which blemish the Roman.

Act I: *As in Terence, 26-154, except at 40-7*:

'...Besides, the boy isn't even my real son, but my
brother's; for, what some think a blessing, I never
married; he did; I adopted one of two sons he had; I've
brought him up from a baby, I've supported him...'

*and without generalization in 65-77, the gist in Menander
simply being:*

'...he is my only happiness, and that happiness is all
I value; I want him to reciprocate my love, so I indulge
him and avoid playing the stern father or prying, for I
want to encourage frankness in him, and dishonesty begins
at home. My brother disagrees with all that; he keeps
criticizing my leniency, but he's no judge, he's far too
strict. Ah, here he comes: I daresay it will be the same
old story...

Prologue-narrative: *after 154, spoken by (e.g.) 'Brotherly
Love' (cf. p. 39-40):*

'These old men were sons of a peasant whose land was
insufficient to divide; the younger left and made his
fortune; he settled here in Athens as a bachelor; a good
man and wise. His brother made a virtue of necessity in
living the farmer's life and by thrift and hard work has
in fact made a good deal of money; honest, earnest, but
less intelligent, and volatile, as you have seen. He
let his brother adopt one of his (identical twin? cf. p. 38)
sons because (....); the mother is dead.

'The boys have been brought up in contrasting ways,
but are close and of good basic character. But our rich
friend is wrong about his boy's frankness. You heard
what he said about his son's wanting to wed (151). Well,
nine months ago the young man got drunk at the festival
of (....); he encountered a girl, and...need I say more?
She is pregnant; but she had wrested a ring from her
assailant and that subsequently served as mutual proof
of identity' (*How Menander explained that remains
entirely obscure*). 'Full of shame, the young man
approached the girl's mother, a widow, and her guardian.
They agreed to let him marry the girl and he promised
to approach his father and ask the necessary permission;
they agreed to discretion to protect the families'
reputations. The young man has secured accommodation
for mother and daughter here next door.

The young man's shame, however, is such that he cannot
bring himself to confess his base deed to a father who
has been so good to him; he has procrastinated, tried,
and failed, as you have heard (151), and thus got
himself into the position of deceiving all those nearest
him' (*except perhaps Ctesipho??*).

'But the other boy has his own troubles. The farmer is
wrong about him too; for he is madly in love with a
musician owned by a procurer; this villainous fellow has
arranged to take his girls to (*Paphos in?*) Cyprus in time
for the festival (*of Aphrodite?*) and its market in love,
and is due to sail today. The young man was desperate;
his brother found out that he was going to kill himself
for love, and to help him and divert the old farmer's
suspicions and condemnations he has taken the lead in
raiding the procurer's house last night. But here they
come, both brothers with the girl and the missing staff
sent last night to escort the rich man's son. I'm off,
but leave my spirit here'.

Act I continued: *155-287, entirely re-written by Terence
using material from Diphilus' 'Partners in Death' (7 ff.,
155-96), a link-speech of his own (196-208), and then
re-joining Menander (208-87) but writing in Ctesipho's
part (252 ff.). One outline:*

'*Enter Aeschinus, Ctesipho, the girl, and retinue
(cf. 26 f.)*

CT. Thank you, Aeschinus. AE. Inside, quick, to tell
father the truth - I'm sure he'll understand and pay
that villain off. CT. Yes, I daresay he's coming any
minute.

Exeunt into Micio's; enter Sannio.

This is the place - I'll get my own back! If only I
weren't so pressed for time! I'll try bluffing it out.

Enter Syrus from Micio's

SY. (*Speaking back*) Your father's off looking for you
- don't worry, I'll deal with Sannio. Ah, what's all
this I hear...'

(*Then, much as in Terence 209-28; then*)

'...besides, I gather you're in a hurry to be off to
Cyprus. SA. Damn! They know! SY. If you insist on
prosecuting, you'll have to cancel the venture. SA.
Blast! Aeschinus has set the whole thing up!...

*(Then, as in 239-251; then, enter Aeschinus as in 265 ff.,
but without Ctesipho:)*

'*AE*. Is Sannio here? *SY*. Yes, and I've sorted him out.
AE. Right: let's go to town to find father and settle.
(Exeunt)'.

C H O R U S

Act II: *287-510: Essentially as in Terence but starting as
follows:*

'*Enter Sostrata from next·door*

SO. What to do? Her pains have started, Geta's out, no-
one to go to the midwife! Oh dear, Oh dear! *(Pauses)*
Now calm yourself: no need to panic; there's plenty of
time, you know what needs to be done, and thank goodness
we can rely on Aeschinus.

Enter Geta from town

GE. Disaster! Disgrace! Where's my mistress? *SO*. Geta,
here! *GE*. Aeschinus has abandoned us: I've just seen
him, his father, Syrus and Sannio settling in the market
for a slave-girl people say Aeschinus abducted last night.
SO. Can it be true? He *swore*... *(weeps)* No, this won't
do: I've got to be sensible. The facts prove he and his
father are against us. If we make a fuss, he'll deny it
all, and our reputation will be in shreds. And if he
doesn't, this is no basis for a marriage. So give in
then...? No, no, no! We must stand up for what's right
in this world! *(fr. 7 K.-Th. would aptly fit here, cf.
p. 265.)* We must fight back! Things couldn't be worse
than they are! No dowry, no prospect of her marrying
anyone else! And I can prove it was him! Here's the
ring she got off him! So we *must* prosecute. Geta, go
and tell my brother Hegio what's happened and bring him
here urgently. But first things first — take the road
through town to his farm and see if you can raise a
midwife: if not, don't waste time looking, I can cope.
(Exeunt)'

*In 355-446 Terence follows Menander very closely and so
in 447-510 except that in Menander it will have been
clear that Hegio is the women's legal 'master' and that
only this morning's news, not the rape, pregnancy, and
arrangement with Aeschinus, is fresh to him, cf. pp. 36-8.*

C H O R U S

Act III: *516-91: Essentially as in Terence. Then perhaps:*
'*Enter Micio and Hegio from town*

MI. There's no call to *thank* me for doing what's right.
I've explained the meaning of Aeschinus' abducting the
girl and my harbouring her, and you've told me what
Aeschinus should have confided in me months ago. He
was evidently too ashamed to speak out. There's another
matter I should have liked to raise under happier
circumstances, but it can't wait. I want your permission
to marry Sostrata. I realise that there is a wide gulf
between us in wealth but I value character more highly.
I trust neither you nor she will take this as insulting
or frivolous: it is sincerely meant and the practical
thing to do for the best. *HE.* I know you as a good and
honourable man and I have no false pride: I agree. As
their guardian, I should like you to come with me to
explain about Aeschinus and to make your proposal in
person. But we must be tactful: people in difficult
circumstances are apt to take things the wrong way.
Perhaps you would prefer me to speak to her first? *MI.*
No: one can't apologize, reassure, or propose by proxy
in these circumstances: it's up to me. *HE.* Well, come
along.

Exeunt to Sostrata's; then enter Aeschinus from town'.

*In 610 ff., Terence follows Menander in substance except
that it should be Geta, not Canthara that Aeschinus has
met in town (617 ff.): the encounter between Micio and
Aeschinus (635-706) is also pure Menander. But at the
end (707-12) Aeschinus in Menander may have praised Micio
more appropriately as a person than an inverted father-
figure, on the lines:*

'*AE.* Tremendous! Great! What a graceful thing a man
is, if he be a man! And from now on I mean to match
him as best I can in kindness and consideration as a
man and friend!'

C H O R U S

Act IV: *713-854, exactly as in Terence, except that we
already know, unlike Demea, that Micio is going to
marry Sostrata, cf. Act III.*

C H O R U S

Act V: *855-997, expanded and altered in emphasis by*
Terence

'Enter Demea from Micio's

DE. Well, you're never too old too learn. I admit my
way has failed. His life has been one long holiday of
sociability and contentment, mine a conscientious struggle
against poverty and to do my social duty. The result?
He wins all, I lose. So 'friends say not mine and thine
but ours', eh? (*cf. 804*) Well, I accept the challenge.
I'll adopt his weapons of liberality and cheeriness and
take things to their logical conclusion. Let's see how
he likes some of his own medicine when *I* start giving
away some of 'ours'!

Enter Geta from Sostrata's

GE. I'll ask when they want to fetch you both, Ma'am.
DE. Ah...What's your name? *GE*. Geta, Sir. *DE*. Yes of
course. Well, er, Geta, my dear fellow, I'm very
impressed with what I have seen of your conduct and I'd
like to see you right. *GE*. Much obliged, sir! *DE*.
(*Aside*) Instant popularity! Good!

Enter Aeschinus from Micio's

AE. Will they ever be ready? I can't wait! *DE*. My dear
boy, will you take a suggestion from an old man? Go and
tell them to breach the garden wall and bring your bride
across that way. After all, she can't be feeling very
well! *AE*. Father, that's brilliant! And so thoughtful!
(*Exit into Micio's*). *DE*. Geta, you go in and explain.
(*Exit into Sostrata's*). *DE*. (*Alone*) Great! So I'm
brilliant! The end of his privacy - so what? *Now* let's
see him squander the odd couple of thousand!

Enter Micio with Aeschinus

MI. Demea's idea? Really? *DE*. Really, and it's up to
us to unite the families in every possible way. *MI*. I
quite agree. *DE*. Of course, that will mean you marrying
Sostrata. *MI*. Well, as a matter of fact, I'd already
thought of that: I've already spoken to Hegio and
Sostrata, and was planning a little surprise. *AE*. Father,
I'm delighted! *DE*. (*Crestfallen*) Oh...er...capital.
But yes, what about Hegio? There's that land of yours -
I mean 'ours': let's give him the income from that to
live on. *MI*. An excellent suggestion, Demea. But I've
already thought of that. Isn't it extraordinary how
great minds think alike?

AE. Marvellous! You both think alike! You're the best
best fathers in the world! Ctesipho will be delighted!
DE. Er...quite. (*To impress Aeschinus*) But, Micio, what
about Geta? Don't you think his good service deserves
reward? Tell you what, I'll pay for him. After all you
did pay for Ctesipho's er...young lady. *AE.* Brilliant!
How generous you both are! *MI.* Come on then - torches
to the garden! And may the noble laughter-loving lass
called Victory go ever with us with her blessing! [*67*]
Exeunt'.

8. 1. 1. It is important to emphasize the hypothetical
nature of this reconstruction, deduced from the evidence
reviewed on pp. 31-56 and it is offered in no dogmatic
spirit. To prevent misunderstanding it should also be
said that though it is necessary to use specific words
and phrases here, one does not pretend thereby to be
restoring anything more specific than the gist and
direction of a passage in the lost Menander. Our main
business is with Terence; but as we have seen (pp. 16-30)
we can only go so far in appreciating Terence *without*
reference to his model. From this point of view, it is
useful at least to identify those parts of his play which
are to be seen as faithful translation; and it would take
us a good deal further if we can estimate by how much
Terence is departing in the rest.

8. 1. 2. It will be convenient to note finally where this
scenario differs from those of Rieth/Gaiser (1964) and of
Grant (1971 a, 1973 a, 1975 b, 1980). It agrees with
theirs as to the five-act structure.

In Act I: it differs from Rieth/Gaiser (1964) and agrees
with Grant (1980) in identifying 26 ff. as the start of
Menander's play without previous scenes (Syrus, the young
men, prologue); it differs from Grant (1980) mainly in
not seeing Syrus as directly involved in the raid, and
from Martin (1976) in having the postponed prologue deal
with Aeschinus' affair as well as Ctesipho's. It differs
from all of them in postulating the expansion of Micio's
opening speech.

In Act II: it agrees with Grant (1973) in deleting the role
of Canthara; and goes a little further with respect to
the roles of Sostrata and Geta.

In Act III: it tentatively supposes that Terence has cut a
theme in Menander (cf. Leo (1913) 245).

In Act IV: it agrees with the general opinion that this
is more or less pure Menander; not only in substance, but
in metrical form and proportion.

In Act V: No-one has risked a precise programme for Menander's
last act. This one offered here depends on (i) the idea
that Menander wrote the act for three players, not four
(Sandbach (1966) 48 deletes Aeschinus); (ii) the thematic
importance of 804; (iii) what seem the necessary
implications of Donatus' note on 938 (see p. 264, p. 56
f.; Rieth (1964) 118-20).

1. So Quintilian *Inst.* 10.1.99., cf. Beare (1964) 93.
    See the *OCD* for basic biographies of those here
    introduced in capital letters.

2. New Comedy and Menander: *CHCL* i 398-425, ii 77-9,
    96-105, Arnott (1975, 1979), Sandbach (1973), (1977),
    Hunter (1985), Brown (1986).

3. Caecilius: Leo (1913) 217-26, Warmington (1940) 468-
    561 (text, translation), Wright (1974) 87-126, *CHCL*
    ii 115 f.

4. Luscius Lanuvinus: Garton (1972) 41-139, Wright (1974)
    78-80

5. Beare (1964) 128-36, *CHCL* ii 82 ff.

6. The *Palliata*: Duckworth (1952), Beare (1964), *CHCL* ii
    77-127.

7. Duckworth (1952) 384-441; English and French descendants
    of *Brothers*, *ibid.* 400, 405 f., 428 f., 431.

8. Volcacius Sedigitus ap. Gellium *N.A.* 15. 24; Beare
    (1964) 117 f.

9. Varro *De sermone latino* 5 fr. 60 (Charisius p. 315
    Barwick); Varro ap. Donatum *Vita Terenti* 3 (quoted
    p. 263).

10. Caesar and Cicero: Donatus *Vita Terenti* 7, Leo (1913)
    253; Quintilian *Inst.* 10. 1. 99.

11. Goldberg (1981) 103-4, Reeve (1983) 412-3.

12. *CHCL* ii. 101-3.

13. Gellius *N.A.* 2. 23; Wright (1974) 87-126

14. Nineteen ancient 'iudicia', see K.-Th. (1959) 7-11.

15. Syrianus *in Hermog.* 2. 23 Rabe; Pfeiffer (1968) 190 f.

16. Quoted from a lost source in Donatus *De comoedia* 5.
    1 (p. 22. 19 Wessner).

17. Quintilian *Inst.* 10. 1. 69.

18. Gellius *N.A.* 2. 23

19. In *Brothers*, the dramaturgy at 26 ff., 141 ff., 364 ff.,
    435 ff., 486 ff., 540 ff., 635 ff., 775 ff. is typical
    of Menander's economy and originality in handling the
    'syntax' of the theatre.

20. This is to state a difference of kind, not a disparagement;
    and it is not suggested that Menander never nodded.
    Cf. Brown (1983).

21. Horace *A.P.* 189 f., Beare (1964) 196-218.

22. See Appendix III.

23. This has a technical sense, cf. p. 25, 54 f.

24. *Contra* the view or assumption in much recent writing
    on *Brothers* that there are 'faults' in the Micio of
    26-854 which the Roman audience was to weigh in the
    balance against 'good things' in Demea by virtue of
    which the reversal of favour in 855-997 would be made
    smoother (p. 51). This involves fundamental confusion
    over the categories of criticism appropriate to New
    Comedy and the *Palliata*, which, even from the pen of
    the maturing Terence, was still the *Palliata*. See
    notes 25 and 64.

25. Martin (1976) 16-29, esp. 27-8, and on 911, 915, 922;
    Bonner (1977) 19; Goldberg (1981) (quoting Pöschl (1975)
    with approval) 'Micio...undergoes not real humiliation
    but only the teasing that comic heroes often endure.
    He has after all converted Demea to his way of
    thinking'. Has he?

26. The case for postulating expository prologues in all
    of Terence's originals depends not on generalizations
    about New Comedy (all of which would be false) but on
    examination of the exposition of each particular
    play as Terence presents it. See (with caution)
    Lefèvre (1969). On the social background to Menander,
    see Sandbach (1973) 21-35, Casson (1976) 29-59.

27. On Aemilius Paullus and Scipio Aemilianus see Astin
    (1967) 12 ff., Walbank on Polybius 31. 21. 4.

28. Astin (1978) 104 f.

29. Horace *Ep.* 2. 1. 156.

30. *CHCL* ii. 60-76, Skutsch (1985) 1-69.

31. Livy 44. 37. 5-9, Walbank on Polybius 39. 16. 1-3.

32. Suetonius *gramm.* 2.

33. Cato fr. 15 Jordan = Julius Victor p. 374 Halm.

34. Suetonius *rhet.* 1.

35. Long (1974) 210-216.

36. Walbank on Polybius 33. 2/Gellius *N.A.* 6. 14.
    8-10 with further references to the sources.

37. Long (1974), Rist (1972).

38. Vischer (1965) 60-88.

39. Dodds on Plato *Gorgias* 485 e - 486 d, Walbank on
    Polybius 31. 31.

40. Virgil *Georgics* 4. 125 ff.

41. Polybius 31. 23. 6 ff.

42. Plutarch *Aemilius* 6.

43. Plutarch *Cato Maior* 20.

44. Bonner (1977), Booth (1978).

45. Astin (1978).

46. Crook (1967 a, b), Watson (1971) 28-34, Gratwick
    (1984) 42-5, Lacey (1986) 121-144.

47. Nicoll (1963). There is of course no genetic
    relationship.

48. Quintilian *Inst.* 10. 1. 99.

49. Cf. n. 26.

50. Watson (1971) 35-42.

51. MacDowell (1978) 84-101.

52. MacDowell (1978) on *Aspis* 258-73, Brown (1983).

53. See p. 26 ; otherwise Grant (1971 b) 201.

54. So Gaiser (1964) 135-9.

55. Donatus *Ad. praef*. 4.

56. Marti (1959).

57. *CHCL* ii. 78-9, Beare (1964) 137-48, 366-8.

58. Sandbach (1975 a), (1978) 78-80.

59. Fantham (1968), Grant (1980) with references.

60. Cf. n. 13.

61. Grant (1973 a) 70-5, Webster (1974) 115.

62. (The idea of marrying Sostrata) '...bei Menander dem Alten von vornherein genehm war; woraus zu schliessen ist, dass Menander diesen Gedanken irgendwie vorbereitet und annehmbar gemacht hatte', Leo (1913) 245.

63. Rieth (1964) had written his study of *Brothers* during the 1939-45 war and was killed in 1944; Menander's *Dyskolos* only became known in 1959. Parallels had already been drawn between the ends of *Brothers* and *Dyskolos* (Thierfelder (1960), Arnott (1963)), but Gaiser (1964) 120 n. 165 was right to insist that the cases are different, and an inadequate basis for the subsequent tendency among critics to minimize the *a priori* probability that Terence's changes are substantial.

64. Views of the characters of Micio and Demea are of course intimately connected with views of the end of the play. At the risk of some over-simplification and with the *caveat* that the emphases of the different writers differ, we may categorize recent opinion in three groups. There are those who, seeing Micio and Demea as both representing faulty extremes, find more or less fault in Micio as well as more or less virtue in Demea: Thierfelder (1960) 107 ff., Johnson (1968), Fantham (1971) 991-4, Tränkle (1972), Lloyd-Jones (1973), Grant (1975 b), Martin (1976), Lord (1977), Campagno (1978), Grimal (1982), Orlandini (1982), Callier (1982) Blanchard (1983). For these writers there is no need to postulate that Terence has changed the ending very much. Others hold that there is, because they think that in Menander Micio was definitely

in the right and Demea more or less wrong. These
include Dorey (1962), Rieth and Gaiser (1964), Sandbach
(1966), Ludwig (1968) 177, Büchner (1974), Pöschl
(1975), Brown (1986), and the present editor. Those
more or less agnostic but well worth reading include
Arnott (1963) and (1964), Garton (1976), Greenberg (1980),
Goldberg (1981), Hunter (1985).

65. Greek adoption: MacDowell (1978) 99-100; Roman: Watson
(1971) 30-3. It is doubtful whether a Roman of
Terence's time who had never tried to get a natural
heir by marrying could in fact adopt (*ibid.* 31, n. 2),
though this was permitted in the later Roman law.

66. Publilius Syrus P 18.

67. Menander's usual *envoi* and not only his, cf. Sandbach
(1973) on Menander *Dyskolos* 968 f.

A: *Codex Bembinus*, rustic capitals, 5th c.; lacks lines 915-997; full photographic reproduction, Prete (1970).

γ: the agreement of *CPFE* (or three of them), minuscule Mss. of the 9th-11th c. *CPF* are the oldest of the illustrated Mss., cf. Jones and Morey (1931); *F* is reproduced in full in Bethe (1903); Questa (1984) plates 16-20 gives the song 610-7 as set down in *ACPF*.

δ: the agreement of *DGL* (or two of them), minuscule Mss. of the 10th-11th c. *V* (*periocha* and 26-158 only) and *p* (only occasionally cited) also belong to this class; for *f* (only cited at 522) see Raasted (1957).

Σ: the agreement of γ and δ, collectively called the Calliopian Mss., cf. the subscription at 997; the recension of Calliopius is the source of all the 650-odd surviving Mediaeval Mss. except *A*; when he lived is quite uncertain and Σ may or may not be his work and may or may not be older than *A*.

J: 'Joviales', a 6th c. hand correcting *A* from a Calliopian source, in effect our earliest systematic witness to that tradition.

For the 'family-tree' see Appendix I: for more detail of the individual Mss., Reeve (1983), Grant (1986).

A^1: the first hand in *A*; A^2: corrections by the first hand.

C^1, D^1, etc.: the first hand in *C*, *D*, etc.; C^2, D^2, etc.: corrections in these Mss. by the first or another hand.

ω: the agreement of *A* and Σ, but not necessarily of external witnesses to the text, of whom the most important is

Don.: Donatus (c. 350 A.D.). Other late grammatical sources (c. 300-600 A.D.): Nonius, Arusianus Messius, Charisius, Lactantius Placidus, Priscian, Eugraphius, see the list of works cited, p. 284 ff., as also for the names of those to whom conjectures are attributed.

Readings in *ACPFEDGL* are mostly cited on the negative principle that (e.g.) 'ipse eripit *A*' (app. crit. to line 4) implies that 'ipse erit' (text of line 4) is the reading of Σ. But in 915-997 where *A* is lost e.g. 'facto sit δ' (app. crit. to line 996) implies that 'factost' (text of line 996) is the reading of γ.

For the metrical abbreviations used in the apparatus and explanation of the dots and spaces in the text see Appendix IV, p. 281, and for the meaning of the *DOTS UNDER THE LINES, PROSODICAL MARKS,* and *TRIPLE SPACING IN THE TEXT,* see Appendix IV, pp. 270-1; 274-6; 283.

INCIPIT PROLOGVS

F: fol. 50

GRAECA MENANDRV
ACTA LVDIS FVNERALIBVS LVCIO AEMELIO PAVLO
QVOS FECERE Q. FABIVS MAXVMVS P. CORNELIVS AFRICANVS
EGERE L. HATILIVS PRAENESTINVS LVCIVS AMBIVIVS TVRPIO
MODOS FECIT FLACCVS CLAVDI
TIBIIS SARRANIS TOTA
FACTA VI
MARCO CORNELIO CETHEGO LVCIO GALLO COS.

G. Sulpicii Apollinaris periocha

1 duos cum haberet Demea adulescentulos,

   dat Micioni fratri adoptandum Aeschinum,

   sed Ctesiphonem retinet. hunc citharistriae

   lepore captum, subduro ac tristi patre,

5 frater celabat Aeschinus: famam rei, ¦

   amorem in sese transferebat. denique

   fidicinam lenoni eripit.   uitiauerat

   idem Aeschinus   ciuem Atticam   pauperculam

   fidemque dederat hanc sibi uxorem fore.

10 Demea iurgare, grauiter ferre; mox tamen

   ut ueritas   patefactast, ducit Aeschinus

   uitiatam, potitur Ctesipho   citharistriam.

Index ut in A praeter Adelphos; Paulo modos fecere Lucius F.;
Ambibius; serranis; *et ita discriptus*: Adelphos/; funeralibus/;
fecere/; Cornelius/; Praenestinus/; fecit/; VI/; cos/. Σ *autem
fere sic*: Incipit Adelphoe acta ludis funebribus quos fecere
Q. Fabius Maximus P. Cornelius Africanus Aemilii Pauli egere
L. Atilius Praenestinus Minutius Prothymus (*C*; funebribus Q.
Fabio Maximo P. Cornelio Africani Aemelii Pauli aedilibus
curulibus quos fecere L. Atilius Praenestinus Minutius
Prothymus *DEFG*) modos fecit Flaccus Claudi tibiis sarranis
facta graeca Menandri Anicio M. Cornelio cons.

Periocha G. S. A p. *A*: argumentum Σ.   4 captus *A*. subduro
scripsi: sub duro *uulgo*.   5–6 famamque amoris in se Σ.
7 eripit lenoni *A*, lenoni eripuit Σ.   8 eidem *A*. ciue *A*.
10 et grauiter Σ *praeter C*.   11 et ueritas *A*.   11–12 ducit
Aeschinus/ a se uitiatam ciuem atticam uirginem/ uxorem
potitur Ctesipho citharistria/ exorato suo patre duro Demea Σ.

The Greek model, Menander's. Put on at the Funeral Games
which Q. Fabius Maximus and P. Cornelius Scipio Aemilianus
Africanus celebrated for L. Aemilius Paulus. Principal
actors L. Hatilius of Praeneste and L. Ambivius Turpio.
Flaccus servant to Claudius performed the music on
the Tyrian double-pipe throughout. The dramatist's
sixth work, in the consulship of M. Cornelius Cethegus
and L. Anicius Gallus (*160 B.C.*).

The Summary by G. Sulpicius Apollinaris

Demea, having two lads, gave one of them, called Aeschinus,
to his brother Micio to adopt, but kept the other, called
Ctesipho. Demea being somewhat harsh and grim, Aeschinus
undertook to conceal his brother Ctesipho's falling for
the charms of a *cithara*-player; (5) he went about taking the
romance and the gossip about it all on himself. This results
in his seizing the girl from her wicked master. But this
same Aeschinus had already wronged a poor defenceless girl,
an Athenian citizen, and given his word that she should be
his bride. (10) Moral outrage and deep objections on Demea's
part; but eventually when the truth has come out, Aeschinus
marries the girl he had wronged, and Ctesipho wins his
cithara-player.

Dramatis personae

MICIO, an old gentleman
DEMEA, an old farmer
SANNIO, the villain
AESCHINVS, a young man
SYRVS, servant to Micio
CTESIPHO, a young man

SOSTRATA, a widow
CANTHARA, an old nurse
GETA, an old servant
HEGIO, an old farmer

Extras: Storax, Parmeno, Dromo (*et al.*), *servants in
Micio's household; a young cithara-player*; Pamphila,
daughter to Sostrata.

1   Postquam pŏetă sensit scripturam sŭam

     ăb ĭniquis obseruari ĕt aduorsarĭos

     răpĕre in peiorem partem quam acturi sŭmûs,

     indĭcĭo de se ipse ĕrĭt, uos ĕrĭtis iudĭces

5   laudin an uĭtĭo duci factum ŏportĕat.

     Sÿnăpŏthnescontes Diphĭli   comoedĭast;

     ęam Commŏrĭentes Plautus fecit fabŭlam.

     in grąeca ădŭlescens est qui lenoni erĭpit

     mĕrĕtricem in prima fabŭla: ęum Plautus lŏcum

10   rĕliquĭt intĕgrum, ęum hic lŏcum   sumpsit sĭbî

     ĭn *Adelphos*; uerbum de uerbo expressum extŭlit.

     ęam nos acturi sŭmŭs nŏuam: pernoscĭtê

     furtumnĕ factum existŭmetĭs, an lŏcum

     rĕprĕhensum qui praetĕrĭtus neglĕgentĭast.

15   nam quŏd ĭsti dicunt mălĕuŏli, hŏmĭnes nobĭles

     ĕum adiutare adsĭdŭeque una scribĕrê,

     quŏd ĭlli mălĕ dictum uehęmens esse existŭmant,

     eam laudem hic ducit maxŭmam,   quom illis plăcet

     qui uobis unĭuorsis et pŏpŭlo plăcent,

20   quorum ŏpĕra in bello ĭn otĭo in nĕgotĭo

     suo quisquĕ tempŏre usust sĭnĕ sŭperbĭa.

      dehinc ne exspectetĭs argumentum fabŭlae;

1-154 *ia⁶*.   4 ipse eripit *A*.   eritis *om. C¹*.   de sese ipse
erit. uos iudices *Bentley*.   5 id factum *Aδ*.   15 maledici *A*.
16 hunc adiutare *Don*.   21 usus est ω.

PROLOGUE

Since our dramatist realised that his writing was being

pounced on by hostile critics and that rivals were putting

the play which we are about to perform in a very bad light,

he is going to put himself in the dock, and you are going

to judge (5) whether what he has actually done should be

held to his credit or blame. *Synapothnescontes* is a comedy

by Diphilus; Plautus rendered it as the farce 'Partners in

Death'. In the original there is a young fellow who at the

start of the play kidnaps a girl from her evil master.

Plautus (10) left that scene untouched; Terence has taken

possession of that scene for his *Brothers*; he has reproduced

it rendering word for word. We are producing the play for

the first time: consider carefully whether in your judgement

this is a case of theft, or the rescue of a scene which was

passed over through failure of discrimination. (15) Now as

to the charge of certain ill-disposed persons, that

prominent Romans keep helping our dramatist and closely

collaborate with him in writing. What they reckon a

devastating insult, Terence counts the best possible praise:

he enjoys the approval of men who enjoy the approval of every

last man here, and of all true Romans, (20) men whose

service in war, in peace, in enterprise each of us has

experienced when he needed it most and without the least

condescension. And next, the background to the play? No;

sĕnes qui primi uĕnĭent, ĕi̯ partem ăpĕrĭent,

ĭn ăgendo partem ostendent.   făcĭte aequănĭmĭtas

25   pŏetae ad scribendum augĕat   industrĭam.

                                                        (i.1)

MI.   Stŏrax?   non rĕdĭi̯t hac nocte a cena Aeschĭnus

nĕquĕ quisquam seruŏlorum qui aduorsum ĭe̅rant.

prŏfecto hoc uere dicunt:˙si absis uspĭam ¦

† aut ĭbĭ si cesses, euĕnire ĕă sătĭŭs est

30   quae in te uxor dicĭt et quae ĭn ănĭmo cogĭtat

irătă, quam illa quae părentes prŏpĭtĭi. ¦

uxor, si cesses, aut te ămarĕ cogĭtat

aut †tete ămari aut potare atque ănĭmo obsĕqui

et tĭbĭ bĕne essĕ soli quom sĭbĭ sit măle̅. ¦

35   ĕgŏ, quĭă non rĕdĭit filĭus - quae cogĭto et

quĭbŭs nunc sollĭcĭtor rebus!   ne ille aut alsĕrit

aut uspĭam   cĕcĭdĕrit aut praefregĕrit

ălĭquid!   uah, quemquamne hŏmĭnem ĭn ănĭmum

                                              instĭtŭĕre aut

părarĕ quod sit carĭus   quam ipsest sĭbi! ¦

---

23 ii ω *nisi* hi(i) *CF*.   26 Astorax *A*.   27 aduersum *AG*.
29 aut ubi si *edd. uett.*, atque ibi si *Sydow;* an ut ibi sic
cesses? 30 dixit δ.   33 aut te aleari *Favet.*   ac potare *Don.:*
aut ω.   34 *om. A.*   35/6 cogito/ et *APF.*   37 prae- *suspectum*
(per- *edd. uett.*).   37/8 aliquid uah/ quemquamne *APF.*   39 sit
sibi *CE*.

it's the old fellows who come on first who will partly

expound, partly act that out. Make sure that your sense of

fair play intensifies our playwright's dedication to the pen!

(The scene is a street in 'Athens'; two houses face us; one

side entrance leads to the town, the other to the country.

It is just after dawn. MICIO enters from what is evidently

the wealthier house. He peers anxiously towards town, and

calls.)

(26) Storax? *(Pauses)* Aeschinus not back from dinner

last night, none of the staff who went to fetch him either.

It's quite true what they say: if you're out somewhere or

linger there, better the things an angry wife suspects and

scolds you for than anything fond parents think might be

happening! If you're out late, a wife suspects there's

someone else, or you're gambling, or you're drinking and

enjoying yourself; you're the only one that gets any fun,

she's the only one that doesn't. (35) But as a father –

the things I imagine...dreadful, terrible things... just

because Aeschinus hasn't come home! *(Shivers at the chill*

morning air). Has he caught cold? Tripped somewhere...

broken something? God forbid! *(Wry laugh)* It's quite daft:

fancy anyone taking on a responsibility that comes to mean

more than life itself, and actually doting on it!

40   atque ex me hic natus non est, sed ex fratre: is adeo

dissimili studiost iam inde ab adulescentia.

ego hanc clementem uitam urbanam atque otium

secutus sum, et quod fortunatum isti putant,

uxorem numquam habui. ille contra, haec omnia:

45   ruri agere uitam, semper parce ac duriter

se habere; uxorem duxit, nati filii

duo. inde ego hunc maiorem adoptaui mihi.

eduxi a paruolo, habui, amaui pro meo.

in eo me oblecto, solum id est carum mihi.

50   ille ut item contra me habeat facio sedulo.

do; praetermitto; non necesse habeo omnia

pro meo iure agere. postremo alii clanculum

patres quae faciunt quae fert adulescentia,

ea ne me celet consuefeci filium.

55   nam qui mentiri aut fallere insuerit patrem aut

audebit, tanto magis audebit ceteros.

pudore et liberalitate liberos

retinere satius esse credo quam metu.

40-1 fratre meo/ is *A*.   44 *an* moenia *(= munia).?*   50 adsedulo *A*.   51 omnia *om. A*.   53 *an* qua fert?   55-6 insueuerit patrem/ aut *A*.   insueuit *V*.   institerit *Lindsay-Kauer*.

(40) Besides, the boy isn't even my real son, he's my
brother's; and my brother, he has had values different from
mine ever since we were young. I have gone for a civilized
life of ease here in the city, and I have never married –
an enviable status, according to certain people. My
brother? The opposite. He went for all this: (45) a life
of work on the land, the constant practice of thrift and
austerity. He did marry: result, two boys. I adopted
Aeschinus, the elder of them, I've brought him up from a
toddler, I've supported him, I've loved him as my own.
My happiness lies wholly in that, and that happiness is the
only thing I care about. (50) I do my honest best to make
him feel the same about me. I fund him; I pass things over;
I do not think it essential to transact everything by the
letter of a father's legal rights. In short, the things
other boys get up to, pathetically deceiving their fathers,
the things which young manhood brings, these are precisely
what I have trained my son *not* to hide from me. (55) For
the youngster who's bold enough to lie to his father even
once, let alone make a habit of it, will be more than bold
enough to cheat anyone else. I believe it is better to
control the rising generation by being generous and by
creating respect, not dread.

haec fratri mecum non conueniunt neque placent.

60   uenit ad me saepe †clamitans† 'quid agis, Micio?

quor perdis adulescentem nobis?   quor amat?

quor potat?   quor tu his rebus sumptum suggeris,

uestitu nimium indulges?   nimium ineptus es!'.

nimium ipsest durus, praeter aequomque et bonum;

65   et errat longe mea quidem sententia

qui imperium credat grauius esse aut stabilius

ui quod fit, quam illud quoi amicitia adiungitur.

mea sic est ratio et sic animum induco meum.

malo coactus qui suom officium facit

70   dum id rescitum iri credit, tantisper cauet;

si sperat fore clam - rursum ad ingenium redit.

ill' quem beneficio adiungas ex animo facit,

studet par referre, praesens absensque idem erit.

hoc patriumst, potius consuefacere filium

75   sua sponte recte facere quam alieno metu.

hoc pater ac dominus interest. hoc qui nequit,

fateatur nescire imperare liberis.

---

60 ω *Don., Cic. Inv. 1. 27 (cf. An. 144)*: clamans *Guyet,*
increpitans *ego*.   62 putat *A*.   sumptus Σ.   63 indulgis *A*.
inceptus *A*.   64 durus est γ.   67 quoi *Grant:* quod ω.
70 id *del. Grant (cf. 5)*.   pauet *A*.   71 rursus *Jδ*.
73 -que *suspectum*.   75 recte *om. A*.   77 se nescire γ,
nescire se *Jδ*.

My brother does not share this view. He does not
approve. (60) He keeps coming here shouting, 'Micio!
What's the idea? Why spoil the boy and bring shame on us all?
Why these girls? Why these wild parties? Why foot all
those bills, and pander to his grotesque ideas of style!
It's grotesque how wrong you are!'. But *he's* grotesquely
strict - quite beyond anything right or reasonable.
(65) And in my view it's a fundamental mistake to think
that power based on might is more real or better grounded
than power which essentially involves friendship.

This is my theory and this is my conviction. If
someone is forced to behave properly by punishment, (70)
then he watches his step just so long as he thinks any
hanky-panky would be found out. But if he is pretty sure
it could be kept quiet, then he reverts to his true nature.
Whereas, if you get someone's confidence by kindness, then
he acts sincerely; he can't wait to repay in the same coin;
he'll be the same whether you're there or not. Training a
son to do what is right (75) because he wants to, not for
dread of someone else - that is being a real father: that
is the difference between a father and a tyrant; and if
there is anyone who can't cope with that, he should face
the fact that he does not master the art of ruling the
unruly. (*Looks to side entrance*).

sĕd estne hic ipsus de quo ăgebam? et certe ĭs est.

nescĭŏquid tristem uĭdĕo. credo iam ut sŏlet

80   iurgabit.

(i.2)

saluom te aduĕnirĕ, Demĕâ,

gaudemŭs. *DE.* ĕhem ŏpportune: te ipsum quaerĭto.

MI. quid tristĭs es? *DE.* rŏgas me, ŭbĭ nobis Aeschĭnus

sic det, quid tristĭs ĕgŏ sim? dixin hoc fŏrê?

MI. quid fecit? *DE.* quĭd ĭllĕ fecĕrit?

quem nĕquĕ pŭdet

85   quicquam, nec mĕtŭit quemquam, nĕquĕ legem pŭtat

tĕnerĕ se ullam? nam illă quae antehac factă sunt

ŏmitto: mŏdŏ quid dissignauit! *MI.* quidnam ĭd est?

DE. fŏres effregĭt atque ĭn aedis inrŭĭt

ălĭenas; ipsum dŏmĭnum atque omnem famĭlĭam

90   mulcauĭt usque ad mortem; erĭpŭit mŭlĭĕrem

quam ămabat. clamant omnes indignissŭme

factum esse. hoc aduĕnĭenti quot mĭhi, Micĭo,

dixere! ĭn orest omni pŏpŭlo! denĭquê

si confĕrendum exemplumst, non fratrem uĭdet

---

78 ipse *ADV.* 82 rogitas me γ. 83 sic det *scripsi*: siet
ω. sum *GLVE Don. ad 789.* d. h. f. *Demeae Spengel: Micioni
uulgo.* 84 quid is fecit δ. 85 neque *G.* 87 designauit
AEF[2]. 92 *ita Don.*: quod ω.

Well, isn't that the very man? Speak of the devil!

(enter DEMEA from country). Yes, it is him. He looks

annoyed for some reason. Moral outrage as usual, I

expect. (80) *(Affably)* Good morning, Demea; we're

all glad you've arrived safely.

DE. Ah – it's you: good. You're the one I'm after.

MI. What's the matter?

DE. The matter? Stupid question, when Aeschinus deals with

us like this! Didn't I say this would happen?

MI. What's he done?

DE. Done? Done? That vandal has no conscience (85), no

respect, no idea that any law might apply to *him*!

Forget his previous achievements – what he's just

brewed is something really special!

MI. What exactly *is* it?

DE. *(Savouring the charges)* One, breaking a complete

stranger's door off its hinges; two, invading his

premises; (89-90) three, thrashing the proprietor and

his staff practically to death; four, absconding with

the female he had been seeing. *(Warming up)* They're

shouting from the rooftops it was absolutely

disgraceful! Hundreds of people have told me on my

way here, Micio! It's the talk of the town! But the

point is this – if I really have to provide him with

a model – can't he take note of his brother,

95   rej dare operam,   ruri esse parcum ac sobrium.

nullum huius simile factum. haec quom illi, Micio,

dico, tibi dico: tu illum corrumpi sinis.

MI. homine inperito numquam quicquam iniustiust;

qui nisi quod ipse fecit, nil rectum putat.

100   DE. quorsum istuc? MI. quia tu, Demea, haec

                            male iudicas.

non est flagitium, mihi crede, adulescentulum

scortari neque potare: non est - neque fores

effringere. haec si neque ego neque tu fecimus

non siit egestas facere nos. tu nunc tibi |

105   id laudi ducis quod tum <haud> fecisti inopia? |

iniuriumst! nam si esset unde id fieret,

faceremus. et tu illum tuom,   si esses homo,

sineres nunc facere dum per aetatem decet,

potius quam ubi te exspectatum eiecisset foras,

110   alieniore aetate post faceret tamen.

DE. pro Iuppiter,   tu homo adigis me ad insaniam!

non est flagitium facere haec adulescentulum? MI. ah

ausculta, ne me optundas de hac re saepius.

tuom filium   dedisti adoptandum mihi. |

---

95 *uel* rei dare operam, ruri ess' parcum...   96 f. s. Σ.
98 est *om.* A Don., *an recte?*   99 qui sini A.   104 *p:* siid *A,*
siuit *cett.*   105 *suppleui.* tunc δ.   107 homo *om.* A.
108 seneres A. decet *JδF:* licet Aγ.   111 adigis AD[1] GV *Charisius*
redigis/-es *cett.*

(95) working for his future, living a life of thrift
and sobriety on the farm?   No such nonsense from him!
(*Grasps Micio*) In blaming Aeschinus I am blaming you,
Micio: your leniency is that boy's ruin!

MI.   (*Detaching himself: calmly*)   There's no-one more unfair
than a man of limited horizons: he thinks nothing can
be right unless he's done it himself.

DE.   (100) What do you mean by that?

MI.   I mean, Demea, that you are misjudging the case.
Believe you me, there's nothing terrible about a young
lad meeting girls or drinking with friends.   There
really isn't! Nor about breaking down a door.   If
neither you nor I did all that, it was our poverty
that prevented us.   (105) Are you congratulating
yourself now for what you *didn't* do then for lack of
money? That would be outrageous! Yes, if we had had
the wherewithal, we'd have done all that.   And if you
really understood, you'd be letting that lad of yours
do all that now, while it still goes with his age,
rather than have him doing it anyway, later on, at a
less appropriate age, (110) when he's finally got shot
of you at long last!

DE.   Good God! 'Understanding' indeed! You fool, you're
driving me mad! Nothing terrible in a lad doing this?

MI.   No Demea, hear me out, to save you going on and on
thumping at me about it. You gave me your boy to adopt.

115   is meus est factus. siquid peccat, Demea,

mihi peccat; ego illi maxumam   partem fero.⌐

obsonat, potat, olet unguenta? de meo;⌐

amat? dabitur a me argentum, dum erit commodum.⌐

ubi non erit, fortasse excludetur foras.

120   fores effregit? restituentur. discidit

uestem? resarcietur. est dis gratia⌐

†et unde haec fiant: et adhuc non molesta sunt.

postremo aut desine, aut cedo quemuis arbitrum:

te plura in hac re peccare ostendam! DE. ei mihi,

125   pater esse disce ab illis qui uere sciunt!

MI. natura tu illi pater es, consiliis ego.

DE. tun consulis quicquam...? MI. ah si pergis,

                                          abiero.

DE. sicin agis? MI. an ego totiens de eadem re

                                          audiam?

DE. curaest mihi. MI. et mihi curaest. uerum, Demea,

130   curemus aequam uterque partem: tu alterum,⌐

ego item alterum. nam ambos curare - propemodum

---

116 feram Σ *Don.* 117 scortatur potat *Varro LL 7. 84, cf.* 102, 60 *supra.* 121 et est ALVF[1]. 121-2 ω *Don. ut uid.:* est d.g./est unde *Spengel,* et - d. g. -/ est unde *Umpfenbach.* *malim* est d.g./<quom> est unde, *cf.* 139. non *om.* A. modesta A. 125 ab aliis *Don.* 127 consiliis A (?), consilis Σ: *an* consili *uel* consulas? a si APC[1]F[1], *item* 132.

(115) He became *my* son. If he makes any mistakes,
Demea, those mistakes are my affair. And I am prepared
to put up with most things in that area. Choice menus,
wine, good grooming? At *my* expense. Girls? I'll
fund him as long as it suits, and when it doesn't, well,
maybe he will be out in the cold. (120) A door broken
off its hinges? It'll be rehung. Someone's clothes
torn? They'll be replaced. Praise be, I have the
means for all this, and so far it has been no burden.
In a word: either shut up, or name an arbiter - the
choice is yours. I'll prove it's you that are more
wrong than anyone in all this.

DE. For Heaven's sake, (125) learn how to be a father from
those who really know!

MI. You gave him life, but I, his principles.

DE. Principles? What could *you* tell...

MI. *(Making as if to leave)* No! If you go on, I shan't be
here.

DE. *(Restraining him)* Is that your attitude?

MI. *(Breaking loose)* Yes! Why should I go on for ever
listening to the same old story?

DE. It concerns me. MI. *(Calmly)* And it concerns me.
But, Demea, (130) let us each concern ourselves an
equal amount: you with your boy, I with mine. For
concerning yourself with both is virtually - *(Micio*

132   reposcere illumst quem dedisti. *DE.* ah Micio,

136   irascere? *MI.* an non credis? *DE.* repeto quem dedi?

133   *MI.* mihi sic uidetur. *DE.* quid istic? si tibi

                                             istuc placet,

profundat perdat pereat: nil ad me attinet.

135   *MI.* iam si uerbum unum posthac rursum, Demea...

137   *DE.* aegrest: alienus non sum: si obsto...em desino,

unum uis curem? curo; et est   dis gratia

quom ita ut uolo est. iste tuos ipse sentiet

140   posterius... nolo in illum grauius dicere.

(i.3)

MI. nec nil neque omnia haec sunt quae dicit tamen.

non nil molesta haec sunt mihi. sed ostendere

me aegre pati illi nolui. nam itast homo:

quom placo, aduorsor sedulo ac deterreo;

145   tamen uix humane patitur. uerum si augeam

aut etiam adiutor sim eius iracundiae

---

132 est illum γ.   136 *transposui: sic* ω: ...ah Micio!/
MI. mihi sic uidetur. *DE.* quid istic (-uc *EFGV*)? si tibi
istuc placet/ profundat perdat pereat: nil ad me attinet./
iam si uerbum unum (ullum γ) posthac... *MI.* rursum, Demea,/
irascere? *DE.* an non credis? repeto (-n Σ) quem dedi?/
aegrest...   137 hem Σ (*om.* PCF[1]).   139 ipse se *A*.   140 g.
quicquam d. δ.   141 *ita Don.;* ...dicit; tamen/ non...*uulgo*.
144 quod *A,* cum Σ.   146 eius sim *Don.*

bellows) to demand back the son you gave me!

DE.   What, Micio, (136) getting angry?

MI.   Yes! Don't you believe what I say?

DE.   Asking back the son I gave you? Am I?

MI.   (133) That's how it looks to *me*.

DE.   Very well: if that's what you want, (134) let him stew
in his own juice, the wastrel; he's no boy of mine.

MI.   (135) Now if I hear another word from this moment on,
Demea...

DE.   (137) It's hard: I'm *not* an outsider: if I do try to
block you...all right, that's it, I've done. You want
me to concern myself with one? I already do; and,
praise be, he is the way I want him. That lad of yours
will find out for himself all too late... (140) Well,
I choose not to blame *him* any more harshly *(exit Demea
to town)*.

MI.   *(Calmly, slowly)* What he says is neither spot-on, nor
yet wholly off-target. It's definitely worrying. But
I didn't want him to see that I'm bothered. For this
is his style of reasonability: when I want to calm him
down, I have to do my very best to stand up to him and
frighten him off: (145) even then, his reaction is
barely that of a creature that thinks. Whereas if I
were to encourage his bad temper, or even imply approval,

I really would be

insaniam   profecto cum illo. etsi Aeschinus

non nullam in hac re nobis facit iniuriam.

quam hic non amauit meretricem, aut quoi non dedit

150   aliquid? postremo, nuper - credo iam omnium

taedebat - dixit uelle uxorem ducere.

sperabam iam deferuisse adulescentiam:

gaudebam. ecce autem de integro! nisi...

quidquid est,

uolo scire atque hominem conuenire, si apud forumst.

(ii.1)

155   SA. obsecro populares, ferte

misero atque innocenti auxilium,

156   subuenite inopi! AE. otiose

nunciam: ilico hic consiste.

157   quid respectas? nil periclist:

numquam dum ego adero hic te tanget.

158   SA. ego istam inuitis omnibus... AE. quam-

159   quamst scelestus non committet

hodie umquam iterum ut - uapulet!

160   SA. Aeschine, audi, ne te ignarum

fuisse dicas meorum morum:

---

153 *distinxi.* 155-9 *systema trochaicum xviii metrorum cum*
catalexi. 158 omnibus/ *AE.* quamquamst *uulgo.* 160-1 *syst.*
troch. viii metrorum cum catalexi.

as raving mad as he. *(Pauses)* And yet Aeschinus is
doing the family definite damage in all this. Which
beauty in Athens hasn't attracted his attention? Who
is there (150) he *hasn't* spent money on? But the
latest thing – I suppose he was getting bored with them
all – was last week: he spoke of wanting to marry and
settle down. I was pretty sure he'd finished sowing
his wild oats: I was really very pleased. And now
here we go again! *(A doubt occurs to him)* Unless...
(Coming to a decision) Whatever the facts, I intend to
see the young man and find out, supposing he's in town.
(Exit to town. Rumpus off-stage at the other side.
Enter AESCHINVS with a pretty girl from the country-
entrance, closely followed by three or four of Micio's
staff, restraining SANNIO)

SA. (155) Help! I'm an Athenian! Help me, someone! It's
robbery! I haven't done a thing! Help! I'm not strong
enough to stop them! Help!

AE. *(To the girl)* Take your time now: stop just here. Don't
look back – there's no danger. He'll never lay a finger
on you while I'm with you.

SA. In spite of you all I'll get her...

AE. However disgusting he is, he'll never risk another going
over today.

SA. (160) Listen, Aeschinus, to stop you saying you didn't
know my mettle.

leno ego sum...*AE.* scio. *SA.* at ita ut usquam

fuit fide   quisquam optuma;

162   tu quod te posterius purges,

hanc iniuriam mi nolle

163   factam esse, huius non faciam. crede hoc,

ego meum   ius persequar!

164   neque tu uerbis solues umquam

quod mihi re male feceris.

165   noui ego uostra haec 'nollem factum';

iusiurandum dabitur te esse in-

166   dignum iniuria hac - indignis

quom egomet sim acceptus modis.

167   *AE.* abi prae strenue ac fores aperi.

SA. ceterum hoc nihili facis?

168   *AE.* i intro nunciam. *SA.* at enim non sinam...

AE. accede illuc, Parmeno -

169   nimium istuc abisti. hic propter hunc

adsiste: em sic uolo.

---

162 s., 165 s. *syst. troch. ut 161 s.*; 167-9 *tr*[7]. 165 *sic
Rosivach*: 'nollem...hac' *omne pro prosopopoeia uulgo.* esse/
indignis ω. 166 *laborat; exspectes* te esse indignam
iniuriam hanc, *cf. 349. sane 165-6 abesse possunt sine de-
trimento.* 167 nihil ω: -i *Don.* 168 nunc tu iam δ, iam nunc
tu γ. at *om. Ap.*

My business is girls and punters...

AE. I know.

SA. ... but I'm straight, the straightest as ever was in
the trade. As for what you'll be coming up with later
on as your apology, that it's a shame I had this
aggravation - here's what I give for that *(rude gesture
and/or spits).* I'm telling you, I'll have the law on
you! Mere talk from you isn't going to pay off the real
harm you've done me. (165) I know your sort and your
'deepest regrets' stuff: I'll be given *your* solemn word
this aggravation was dreadfully out of character - when
I've had this dreadful service!

AE. *(Ignoring him; to the girl)* Go ahead - be brave, open
the door.

SA. So my warning means nothing?

AE. In you go - now!

SA. Oh no you don't! *(grabbing at girl)*

AE. *(protecting her)* Parmeno, quick! Over there! (169)
Too far your side! Stand close beside him! There,
that's what I mean.

170   căuĕ nuncĭam ŏcŭlos a mĕis ŏcŭlis

                                        quoquam demŏuĕas tŭos

      ne mŏrā sit, si innŭĕrim, quin pugnus

                                        contĭnŭo in mala haerĕat.

      SA. istuc uŏlo ergo ipsum expĕriri. em

                                        serua! *PA.* ŏmittĕ mŭlĭĕrem. ¦

      SA. o făcĭnŭs indignum! *AE.* gĕmĭnabit,

                                        nĭsĭ căues.   *SA.* ĕi, mĭsĕrĭam!

      AE. non innŭĕram;   uerum ĭn ĭstam partem pŏtĭus

                                        peccato tămên.

175   i nuncĭam!   *SA.* quĭd hoc rĕist?   regnumne,

                                        Aeschĭne, hic tu possĭdes?

      AE. si possĭderem, ornatŭs esses ex tŭis –

                                        uirtutĭbus.

      SA. quid tĭbĭ rĕi mecumst?   *AE.* nil.   *SA.* quid,

                                        nostin qui sim?   *AE.* non desidĕro.

      SA. tĕtĭgin tui quicquam?   *AE.* si attĭgisses,

                                        ferres – infortunĭum.

      SA. qui tĭbĭ magis   lĭcet meam hăberĕ pro qua ĕgo

                                        argentum dĕdi?

180   responde!   *AE.* ante aedis non fecisse ĕrĭt melius

                                        hic conuicĭum.

170–83 *ia⁸*.   172 hem *DG*.   em serua *Sannioni dedi*: AE. em
serua. PA. omitte mulierem *A*.   (h)em serua omitte mulierem
Parmenoni $C^2D^1E^2FP^2$, *Aeschino* $C^1D^2E^1GP^1$ (hem *DE?G*).   173 o
miserum facinus Σ.   ei misero mihi *A*.   179 quid tibi
$A^1D^1L^1P^1E^1$.

Now pay attention! Don't shift your eyes anywhere

away from mine, so if I nod, your fist will be

simultaneously planted in his jaw, no humming or hawing.

SA. Well, that's the very thing I'd like to try. On

guard! *(Aeschinus nods)*

PA. Leave the lady alone.

SA. Ouch! It's not fair!

AE. He'll match that one if you don't look out.

(Parmeno hits Sannio again)

SA. Ow! That hurt!

AE. I didn't nod that time, but you can go on making that

mistake rather than the other. *(To girl)* (175) Inside

now! *(Exeunt the girl and the slaves)*

SA. What is all this? Are you the local dictator?

AE. If I were, you'd be kitted out to match your sterling

qualities.

SA. What quarrel have you got with me?

AE. None.

SA. Well, do you even know who I am?

AE. No, and I can do without, thanks.

SA. Have I laid a finger on anything of yours?

AE. If you had, your prize would be a surprise.

SA. How come *you're* allowed to own a girl who's mine, who

I paid cash for, but *I'm* not? (180) Well?

AE. Better not have a stand-up quarrel here in public.

nam si mŏlestus pergĭs essĕ, iam intro abripĭere

atque ĭbi¦

usque ad nĕcem opĕrĭerĕ loris. *SA.* loris liber?

AE. sic ĕrît.

SA. ŏ hŏmĭnem inpurum! hicin libertatem aiunt

esse aequam omnĭbus?

184   *AE.* si sătĭs iam debacchatŭs es,

leno, audi si uis nuncĭam.¦

185 *SA.* egŏn debacchatus sum autem an tu in me?

AE. mitte ista atque ad rem rĕdi.

186   *SA.* quam rem? quo rĕdĕam? *AE.* iamnĕ me

uis dicĕre id quŏd ăd te attĭnet?

187 *SA.* cŭpĭo, aequi mŏdo álĭquid. *AE.* uah leno

ĭniquá me non uolt lŏqui!

SA. leno sum, fátĕor, pernĭcĭes   communis

ádŭlescentĭum,

periurus, pestis; tămĕn tĭbi a me nulla ortast

iniurĭa.

190 *AE.* nam hercle etĭam id restat. *SA.* illuc quaeso

rĕdĭ quo coepisti, Aeschĭnê.

AE. mĭnis uiginti tu illam emisti (quae res tĭbĭ

uortat mălê):¦

184, 186 ia^{4+4};   185, 187-96 ia^8. 187 modo aequi γ.
189 est orta γ. 190 hoc restat *A*.

(seeming more friendly). For if you go on being a pest, you'll presently be hauled inside, and in there you'll very near fatally disappear under - their lashes.

SA. Lashes? I'm an Athenian!

AE. That's how it will be.

SA. You disgusting filth! And they call this a democracy!

AE. If your drugs have really worn off, Sannio, would you care to listen now?

SA. (185) *My* drugs? *Yours* more like!

AE. Forget that and get back to the point.

SA. What point? Get back where?

AE. Would you like me to discuss a subject of special interest to *you*?

SA. Yes, as long as you don't take advantage.

AE. That's a good one! In *that* trade, and he doesn't want me to take advantage!

SA. Yes I'm in *that* trade, I'm the universal ruination of the young, a liar, a plague, O.K.; but you haven't had any bad treatment from me.

AE. (190) Of course - that's still on your agenda.

SA. Would you mind going back to what you were getting at, Aeschinus?

AE. You bought that girl for two filthy thousand,

argenti tantum dăbĭtur. *SA.* quid si ĕgo ĭllam nolo

uendĕrê?

coges me? *AE.* mĭnĭme. *SA.* namque id mĕtŭi!

AE. nĕquĕ uendundam censĕo

quae lĭbĕrast: nam ĕgŏ lĭbĕrali illam adsĕro

causa mănu.

195 nunc uĭde ŭtrum uis,   argentum accĭpĕre, an causam

mĕdĭtari tŭom.

delĭbĕra hoc dum ĕgŏ rĕdĕo, leno. *SA.* pro sŭpremĕ

Iuppĭter!

197 mĭnĭme miror qui insanire occĭpĭunt ex iniurĭa!

198 dŏmŏ me erĭpŭit, uerbĕrauit,

me inuito abduxit mĕam; ¦

200 hŏmĭni mĭsĕro plus quingentos

cŏlăphos infregit mĭhi; ¦

199 ob mălĕ facta haec, tantidem emptam

postŭlat   sĭbĭ tradĭer.

201 uerum enĭm quando bĕnĕ promĕrŭit,

fīat: suŏm ius postŭlat.

ăgĕ, iam cŭpĭo, si mŏdo ărgentum

reddat. sĕd ĕgo hoc hărĭolor:

ŭbĭ me dixĕro   dărĕ tanti, testis făcĭĕt ilĭco

---

193 cogis *AG.* 197-208(9?) *tr*⁷. 198 domi *A.* 199 *trans-posuit Muretus. an* bene facta?

and that's how much cash you'll get.

SA.   And what if I choose not sell her? You'll make me?

AE.   Oh no, no, no...

SA.   That *was* worrying me!

AE.   ... nor do I hold that there can be any question

of *selling* a free woman. For I claim her at law as

free.   (195) Now consider which you prefer: take

the money, or prepare your defence. Weigh that up

before I come back, Mr Entrepreneur. *(Enters Micio's)*

SA.   Good God in Heaven! I'm not a bit surprised at people

who start going mad after a mugging! *(Produces his*

cashbook, consults it as if checking items). (198)

He's hauled me out of my house; thrashed me: taken

away a girl that's mine without my consent; (200) he's

cracked more than five hundred clouts on my poor old

head. (199) In return for these unkindnesses, he

proposes she should be handed over to him at cost-price.

Well, since he's done me so much good service, I agree:

he's asking what's fair to him. Come on Sannio, you

really want to - *if* he were to pay the money back.

(Pauses) But I can see what's coming: when I've said

I'm selling at so much, he'll produce instant witnesses

to say

uendidisse me: de argento –

somnium: 'mox; cras redi'. |

205   id quoque possum ferre, si modo reddat, quam–

quam iniuriumst.

uerum cogito id quod res est:

quando eum quaestum occeperis,

accipiunda ac mussitanda iniuria

adulescentiumst.

sed nemo dabit; frustra egomet

mecum has rationes puto.

(ii.2)

SY. tace, egomet conueniam iam ipsum; cupide

accipiat faxo atque etiam

210   bene dicat secum esse actum. quid istuc Sanniost

quod te audio

nescioquid concertasse cum ero? *SA.* numquam uidi

iniquius

certationem comparatam quam haec hodie inter nos

fuit;

---

206 *Don.*: inceperis ω. 208 hanc rationem δ. 209 conueniam
ipsum Σ. iam faxo γD^2p, iam *om.* D^1GL. atque etiam *om.* G.
tr^8 *ut est ante* ia^8 *suspectum;* ia^7 D^1. 210 (?209, 211)-27
ia^8. 210 *melius fluat* bene dicat <?ita> secum esse actum
(tr^4). quid istuc Sanniost *(colon 'di boni quid hoc')* quod
te audio (ia^2). 212 *sic* APC^1D^1: haec quae *cett.*

I've sold her; as to the cash? All in the mind; 'by
and by; come back tomorrow'. (205) I could put up
with that too, however unfair it is, *if* he were to pay.
(Pauses) But I have to face the fact: once you're in
the profession, you've got to suffer violence from
young gentlemen in silence. *(Snapping book shut)* No,
nobody's going to pay: this private audit was a waste
of my precious time.

SY. *(Entering from Micio's, speaking back to Aeschinus)*
Quiet, I'll do it, I'll see his nibs now; I'll have
him eagerly agreeing, and (210) saying besides that
he's been well treated. *(Approaches)* Sannio, what's
your side of the story I hear, that you've had a bit
of a barney with the young master?

SA. I've never heard of a worse-matched fight than the one
                                              we had today;

O: fol. 102

ĕgŏ uapŭlando, ill' uerbĕrando, usque ambo

                              defessi sŭmus.

SY. tua culpa. SA. quid făcĕrem? SY. ădŭlescenti

                    morem gestum ŏportŭit.

215   SA. qui pŏtŭi mĕlĭus, quĭ hŏdie usque os praebŭi?

                              SY. ăgĕ, scis quid lŏquar:

pĕcunĭam in lŏco neglĕgĕrĕ maxŭmum interdumst

                              lŭcrum. hui,

mĕtŭisti, si nunc de tŭo iurĕ concessisses

                              paullŭlum atque

ădŭlescenti esses morĭgĕratŭs, hŏmĭnum hŏmo

                              stultissĭmê,

ne non tĭbi īstuc fenerarĕt? SA. ĕgŏ spem prĕtĭo

                              non ĕmo.

220   SY. numquam rem făcĭes: ăbĭ, nescis   ĭnescare

                    hŏmĭnes, Sannĭo.

SA. credo istuc mĕlĭus essĕ; uerum ĕgŏ numquam

                    ădĕo astutus fŭi

quin quidquid possem mallem auferrĕ pŏtĭus in

                              praesentĭa.

SY. ăgĕ noui tŭom ănĭmum: quăsĭ iam usquam tĭbĭ

                    sint uiginti mĭnae,

---

214 agerem γ.   215 quid potui A.   220 inescare nescis
Bothe.

we're both completely worn out, him with bashing, me
with being bashed.

SY. Your fault.

SA. What should I have done?

SY. The thing to do was go along with the young chap.

SA. (215) How could I more than I did? I've been offering
him my chin all day!

SY. Come on, you know what I mean. In the right circumstances,
not bothering about money can sometimes maximize profits!
(Laughs) Were you afraid that if you had now let go a tiny
bit of what's fair to you and gone along with the young
chap it wouldn't come home with interest? You must be
the most naïve man in the world!

SA. I don't invest in futures.

SY. (220) You'll never be a success; no good, son, you don't
understand the art of hooking people.

SA. Your way may be better, granted: *(ironically)* but then
I have never been *that* sharp - to the extent of *not*
preferring to get off *(scratching palm)* with whatever
I could in hard cash!

SY. Come on, I can read your mind: as if you had any chance
at all now of your two thousand

dum huic \<ne\> obsequare! praeterea autem te aiunt

proficisci Cyprum... SA. hem?

225   SY. ...coemisse hinc quae illuc ueheres multa,

nauem conductam; hoc, scio,

animus tibi pendet. ubi illinc spero redieris

tamen hoc ages.

SA. nusquam pedem! perii hercle: hac illi spe hoc

inceperunt. SY. timet:

inieci scrupulum homini. SA. o scelera! illuc uide

ut in ipso articulo oppressit. emptae mulieres

230   complures et item hinc alia quae porto Cyprum.

nisi eo ad mercatum uenio - damnum maxumumst.

nunc si hoc omitto - actum agam ubi illinc rediero.

nil est: refrixerit res - 'nunc demum uenis?

quor passu's? ubi eras?' - ut sit satius perdere

235   quam aut hic manere tam diu aut tum persequi.

SY. iamne enumerasti quoad te rediturum putes?

SA. hoccin illo dignumst? hoccin incipere Aeschinum,

per oppressionem ut hanc mi eripere postulet?

SY. labascit. unum hoc habeo: uide si satis placet.

224 *suppleui*. in C. *DL*.   228-53 *ia*^{6}.   228 illud *Aδ*.
229 *uel* ut in ipso; *cf. 231; 237*.   232 ac tum agam *Bentley*
duce ignoto ne hietur.   234 *malim* quid passu's?   235 *Kauer*;
quam aut nunc *A*, quam aut hic nunc γ, quam hic nunc δ.
236 quoad *Phillimore*: quod *CPF*^{1}*J*. id quod *cett.* (*om.* quod *D*^{1})
quot *Lindsay-Kauer*.   237 -ne ω, *et sic passim in similibus*.

as long as you *fail* to fall in with him! Besides, the
word is, you're off to Cyprus...

SA. Eh? (225)

SY. You've bought in a lot of stuff here to take there,
and booked passage: your thoughts are all on that - I
understand. But when you get back, as I do hope you
will, you'll see to this business.

SA. I'm not moving a foot anywhere! *(Aside)* I've had it!
This is what they were banking on all along!

SY. *(Aside)* He's afraid: I've caught him on the hop.

SA. *(Aside; as if doing sums)* Damnation! Just see how he's
landed right on the crucial point! I've bought a dozen
girls (230) and other local stuff to take to Cyprus.
If I don't get to the big event there, total disaster.
If I forget about this Aeschinus-thing for now - I'd
be wasting my time when I get back from Cyprus. No
good: it will all have gone off the boil. 'Oh so *here*
you are at last! Why didn't you make a move? Where
were you?'. On balance, I'll be better off losing her
(235) than either staying here that long or prosecuting
later.

SY. Have you worked out yet what date you reckon you'll be
back?

SA. *(Blustering)* Can he stoop to this? Was this the gentleman's
scheme, to rob me of the girl by making me go broke?

SY. *(Aside)* He's on the edge. *(Aloud)* I've got one idea:
                              see if it suits you.

240 pŏtĭus quam uĕnĭas in pĕrĭclum, Sannĭo,

seruesne an perdas totum, diuĭdŭom fắcê:

mĭnas dĕcem   conradĕt ălĭcunde. *SA.* ẹi mĭhi, |

ĕtĭam de sortĕ nunc uĕnĭo in dŭbĭum mĭser?

pŭdet nil? omnis dentis lăbĕfecit mĭhi,

245 praetĕrĕa cŏlăphis tubĕr est   totum căpût:

ĕtĭam insŭper   defrudet? nusquam ăbĕo. *SY.* ut lŭbet.

numquid uis quin ăbĕam? *SA.* immo hercle hoc quaeso

Sўrê: |

ŭtŭt haec sunt actă, pŏtĭus quam litis sĕquar,

meum mĭhi reddatur saltem quanti emptast, Sўrê.

250 scĭŏ te non usum antehac ămĭcĭtĭa mĕa:

mĕmŏrem me dices esse et gratum. *SY.* sedŭlo

făcĭam. sed Ctesĭphonem uĭdĕo: laetŭs est

de ămica. *SA.* quid quod te oro? *SY.* paullisper măne.

(ii.3)

254   *CT.* abs quiuis homĭnĕ quom est ŏpus

benĕfĭcĭum accĭpĕrĕ gaudĕas;

255   uerum enĭmuero id demum iŭuat

si quem aequomst făcĕre is bĕnĕ făcît.

---

240 periculum *A.*   245 colafis γ.   246 defraudat *A,* defrudat δ*E.*   248 facta Σ.   250 esse usum Σ.   254-6 *ia*$^{4+4}$.
254 quouis *J.*   255 bene facere γ*D*^{2}*L*^{1}.

(240) Instead of exposing yourself to the risk of keeping or losing the lot, my friend, split the difference: he'll scrape a thousand together from somewhere or other.

SA. Oh no! Have I now got to start worrying even about the cost-price? It's just not fair! Has he no shame? He's slackened all my teeth; (245) besides that, my head's swollen all over with his clouts; on top of all that is he to swindle me? I'm not budging!

SY. *(Shrugging)* It's your decision. *(Making to leave, timing it carefully)* Anything else you want that er... might keep me here?

SA. *(Breaking)* Yes there is: a favour, Syrus. *(Pauses)* Whatever's to be made of all this bother, rather than me taking him to court, at least let me get back what's mine, Syrus, - I mean the money she cost. (250) I know that up to now you haven't seen me as a friend: one day you'll say I don't forget a favour.

SY. I'll do my honest best. But I can see Ctesipho: he's delighted about his girlfriend.

SA. What about my request?

SY. Just a minute! *(Enter CTESIPHO from town)*

CT. To get help when you need it from any stranger at all is great; (255) but it's utterly tremendous when your saviour is the one who really ought to help!

256   o frater, frater, quĭd ĕgŏ nunc

         te laudem? sătĭs certo scĭo

257   numquam ĭtă magnĭfĭce quicquam dicam, id uirtus

                                   quin sŭpĕret tŭa.|

      ĭtăque unam hanc rem me hăberĕ praetĕr ălĭos

                                   praecĭpŭum arbĭtror,

      fratrem hŏmĭni nemĭni esse primarum artĭum

                                   măgĕ princĭpem.

260   SY. O Ctesĭpho. CT. O Sўre, Aeschĭnŭs

             ŭbĭst? SY. ellum, te exspectat dŏmi. CT. hem.

261   SY. quĭd ĕst? CT. quid sit? illius ŏpĕra, Sўrĕ,

                              nunc uiuo. festiuom căput,

      quin omnĭa sĭbi post putarit essĕ prae meǫ commŏdo?

      mălĕdictă famam meǫm<que> ămorem et peccatum in se

                                   transtŭlit:

      nil pŏtĕ sŭpra.   quidnam forĭs crĕpŭit? SY. mănĕ

                              măne: ipse exit fŏras.

(ii.4)

265   AE. ŭbist ill' săcrĭlĕgus? SA. me quaerit.

                              numquidnam ecfert? occĭdi:

---

256 *an* qui? 257-9, 261-87 *ia*^{8}; 260 *ia*$^{4+4}$. 259 homini
neminem *JγD*, hominem neminem *pG*^{2} (neminem *om. G*^{1}). 262 quin
(qui *DGFE*) omnia *ΣJ*: qui ignominia *A*. 263 -que *addidi*:
laborem *JGLp*, amorem *cett.*, *cf. periocha 6*. 264 *sic Don.*:
potest ω. 265 men(e) *Σ*. ecfert *p*: effert *cett.* (of- *G*).

My dear, dear brother! There just aren't words
extravagant enough to match your brilliance! All I can
say is the one thing that marks me out in all the
world - that no-one ever had a brother more amazing
for his amazing talents!

SY. (260) Hi, Ctesipho!

CT. Syrus, hi! Where's my brother?

SY. *Voilà* - he's at home, waiting for you.

CT. What?

SY. What's the matter?

CT. The matter? Don't you realise, Syrus? It's thanks to
him I'm still alive! How fantastic can anyone be?
Why, everything from his angle has counted second to
my convenience. The hostile remarks, the gossip, my
affair and my going wrong - he's taken it all on
himself. Nothing could beat it! *(Startled, scuttling
at noise within)* The door - what does that mean?

SY. Wait, wait, it's your brother coming out.

AE. *(Entering)* Where is he, the ghoul? (265)

SA. He's after me. Has he got any cash with him? Oh, no,

that's the end:

nil uideo. *AE.* ehem opportune: te ipsum quaero.

quid fit, Ctesipho?

in tutost omnis res: omitte uero tristitiem tuam.

CT. ego illam hercle uero omitto qui quidem te

habeam fratrem: o mi Aeschine,

o mi germane! ah uereor coram in os te laudare

amplius,

270 ne id adsentandi mage quam quo habeam gratum facere

existumes.

AE. age inepte, quasi nunc non norimus nos inter nos,

Ctesipho.

hoc mihi dolet, nos paene sero scisse et paene

in eum locum

redisse ut si omnes cuperent nil tibi possent

auxiliarier.

CT. pudebat. *AE.* ah stultitiast istaec, non pudor.

tam ob paruolam

275 rem paene e patria... turpe dictu. deos quaeso ut

istaec prohibeant.

CT. peccaui. *AE.* quid ait tandem nobis Sannio?

SY. iam mitis est.

---

267 tristitiam ΣJ.   268 hercle *om.* A *(corr. J)*: facile Σ
(f. hercle *DL*).   272 sed hoc Σ. et in eum rem locum
Bentley.   273 nihil tibi A^2, *Eugraphius*: tibi nihil A^1Σ.
275 ex Σ.

I can't see anything.

AE. *(To Ctesipho)* Ah good: it's you I want. All right,

Ctesipho? The whole consignment's safe in port:

(Nodding to house) you really can forget your blues.

CT. Yes, with a brother like you, I really can: God bless

you, Aeschinus, you're, you're...no, I can't say more

to your face, it's too embarrassing...maybe you'd put

it down to flattery rather than think I do it because

I think it's a pleasure to do it... (271)

AE. Come on, don't be silly: as if you and I didn't know

each other, Ctesipho! My only regret is that we found

out almost too late and almost got into the position

that if the whole world had been on your side, it

couldn't have done any good.

CT. I was ashamed...

AE. No, that wasn't shame, that was being daft! Leaving

Athens over such a tiny scrap! *(Nodding to house)*

It doesn't bear speaking about. Let's hope that's an

end to any such ideas of yours. (276)

CT. Yes, I was wrong.

AE. Well, what's Sannio's final word?

SY. *(Glancing at Sannio)* He's agreeable now.

AE. ĕgo ad fŏrum ibo ŭt hunc absoluam: tu intro

        ăd īllam, Ctesĭpho.

SA. Sy̆re, insta. *SY.* ĕamus; namque hic prŏpĕrat

   in Cy̆prum. *SA.* ne<c> tam quĭdem;

quamuis ĕtĭam mănĕo otĭosŭs hic. *SY.* reddetur,

         ne tĭme.⎪

280   *SA.* ăt ŭt omnĕ reddat... *SY.* omnĕ reddet; tăcĕ

    mŏdo ac sĕquĕre hac. *SA.* sĕquor.

CT. heus heus Sy̆re. *SY.* hem? quĭd ĕst? *CT.* obsĕcro

     herclĕ te, hŏmĭnem istum inpurissĭmum

quam primum absoluĭtotĕ, ne si măgĭs irritatus sĭet,

ălĭqua ad pătrem hoc permānet atque ĕgŏ tum

       perpĕtŭo pĕriĕrim.

SY. non fīet; bŏno ănĭmo esto; tu cum illa intus

      te oblecta intĕrim.

285   et lectŭlos   iubĕ sterni nobis et părari cetĕrā.⎪

  ĕgŏ iam transacta re conuortam me dŏmum   cum opşonĭo.⎪

CT. ĭtă quaeso. quando hoc bĕnĕ successit,

     hĭlăre hunc sumamus dĭem.

---

278 *suppleui* (non *Madvig*). 279 quam uis; etiam *Don.*; maneo
etiam *A*. 281 hem *om. A*. hercle te *JCP*: te hercle *A*, te
om. cett. 283 tum *Ap*: tunc *cett.* 284 es *AC[1]*. tu *om. DGo*
te intus Σ. 287 hoc *om.* Σ.

AE. I'll go to town to pay him off; Ctesipho, indoors to your one and only.

SA. Syrus, attack!

SY. Let's go; for our friend is in a hurry for Cyprus.

SA. Yes, but not so much of a hurry; I can go on staying, free as you like, here in Athens.

SY. You'll be paid, don't worry.

SA. (280) But the *total* payment is...

SY. ...what you'll get: just keep quiet and come this way.

SA. I'm coming. *(Leaving for town)*

CT. *(From house)* Hsst! Syrus!

SY. Eh? What's up?

CT. For goodness' sake, pay that filthy villain off as quick as you can so if he gets any more prickly the story can't somehow soak through to father - that would mean my definite destruction!

SY. That won't happen. Keep your spirits up; while we're away, amuse yourself with her indoors (285) and tell the staff to arrange the dining-room and get all the rest ready. On completion of present negotiations I shall report back home with - the goodies.

CT. Jolly good! As it's all turned out well, let's 'down the day with merriment' *(Exeunt; Syrus may be accompanied by a couple of silent extras)*

(iii.1)

SO. obsĕcro   mĕă nutrix, quid nunc

                              fīet? CA. quid fīat rŏgas?

recte ĕdĕpol spero. mŏdŏ dŏlores,

                              mĕă tu, occĭpĭunt primŭlum:

290   iam nunc tĭmes,   quăsĭ numquam adfŭĕris,

                              numquam tutĕ pĕpĕrĕris?

SO. mĭsĕram me! nemĭnem hăbĕo – solae sŭmŭs, Gĕta

                              autem hic non ădest –

nec quem ăd obstĕtricem mittam,

                              nec qui accersat Aeschĭnum.

CA. pŏl is quĭdem   iam hic ădĕrit; nam numquam

                              unum intermittit dĭem

quin semper uĕnĭat. SO. solus mĕarum mĭsĕrĭarumst

                              rĕmĕdĭum.

295   CA. e re nata mĕlĭus fĭĕri haud pŏtŭit quam

                              factumst, ĕrâ,

quando uĭtĭum oblatumst, quŏd ăd illum attĭnet

                              pŏtissĭmum,

talem, tali ingĕnĭo atque ănĭmo,

                              natum ex tanta fămĭlĭa.

---

288 *tr⁷*.   fiet rogas γ.   289-91 *ia⁸*.   292 *tr⁷*.
293-4 *ia⁸*.   295-8 *tr⁷*.   295 erae natae Σ.   296 quando Σ:
quom *A*.   297 ingenio *Bentley*: genere ω.

(Enter SOSTRATA and CANTHARA from the second house)

SO.   Nanny dear, *please* - what's the next stage?

CA.   The next stage? An easy delivery I hope. Her

contractions are only just coming on, dearie:

(290) are you worried already, as if you'd never

assisted, never had a baby yourself?

SO.   I can't think straight! I've no-one - we're on

our own, our Geta is out - either to send for the

midwife or to fetch Aeschinus.

CA.   Why, he'll be here by and by. He never lets a day go

by without coming regular.

SO.   He's the only one who can be the cure of my troubles.

CA.   As things were set, his being involved of all people

has turned out for the best, Ma'am, given she's been

got into trouble I mean, such a nice young man, such

a fine character, and such an important family!

C: fol. 55

SO. ĭtă pŏl est ut dicis: saluos

nobis dęǫs quaeso ut sĭet.

(iii.2)

GE. nunc illŭd est quom si omnĭa omnes

sŭă consĭlĭă confĕrant

300 atque huic mălo sălutem quaerant, auxĭli

nil adfĕrant,

quod mihique ĕraeque filĭaeque ĕrilist.

uae mĭsĕro mĭhi!

tot res rĕpentĕ circumuallant se unde emergi

non pŏtest:

uis ĕgestas iniustĭtĭa solĭtudo infamĭâ.|

hoccin saeclum! o scĕlĕra, o gĕnĕră

săcrĭlĕga, ŏ hŏmĭnem inpĭum!

305 SO. me mĭsĕram, quidnam est quod sic uĭdĕo tĭmĭdum

et prŏpĕrantem Gĕtam?

GE. quem nĕquĕ fĭdes nĕquĕ iusiurandum nĕque

illum mĭsĕrĭcordĭâ

---

299 cum D^1, quod cum G: quod cett. 299-302 ia^8. 302 se
AD^1L, Don.: om. cett. 303-4 tr^7., 305-12 ia^8. 306 an illim?

SO.   Yes, you're quite right of course; Heaven protect

him for all our sakes.

(Enter GETA running from the town)

GE.   Now it's come to this, that if all the world

sat down to offer us all their plans (300)

to find a remedy for the mess

which faces the lady, the girl, and me

They couldn't deliver us any resource,

but gloom, pain, misery, tragedy.

So many things suddenly box us in

from which there's no way we'll escape:

Violence, poverty, wrongs, injustice,

friendlessness and loss of face.

Oh what a world! Immorality, villainy,

filth, and *his* base treachery...

SO.   (305) What on earth can it be? Why is Geta in such a

tizzy and fluster? Oh dear, I don't like the look

of this!

GE.   ...whom honour, oath, pity have not availed

repressit nĕquĕ rĕflexit nĕquĕ quod partŭs

                                        instabat prŏpê

quoi mĭsĕrae indigne per uim uĭtĭum obtŭlĕrat.

                                    SO. non intellĕgo

sătĭs quae lŏquatur. CA. prŏpĭŭs obsĕcro accedamus,

                                    Sostrăta. GE. ah

310   me mĭsĕrum, uix sum compos ănĭmi, ĭta ardĕo

                                        iracundĭa;

nil est quod malim, quam illam totam fămĭlĭam

                            dărĭ mi obuĭam ¦

ŭt ĕgo iram hanc ĭn ĕos euŏmam omnem dum aegrĭtudo

                            haec est rĕcens.

313   sătĭs mĭhi ĭd hăbĕam supplĭci –

            dum illos ulciscar <mĕo> mŏdo!

314   sĕni ănĭmam primum exstinguĕrem ipsi qui illud

                            produxit scĕlus;

315   tum autem Sўrum impulsorem – uah, quĭbŭs illum

                            lăcĕrarem mŏdis!

sublimem mĕdĭum †ᴗrimum arrĭpĕrem et căpĭte in

                            terra stătŭĕrem,

        ut cĕrĕbro dispergat uĭam;¦

---

309 satius quae loquitur::proprius A.   312 hanc iram A.
313 ia^{4+4}, 314-6 ia^8.   313 meo add. Bothe.   316 medium
arriperem et capite primum in terram Σ.   primum suspectum.
stuerem A.   317 ia^4.

to repel or restrain, nor even the thought

that her labour was any day due to begin,

that innocent girl that he got into trouble –

she never deserved that wicked assault!

SO. I can't quite make out what he's saying.

CA. Come on, let's move closer, Sostrata.

GE. (310) Grrr! I can hardly control myself, I'm so bloody

blazing! There's nothing I'd like better than to have

the whole clan put right in front of us to spew my

bile all over them while the pain is still piping hot.

I'd reckon that sentence would fit the crime – as long

as I punished them *my* way! The old one first – I'd

snuff out his candle for spawning the monster. (315)

Then Syrus who egged him on – grr, what a mawling I'd

give *him*! I'd heave him in the air by the middle and

stand his head on the ground to spatter the street

with his brains:

adulescenti ipsi eriperem oculos,

　　　　　post haec praecipitem darem.

ceteros - ruerem agerem raperem

　　　　　　　tunderem ac prosternerem.

320　sed cesso eram hoc malo impertiri propere?

　　　　　　　　　　SO. reuocemus. Geta! GE. hem

quisquis es sine me. SO. ego sum, Sostrata.

　　　　　　　GE. ubi east? te ipsam quaerito,

te expeto, oppido opportune

　　　　　　　te obtulisti mi obuiam, |

era... SO. quid est? quid trepidas? GE. ei mihi!

　　　　　　　　　CA. quid festinas, mi Geta? |

animam recipe! GE. prorsus... SO. quid istuc

　　　　　　　'prorsus' ergost? GE. periimus;

325　actumst. SO. eloquere obsecro te quid sit.

　　　　　　　GE. iam... SO. quid 'iam', Geta? |

GE. Aeschinus... SO. quid is ergo? GE. alienus est

　　　　　　　ab nostra familia. SO. hem

perii! qua re? GE. amare occepit

　　　　　　　aliam. SO. uae miserae mihi!

318-9 tr⁷, 320 ia⁸, 321-9 tr⁷. 321 es *om. A.* 322 *Bentley:*
expecto ω. 323 f. quid...recipe *Sostratae Probus dabat,*
Cantharae Asper, v. Don. 324 animam *Ap :* animum *cett.*

As for his nibs, the young one, I'd gouge out his
eyes, and after that, throw him off a cliff. The
staff? I'd batter 'em, shatter 'em, pestle and mortar
'em flat. (320) But I'd better hurry up and share
this disaster with Madam Sostrata.

SO. Let's call him back. Geta!

GE. Let go, whoever you are.

SO. It's me, your mistress.

GE. Where is she? Ah! It's you that I'm after, you that
I desperately need, you're meeting me due on cue,
madam... *(Breaks down wheezing)*

SO. What's wrong? Why are you shaking?

GE. It's terrible! *(Still wheezing)*

CA. Why such a fuss, you silly old man? Get your breath!

GE. Utterly... *(As before)*

SO. Well, utterly what?

GE. ...destroyed; (325) we've had it. *(As before)*

SO. Geta, *please!* Tell us what's wrong!

GE. From now on... *(As before)*

SO. Yes, from now on - what, Geta?

GE. Aeschinus... *(As before)*

SO. Well, what about him?

GE. ...is a stranger to our family. *(Finally recovering)*.

SO. No! Oh no! *(Pauses)* But - why?

GE. He's fallen in love with someone else.

SO. *(Weeps)* No, I can't, I can't...

GE. nĕque ĭd occulte fert: ab lenone

                     ipsŭs erĭpŭit pălam.

SO. sătĭn hoc certumst?   GE. certum; hisce

               ŏcŭlis ĕgŏmet uidi, Sostrăta.   SO. ah

330   me mĭsĕram! quid iam credas aut quoi credas?

                    nostrumne Aeschĭnum

    nostram uitam omnĭum, in quo nostrae spes ŏpesque

                            omnes sĭtae

    ĕrănt? qui sĭne hac iurabat se unum numquam

                     uicturum dĭem?

    qui se in sŭi   grĕmĭo pŏsĭturum pŭĕrum dicebat

                       pătrîs,

    ĭta obsĕcraturum, ut lĭcerĕt hanc sĭbi ŭxorem

                       ducĕrê?

335   GE. ĕră, lăcrŭmas mitte ac pŏtĭus quŏd ăd hanc rem

                   ŏpŭs est porro prospĭcê:

    pătĭamurne an narremus quoipĭam?   CA. au au

                mĭ homo, sanŭn es?

    ăn hŏc profĕrendum tĭbĭ uĭdetŭr usquam?   GE. mĭhĭ

               quĭdĕm non plăcet:

---

329 certumst *AG*, certe *CPF*, certo *D[1]LE*. certum *A*: certe *ΣJ*.
his *A*. 330–42 *ia[8]*. 335 porro consule γ. 336 au...esse
Cantharae AG, Sostratae cett. au *ADE*. 337 proferendum hoc γ.
usquam esse *A*, esse *p*, esse usquam *cett.*: esse *del. Bentley*.

GE. And he's making no secret of it: he stole the girl
from the brothel-keeper for all to see!

SO. Is this quite certain?

GE. Certain; I saw it with my very own eyes, Sostrata.

SO. (330) This is awful! Can't anyone trust anyone about
anything any more? That our own dear Aeschinus should
do this! He was the soul of our family! All our
hope and strength lay in him! Was it really him I
remember swearing he could not live another day without
her, and saying that he would set the baby on his
father's lap, and earnestly ask him for what else but
his blessing on their marriage?

GE. (335) Madam, tears aren't going to help. Instead you ought
to plan ahead what the situation requires. Are we to
put up with it, or tell someone?

CA. Are you completely insensitive? How can you possibly
think of telling under any circumstances?

GE. No, *I* certainly don't think it's a good idea.

iam primum illum alieno animo a nobis esse res

ipsa indicat;

nunc si hoc palam   proferimus, ille infitias ibit,

sat scio;

340 tua fama et gnatae uita in dubium ueniet. tum

si maxume

fateatur, quom amat aliam, non est utile hanc

illi dari.

quapropter quoquo pacto tacitost opus. SO. ah

minime gentium:

343   non faciam. GE. quid ages? SO. proferam.

CA. hem

mea Sostrata,   uide quam rem agis!

344 SO. peiore res loco   non potis est esse quam in

quo nunc sitast.

345 primum indotatast; tum praeterea, quae secunda

ei dos erat

periit: pro uirgine   dari nuptum non potest.

hoc relicuomst:

---

338 alienum AC^1. 339 proferemus Σ. ille *om. A*. 341 amat
D^2EF: amet *cett*. dare *DEF*. 343 ia^{4+2+2}.quid agis Σ. hem...
agis *Cantharae AGP, Getae cett. an* GE. hem. CA. mea...?
344-47 ia^8. 344 nunc siest *A*.

For one thing, the facts show that he no longer has

any feelings for us. As it is, if we do make it public

knowledge, its obvious he'll deny it. Your reputation

and her mode of life will come under suspicion. Then

even if he did admit the truth, since he's in love

with somebody else, it's not in her interest to be

married off to him. For these reasons, whatever line

we take, silence is *essential*.

SO. No, no, no! Absolutely not!

GE. What are you going to do?

SO. I'll make it public.

CA. What? My dear, consider the consequences!

SO. Things couldn't be set worse than they already are.

(345) First, she has no dowry; besides, what should

have been the next best to a dowry has been lost: she

can't be given in marriage as a maiden. This is left.

si infĭtĭas ibit, testis mecum est anŭlus

                                  quem amisĕrat.

postremo, quando ĕgŏ consciā mĭhi sum a me

                                  culpam esse hanc prŏcul,

nĕquĕ prĕtĭum nĕquĕ rem ullam intercessisse

                                  illa aut me indignam, Gĕtâ,¦

350   expĕrĭar. *GE.* quĭd ĭstic? † accedo; ut mĕlĭus

                                  dicas. *SO.* tu quantum pŏtes

ăbi ătque Hegĭoni cognato hūiūs rem enarrato

                                  omnem ordĭnê;

nam is nostro Simŭlo   fuĭt summŭs et nos

                                  cŏluĭt maxŭme.

GE. nam hercle ălĭus nemo respĭcĭet nos.

                                  SO. prŏpĕra tu, mĕă Canthărâ,

curre, obstĕtricem accerse, ut quom ŏpŭs sit ne

                                  in mŏra   nobis sĭet.

(iii.3)

355   *DE.* dispĕrĭi! Ctesĭphonem audiui filĭum¦

una adfŭisse in raptĭonĕ cum Aeschĭno.¦

---

347 miserat *A.*   348 *ia*$^{4+4}$, 349-54 *ia*^{8}.   349 illa *Pp, Don,* :
illam *cett.*   350 ω *Don., Eugraphius, Lactantius, et (sed*
dicis) Priscianus: cedo *Bentley. an diuidendum sic*: ...
Geta, ex/periar.::quid istic? accedo...?   353 nam... nos
Sostratae AL^{1}E^{1}, nam Σ*J*: cum *A.* respicit Σ.   355-516 *ia*^{6}.

If he denies it, I have a witness with me *(produces ring and flourishes it)* - the ring he lost! Since I know in my heart that I am far from any blame in this affair, and that no money or valuables have changed hands in a manner beneath either her or me, Geta - (350) I shall go to law.

GE. Very well; I give way; I only hope...

SO. Off with you, quick as you can, and tell Hegio the whole story in detail. He's a relative of hers; he was very close with my poor dear Simulus, and took real interest in us.

GE. Yes, certainly no-one else is going to want to know us.

SO. Canthara dear, run, fetch the midwife, so she won't be missing when we need her. *(Exeunt, GETA to country, CANTHARA to town, SOSTRATA to her house. Enter DEMEA from town)*

DE. (355) Damn! That's the end of me! I've heard that my boy Ctesipho was along with Aeschinus in the act of seizing the girl! All I

id misero restat mihi mali, si illum potest

qui aliquoi reist, etiam eum ad nequitiem adducere.

ubi ego illum quaeram? credo abductum in ganeum

360   aliquo: persuasit ille inpurus, sat scio.

sed eccum Syrum ire uideo. hinc scibo iam ubi siet.

atque hercle hic de grege illost: si me senserit

eum quaeritare, numquam dicet carnufex.

non ostendam id me uelle.

                                    SY. omnem rem modo seni

365   quo pacto haberet enarramus ordine –

nil quicquam uidi laetius. *DE.* pro Iuppiter,

hominis stultitiam! *SY.* conlaudauit filium;

mihi, qui id dedissem consilium, egit gratias.

DE. disrumpor! *SY.* argentum adnumerauit illico;

370   dedit praeterea in sumptum dimidium minae.

id distributum sane est ex sententia. *DE.* em

huic mandes siquid recte curatum uelis!

SY. ehem Demea, haud aspexeram te. quid agitur?

DE. quid agatur? uostram nequeo mirari satis

375   rationem. *SY.* est hercle inepta, ne dicam

                              dolo, atque

---

358 alicuius *PF¹*.   eum *om. GE*; eum adducere *CFP¹*.   nequitiam
ΣJ.   361 iam hinc scibo *A*.   366 uidi quicquam γ.   368 qui id
APC²: qui (quid *C¹F¹*)Σ.   371 est sane δ.

need now to make my misery complete is if Aeschinus

can seduce him too, the one who's worth something,

into being a drop-out. Where should I try to find

him? I expect he's been taken off to some low dive

(360); that vandal over-ruled him, that's for sure.

Ah, here comes Syrus. *(Enter SYRUS (and extras?) from*

town laden with 'the goodies', cf. 286). I'll find out

from him where he is. But wait a minute· he's one of

the gang. If he notices I'm trying to find Ctesipho,

he'll clam up, the brute.

SY. *(Unaware of Demea)* We've just told the old gentleman

(365) the whole business in detail in its proper light.

I've never seen anyone more delighted.

DE. *(Aside)* Good God! The folly of the man!

SY. He congratulated Aeschinus heartily, and, as for me,

why, he thanked me for coming up with the idea.

DE. *(Aside)* I'm going to burst!

SY. He paid out the cash on the spot (370) and gave us

fifty for expenses. That's been recycled in choice

style. *(Indicating purchases)*

DE. *(Approaching Syrus, out loud)* If you want a job done

right, here's your man, leave it to him!

SY. Er... Demea...I didn't see you. All right?

DE. Right? I simply can't begin to understand the way you

people operate! (375)

SY. Yes, it's off the mark, it's ridiculous, I tell you no

lies.

absurdă. piscis ceterŏs   purga, Drŏmo;

gongrum istum maxŭmum in aqua sinĭto ludĕre

tantisper: ubi egŏ rediero, exossabĭtur;

priŭs nolo. *DE.* haecin flagĭtĭa! *SY.* mihi

                                        quĭdĕm non placent

380   et clamo saepĕ. salsamenta haec, Stephanĭo,

fac macĕrentur pulchre. *DE.* di uostram fĭdem!

utrum, studĭone id sibi habet an laudi putat

forĕ si perdĭdĕrit gnatum? uae misĕro mihi!

uĭderĕ uĭdĕor iam diem illum quom hinc ĕgens

385   profŭgĭet alĭquo milĭtatum. *SY.* Demĕa,

istuc est sapĕrĕ, non quŏd antĕ pĕdes mŏdost

uĭderĕ, sĕd etĭam illa quae futura sunt

prospĭcerĕ! *DE.* quid, istaec iam pĕnes

                                        uos psaltrĭast?

SY. ellam intus. *DE.* ĕho an dŏmist   habĭturus?

                                        SY. credo; ut est

---

377 gongrum *ADE*: congrum *cett.*   378 paulisper *ΣJ, Don. ad An.*
418. uenero Σ.   389 *ita Don.*: est iam ω.

(While saying this, he opens Micio's door and starts
unpacking his purchases, which the staff silently
take in. Calling indoors:)

Clean the rest of those fish, Dromo, but let that

whopper of an eel frolic in the water a teeny bit. When

I'm back, he'll get filleted: (379) not till then.

DE. Such terrible things!

SY. *(Deliberately ambiguous)* I certainly don't like them

and I often say it loud and clear. *(Shouts)* Stephanio!

Make sure these pickled ones get a really good soak!

DE. Heavens above! Which can it be? Is ruining Aeschinus

utterly some scheme of Micio's, or does he think

there's a prize for it? I think it's dreadful! Oh

dear, I can already see the day when Aeschinus will

be a beggar (385) on the road from Athens to join up

as a mercenary!

SY. *(Wiping hands all too near Demea's nose)* There's real

smack in what you say, sir, not only seeing what's at

your feet *(Kicks a dead fish)*, but also spotting in

advance what's really going to happen! *(Cithara-*

music within)

DE. What? Is that *artiste* of yours installed already?

SY. Take a look inside!

DE. *(Recoiling)* What! Is he going to keep her at *home*?

SY. I think so; it would square with

390 dementĭa. *DE.* haecin fĭĕri! *SY.* ĭneptă lenĭtas

pătrĭs et facĭlĭtas prauă... *DE.* fratris me quĭdem

pŭdet pĭgetque. *SY.* nĭmĭum inter uos, Demĕa, ac

— non quĭa ădes praesens dico hoc — pernĭmĭum

intĕrest.

tu quantus quantus nil nĭsî sapĭentĭa es:

395 ill' somnĭum. sinĕres uero   tu illum tŭom

facĕre haec? *DE.* sinĕrem illum? aut non sex totis

mensĭbus

prĭŭs olfecissem quam illĕ quicquam coepĕret?

SY. uĭgĭlantĭam   tŭam tu mĭhĭ narras? *DE.* sic sĭet

mŏdo ŭt nunc est quaeso. *SY.* ut quisquĕ suŏm uolt

esse, ĭtast.

400 *DE.* quĭd ĕum, uidistine hŏdĭe? *SY.* tŭomne filĭum?

abĭgam hunc rus. iamdudum alĭquid ruri ăgĕre arbĭtror.

DE. satĭn scis ĭbi esse? *SY.* oh qui ĕgŏmet produxi...

DE. optŭmest;

metŭi ne haereret hic. *SY.* ...atque iratum admŏdum!

DE. quĭd autem?

---

394 quantus quantu's *edd.* 395 tu *om. AP.* illum tu γ.
397 coeperet *D²GF²E(?) Priscianus 1. 500:* -rit *cett.*
401 hinc *PF²E¹.* 402 quem *δF¹Don.*

(390) his crazy outlook.

DE. Can this be happening?

SY. The father's mistaken leniency and perverse laxness...

DE. I for one am sick and tired of my brother.

SY. There's a big difference between you two, Demea - I'm
not saying this because you're here in front of me -
yes, a big, big difference. Small you may be, but
your juice is sharpness itself. (395) That one? He's
bogus. I mean, would you let your boy do all this?

DE. Let him? Better ask wouldn't I have smelt it six
whole months before he started anything!

SY. You don't need to make a point of your watchfulness to
me, sir.

DE. I just want him to be exactly as he is this minute.

SY. The father's wish is father to the man.

DE. *(Over-casually)* (400). Speaking of whom ... have you
seen him at all today?

SY. Who? Oh, your son. *(Aside)* I'll head him off to the
farm. *(Aloud)* I think he's been busy at something a
good while at the farm.

DE. Are you quite sure he's there?

SY. *(Laughs)* Of course! I was the one that took him out!

DE. That's excellent: I was afraid he might be hanging
around here.

SY. And a fine old temper he was in! DE. *Now* what?

SY. adortust iurgio   fratrem apud forum

405 de psaltria istac. DE. ain uero? SY. ah nil

                                      reticuit.

nam ut numerabatur forte argentum, interuenit

homo de inprouiso: coepit clamare, 'o Aeschine, ¦

haecin flagitia facere te! haec te admittere ¦

indigna genere nostro!' DE. oh lacrumo gaudio!

410 SY. 'non tu hoc argentum perdis, sed uitam tuam'.

DE. saluos sit! spero! est similis maiorum suom!

                                      SY. hui!

DE. Syre, praeceptorum plenust istorum ille.

                                      SY. phy!

domi habuit unde disceret. DE. fit sedulo;

nil praetermitto; consuefacio; denique ¦

415 inspicere tamquam in speculum in uitas omnium

iubeo atque ex aliis sumere exemplum sibi: ¦

'hoc facito'. SY. recte sane. DE. 'hoc fugito'.

                                      SY. callide!

---

404 est *om.* A, est iurgio γ, iurgio est δ. 405 ah *Bothe:*
uah ω, *cf. 445; quod ut pyrrhichum audit Marouzeau utroque in*
loco. ista *Lindsay-Kauer.* 407 o *del. Lindsay-Kauer, cf. 449.*
408 haecine ω, *cf. ad 237.* 409 gaudia A. 411 *distinxi:*sit;
spero; est *Spengel, Stampini:* sit! spero, est *edd. cett.*
suorum FE. 412 -urum plenus es A. 415 inuitast A[1]: -um
uitas Σ. 416 -meresimplum A. 417 facio A.

SY. He set about his brother at the Exchange with moral
outrage (405) about your *artiste*.

DE. Really?

SY. And how! He didn't miss anything out! You see, just
as the cash was being counted, the fellow happened to
drop in unexpectedly. He started shouting, 'For shame,
Aeschinus! How can *you* do such terrible things! How
can you commit acts which disgrace our family!'.

DE. Oh, it makes me weep for joy! (410)

SY. 'It's not this money you're flinging away (*Gestures*),
it's your life'.

DE. Bless him! Hope springs eternal! He *is* like his sires
of yore!

SY. *(Aside)* I don't *believe* this!

DE. Syrus, that lad's full of moral comments like that one.

SY. *(Aside)* Yuck! *(To Demea)* He's had his own special
apprenticeship.

DE. One does one's honest best; I pass nothing over; I
train him; in short, (415) I tell him to look into people's
lives as if into a mirror and take his model from
others: 'Do this in future'.

SY. Quite right!

DE. 'Always avoid *that*'.

SY. Subtle!

DE. 'hoc laudist'. SY. istaec res est. DE. 'hoc

uitio datur'.

SY. prŏbissĭme. DE. porro autem... SY. non hercle

otĭumst

420 nunc mi auscultandi. piscis ex sententĭa

nactus sum: i mihi ne corrumpantur cautĭosʳ.

nam id nobis tam flagitĭumst quam illä, Demêâ,

non fắcĕrĕ uobis quae mŏdŏ dixti: et quod quĕo

conseruis ắd ĕundem istunc praecĭpĭo mŏdum: |

425 hoc salsumst, hoc ắdustumst, hoc lautumst părum; |

illud recte - ĭtĕrum sic mêmento'. sedŭlo

mŏnĕo quae possum pro mĕa   săpĭentĭa:

postremo, tamquam in spĕcŭlum, in pătĭnas, Demêâ, |

inspĭcĕrĕ iŭbĕo et mŏnĕo quid facto usŭ' sit.

430 ĭnepta haec essĕ nos quae facĭmus sentĭo;

uerum quid fắcĭas? ŭt hŏmost ĭtă morem gĕras.

numquid uis? DE. mentem uobis mĕlĭorem dări.

SY. tu rus hinc ibis? DE. recta. SY. nam quid tu

hic ăgas,

---

421 i *om.* A: hi (ii *D¹*) Σ. 422 nam illa A. 424 istunc
(-um *GL*) Σ: ipsum *A*, illis *J*. 427 sententia *CFE*. 429
siet Σ. 430 quae nos (q. facimus n. *G*) δ. 433 abis γ.
recte Σ (*praeter* F²)

DE.   'This is a source of praise'.

SY.   That's just the job!

DE.   'That counts as a failing'.

SY.   Most proper!

DE.   That's only the start...

SY.   *(Interrupting)* I really don't have the time (420) to
      pay proper attention just now. I've got some choice
      fish, and I've strict instructions not to let them go
      off. For it's as terrible for the likes of us not to
      do the things you were just saying, sir, as for you
      important people. I give my colleagues on the staff
      enlightenment in just the same way as you described,
      though not as good of course: (425) *(Mimes tasting)*
      'This needs more salt, this should be crisper, this
      lacks flavour; you've got that perfect, remember to do
      it like that the next time'. I do my honest best to pass
      on all I can kitchen-wise. In a word, I tell them to
      look into the pans, sir, as if into a mirror, and tell them
      what needs doing. (430) I appreciate our ways are off
      line, sir, but then what's a fellow to do? It's the man
      that determines the service he gets. Anything else, sir?

DE.   Yes, a saner outlook in all of you, please!

SY.   Will you be going to the farm?

DE.   Straight there.

SY.   Of course: what difference could one make here

ŭbĭ siquid bĕnĕ praecĭpĭas nemo obtempĕrat?

435   *DE.* ĕgŏ uero hinc ăbĕo, quando is quam ob rem huc

                             uenĕram

rus ăbĭĭt: illum curo unum, ille ad me attĭnet.

quando ĭtă uolt frater, de istoc ipsĕ uidĕrit.

sed quĭs ĭllĭc est   quem uĭdĕo prŏcŭl? estne

                                   Hegĭo

tribulis noster? si sătĭs cerno ĭs hĕrclest. uăha ¦

440   hŏmo ămicus nobis iam inde a pŭĕro - o di bŏni,

ne illiŭs mŏdi   iam magna nobis ciuĭum

paenurĭast -   hŏmo ăntiqua uirtute ac fĭde! ¦

haud cĭtŏ măli   quĭd ortum ex hoc sit publĭce.

quam gaudĕo!   ŭbi ĕtĭam hūiŭs gĕnĕris rĕlĭquĭas

445   restarĕ uĭdĕo, ah, uiuĕre ĕtĭam nunc lŭbet.

oppĕrĭar hŏmĭnem hic ut sălutem et conlŏquar.

(iii.4)

     HE. pro di inmortales, făcĭnŭs indignum, Gĕtă!

quid narras! *GE.* sic est factum. *HE.* ex illan

                             fămĭlĭă

---

434 -ret *AG¹F¹*, *Nonius 372*. 436 ille admeat *A*. 438 procul
quem uideo Σ, *cf. Pl. Rud. 442/50*. 439 tribunus *A*. is *om.* Σ
praeter pJ: bis *A*. uaha *GL:* uah *cett.* 440 o *AGLp: om. cett.*
441 neque *A*. nobis magna *A*. 442 homo *del. Guyet*. 444-5 *uel*
gaudeo, ubi...uideo! ah... 445 uah ω: *corr. Guyet*.
448 quod *Fleckeisen*. illam *A*.

where no-one takes any notice, whatever good counsel
is on offer? *(Exit into Micio's)*

DE.   (435) Yes, I'm leaving all right, since the one for
whose sake I came has gone to the country. *He's* my
one and only concern, *he's* my boy. Since my brother
wants it that way, let him see about the one who
isn't! *(Stops, peers to country)* Who's that I can see
in the distance? Is it...is it Hegio, from our parish?
If my eyes are right - yes, it really *is* him! *(Sighs)*
(440) A friend of ours ever since we were boys - Lord,
what a great dearth there is these days of good men and
true like him - a man of his word, of good old sterling
quality! Him the source of harm to society? Not in a
hundred years! I'm really pleased! When I come across
any of the breed still left with us, it makes me (445)
realize - *(takes deep breath)* - ah life is still worth
living after all! *(enter HEGIO and GETA)* I'll wait
for him here to say hello and have a chat.

HE.   Heavens help us, what a disgraceful business, Geta!
What a story! •

GE.   No story, sir - the truth.

HE.   *That* family the source of such a

tam inliberalĕ făcĭnŭs esse ortum! o͜ Aeschĭnē

450 pŏl haud păternum istuc dĕdisti! *DE.* uĭdĕlĭcet

de psaltrĭa hac audiuĭt: ĭd ĭlli nunc dŏlet

ălĭeno; pătĕr - is nihili pendĭt. ei mĭhi,

utinam hic prope adesset alicubi atque audiret haec!

HE. nĭsĭ făcĭent quae illos aequomst, haud sic

aufĕrent.

455 *GE.* in te spes omnĭs, Hegĭo, nobis sĭtast:

te solum hăbemus, tu es pătronus, tu pătēr.

illĕ tĭbi mŏrĭens nos commendauit sĕnex:

si desĕris tu, pĕrĭĭmus. *HE.* căuĕ dixĕris:

nĕquĕ făcĭam nĕquĕ me sătĭs pĭe posse arbĭtror.

460 *DE.* ădibo. saluere Hegĭonem plurĭmum

iŭbĕo. *HE.* oh te quaerebam ipsum: salue Demĕā.

DE. quĭd autem? *HE.* maior filĭus tŭŏs Aeschĭnus,

quem fratri ădoptandum dĕdisti, nĕquĕ bŏni

nĕquĕ liberalis functŭs offĭcĭumst uĭri.

465 *DE.* quĭd ĭstuc est?

---

449 exortum *A,* est ortum *J.* 452 is Σ *Don:* eius *A* (est *J*).
456 parens *Don. fort. recte.* tu es pater *D²FE.* 458 caue
dextris *A.* 459 neque id satis *A.*

squalid business! For shame, Aeschinus! (450) You've
dealt one there your father never would!

DE. *(Aside)* He must have heard about that *artiste*. An
outsider, but it pains him: Micio the father - he
doesn't care at all. Oh dear, how I wish that he were
somewhere near listening to this!

HE. If they aren't going to do the decent thing, they won't
get away with it just like that!

GE. (455) *(Kneeling; grasps Hegio's knees as a suppliant)*
All hope for our family lies in you, Hegio; we have
no-one but you, you are our champion, you *are* our
family. As he lay dying, the old gentleman entrusted
us to you. If you desert us, we are undone.

HE. Don't say that! I shan't desert you! How could I
think that was morally possible?

DE. (460) *(Aside)* I'll go up to them. *(Aloud)* Good morning,
Hegio; I trust I find you in the best of health.

HE. Oh - it was you I was after. Good morning, Demea.
(Awkward pause)

DE. Well? What's wrong?

HE. *(Pointing in accusation)* Your elder son Aeschinus, whom
you gave in adoption to your brother, has taken on the
role of a squalid villain.

DE. (465) What's that?

465   *HE.* nostrum ămicum noras Simŭlum atque

aequalem? *DE.* quidni? *HE.* filĭam eiūs uirgĭnem

uĭtĭauĭt. *DE.* hem? *HE.* mănĕ: nondum audisti,

                                                    Demēa,

quŏd est grăuissĭmum. *DE.* an quĭd est

                                              ĕtĭam amplĭus?

HE. uero amplĭus: nam hoc quĭdĕm fĕrundum

                                        ălĭquo mŏdost;

470   'persuasit nox ămor   uinum ădŭlescentĭā; |

humanumst'. ŭbĭ scit factum, ad matrem uirgĭnis

uĕnĭt ipsŭs ultro lăcrŭmans orans obsĕcrans

fĭdem dans, iurans se illam ducturum dŏmum.|

ignotumst tăcĭtumst credĭtumst.   uirgo ex ĕo

475   compressu grăuĭdă factast;   mensis dĕcŭmŭs est;

ill' bŏnŭs uir nobis psaltrĭam,   si dis plăcet,

parauit quicum uiuat, illam - desĕrit.

DE. pro certo tu istaec dicis?

                                        HE. mater uirgĭnĭs

in mĕdĭost, ipsă uirgo, res ipsa, hic Gĕtā

---

465 atque *om. A.*   467 mane etiam nondum δ.   468 an quicquam
Σ*J*, *Don.* etiam *om.* δ.   469 aliquo modo ferendum est δ.
475 m. hic d. e. ω, *Lact. ad Stat. Theb. 1. 576: del. Bentley.*
477 deserat Σ *(praeter p).*   478 certon Σ.

HE.   Simulus, our old friend from away back – you did know

him?

DE.   Of course!

HE.   Your son has shamed the modesty of his daughter!

DE.   *(Gasps)*

HE.   Wait: you haven't heard what's most serious yet,

Demea.

DE.   What? Could there be anything more than that?

HE.   Indeed there is something more. That, at any rate,

one could stomach somehow or other; (470) 'night, love,

wine, youth overcame him; its understandable'.

(Pauses) When he found out the truth, he went without

any prompting to the girl's mother; tears, prayers,

pleas, vows, oaths that he would marry the girl.

Pardon, silence, trust in return. The result of his

(475) attack on the girl, a pregnancy; nine months are

up; that fine gentleman, bold as brass, has got

himself an *artiste,* if you please, to live with, and

is deserting the daughter.

DE.   Are you quite certain of what you say?

HE.   *(Gesturing)* The girl's mother is available, the girl

too, the facts speak for themselves, and besides

                               you've got Geta here,

480   praetĕrĕa, ut captust seruŏlorum, non mălus

        nĕque ĭnera: ălĭt illas, solŭs omnem fămĭlĭam

        sustentat: hunc abducĕ, uinci, quaerĕ rem.|

        GE. immo hercle extorque, nĭsĭ ĭtă factumst,

                                            Demĕâ.

        postremo non negabit: coram ipsum cĕdô.

485   DE. pŭdet: nec quĭd ăgam nec quĭd huic

                                    respondĕam

        scĭo. PAM. INTVS mĭsĕram me, diffĕror   dŏlorĭbus!

        Iuno Lucină, fĕr ŏpem! serua me, obsĕcro!

                                            HE. hem?

        numnam illă quaeso partŭrit?   GE. certe, Hegĭo.|

        HE. ĕm ĭllaec fĭdem   nunc uostram implorat, Demĕâ;

490   quod uos uis cogĭt, id uŏluntate impĕtret.

        haec primum ut fīant deos quaeso ut uobis dĕcet.

        sin ălĭtĕr ănĭmus uostĕr est,   ĕgŏ, Demĕâ,

        summa ui defendam hanc atque illum mortŭom.

        cognatus mĭhi ĕrat; una a pŭĕris paruŏlis

495   sŭmŭs educti; una semper milĭtĭae et dŏmi

        fŭĭmus: paupertatem una pertŭlĭmus grăuem.

---

480 captus est ω. seruorum Ap, *Priscianus 1, 286*   malum A.
484 ipso Σ *(praeter* C^1P^1). 486 *ita G:* Φ *intus D, intus C,*
scio. Z mis... A: *nullae notae cett.*   488/9 hem/illaec ω,
corr. Luck. uostram nunc δ.   490 ius F^1P^2.   491 nobis
C^1E: nos P.   492 uoster animus δ.   494 Aγ^1: paruuli δγ^2.
495 educati ω.

(480) an honest and resourceful fellow as staff go.
He alone is getting them food, he alone is keeping the
whole family going. Arrest him, bind him, hold an
enquiry!

GE. No, put me on the rack if it isn't the truth, Demea!
He won't go on with his denials at the very end! Just
make him be there with me face to face!

DE. *(Aside)* (485) The shame! I don't know what to do or
how to answer! *(A girl screams within)*

PAMPHILA Oh the pain! I can't stand it! Oh Mother in
Heaven, please help me! Watch over me, I pray!

HE. What's this? Is she actually...is she in *labour*?

GE. Yes, sir, for sure.

HE. *(Grasping Demea and pointing)* There, Demea! She's
calling on the honour of your family! (490) Let her
have with good grace what force compels you to grant!
(Lets go; raises hands in prayer) Above all, I pray
heaven that this be resolved as we expect of your
family. *(Pointing an accusing finger)* But if, Demea,
your family has other ideas, I shall champion the girl
and her dead father with might and main. He was my
flesh and blood; we were raised together from infancy:
(495) we were always together in training and on
service; together we shouldered the heaviest of hard
times.

quapropter nitar fáciam expériar, deníquê

ánimam rélinquam pótius quam illas deséram.

quid mihi respondes? *DE.* fratrem conuéníam, Hegío.

500   *HE.* sed, Deméa, hoc tu fácíto cum ánimo cogítes.

quam uos fácillúme agítis, quam estis maxúme

potentes dites fortunati nobíles,

tam maxúme   uos aequo ánimo aequá noscérê¦

óportet, si uos uoltis pérhíberi próbos.

505   *DE.* rédito: fïent quae fïéri aequomst omnïã.

HE. décet te fácéré. Gétá, duc me intro

ad Sostrátam.

DE. non me indicente haec fïunt: utínam hic sit mõdô

defunctum! uerum nïmïa illaec   lïcentïã

prófecto euadét ín alíquod   magnum málum.¦

510   ibo ac réquiram fratrem út ín eum haec euómam.

(iii.5)

HE. bóno ánímo fac sis, Sostráta, ét ístam

quod pótes

fac consolere. égó Micíonem, si apúd fórumst,

---

497 enitar δ.   *Inter* 499 *et* 500 is quod mi de hac re
dederit consilium, id sequar ΣJ, *del. Muretus (cf. Ph. 461)*.
500 gites A[1].   501 maxumi *ACPL*.   506 intro *om.* γ.   507 fient
A.   hoc γG[2]L.   509 euadit A.   510 ac Aδ: et γ.   uomam A.
51!-6 *'in quibusdam non feruntur', Don.*   512 ad f.
Arusianus 451.

On that account I shall move heaven and earth - in
short, I would sooner lose my life than desert them.
(Pauses) Well? What do you say to that?

DE. *(Squirming with embarrassment, indicating town and
making to leave)* Hegio - I'll see my brother.

HE. (500) All right; but always bear this in mind, Demea.
The easier your life is, the more influential, the
richer, the more well-known your family, the more
important it becomes that you make impartial decisions,
if you want to maintain your family's good name.
(Turns away to Sostrata's)

DE. (505) Come back later. Everything that is right to be
done will be done.

HE. It's up to you to do it. Geta, take me in to your
mistress. *(Exeunt ambo; Demea lingers)*

DE. I *said* this would happen. I only hope and pray that
this is where it all stops! But the fact is, all that
wanton license is bound to end in some dreadful disaster.
(510) I'll go and look for Micio to give him this
fresh dose of bad news.
(Exit to town. HEGIO returns from Sostrata's)

HE. Try to keep your spirits up, Sostrata, and comfort her
as best you can. I'll see Micio, if he's in town,

conueniam atque ut res gestast narrabo ordine.

si est facturus ut sit officium suom,

515   faciat; sin aliter de hac re est eius sententia,

respondeat   mi ut quid agam quam primum sciam.

(iv.1)

517   CT. ain patrem hinc abisse rus? SY. iam

dudum. CT. dic sodes. SY. apud uillamst;

518   nunc quom maxume operis aliquid

facere credo. CT. utinam quidem; quod

519   cum salute eius fiat, ita se

defetigarit uelim,

520   ut triduom hoc   perpetuo prorsum e lecto

nequeat surgere.

SY. ita fiat, et istoc siqui potis est rectius.

CT. ita. nam hunc diem

misere nimis cupio ut coepi perpetuom in laetitia

degere.

---

515 eius *om.* A.   517-9 *systema trochaicum xii metrorum cum*
catalexi   518 cum ACF^1: autem D^1GF^2, autem eum L, eum P^2D^2.
aliquid operis δ.   quidem/quod ω, *cf. 158, 165.*   519 -fat- AL.
520 $ia^{8(2+6)}$.   prosum PC^1: prorsus δE.   521 $ia^{8(6+2)}$.
siquid Σ.   522 ia^8.   *ut supra f, Don.:* miser uiuos A, miser
nimis J, misere cupio Σ.   utut A.

and tell him in detail how things stand. In the event

that he *is* going to do what he ought, (515) well and

good. But if he takes any other line, let him give me

a straight answer, so that I'll know what action to

take without any delay. *(Exit to town; enter CTESIPHO*

and SYRVS from Micio's, both wearing garlands and with

drinks)

CT. So father *has* gone to the farm?

SY. Ages ago.

CT. Go on, please!

SY. *(Extemporizing)* He's at the farmhouse. I daresay he's

keeping his hands busy this very moment.

CT. If only he really is! Barring harm to his health, I

hope he gets so tired that he'll be absolutely stuck

in bed today, tomorrow, and the day after that!

SY. (520) I'll drink to that, and better than that if

there's such a thing. *(Offering a toast)*

CT. Cheers! Yes, it's agony how I long to spend this

livelong day enjoying myself as I'd started to!

et illud rus nulla alia causa

tam male odi nisi quia propest;

quod si abesset longius,

525 prius nox oppressisset illi

quam huc reuorti posset iterum.

526 nunc ubi me illi non uidebit,

iam huc recurret, sat scio:

527 ┤rogitabit me ubi fuerim: 'ego hodie

toto non uidi die':

quid dicam? SY. nilne in mentemst? CT. nusquam

quicquam. SY. tanto nequior.

cliens, amicus, hospes nemost uobis? CT. sunt:

quid postea?¦

530 SY. hisce opera ut data sit? CT. quae non data sit?

non potest fieri. SY. potest,

CT. interdius: sed si hic pernocto, causae quid

dicam, Syre?

SY. uah quam uellem etiam noctu amicis operam mos

esset dari!

523-4 *systema trochaicum ui metrorum cum catalexi*, 525-6
item uiii metrorum cum catalexi. 525 illic ΣJ. posse A.
527 rogabit Σ. quem ego Σ. *ia*[8] *uulgo, at me ubi fuerim*
cum hiatu hac sede suspectum; tr[7]? ego hoc te toto *Krauss*.
528-35 *ia*[8]. 528 mente Σ (*praeter* p). nusquam *Bentley*:
numquam ω. 530 non datast A. 531 interdiu Σ. 532 *uel*
Ctesiphoni Don.·

And why I shudder at that word 'farm' is simply because

the place is so near; if it were further off, (525) night

would have come down on him before he could get back

here again. As it is, when he sees I'm not there, I

know he'll be running back here again any minute. He'll

stick to the question where I've been: 'I haven't seen

you all day long!'. What am I going to say?

SY. Can't you think of anything?

CT. Not a thing.

SY. More fool you! Hasn't your family got any dependants?

No friends? No people you stay with?

CT. Yes, but so what?

SY. Their calls on your services!

CT. Which haven't I answered? It just won't work!

SY. Yes it will.

CT. For daytime, it might; but if I stay the night here,

what earthly excuse can I offer him, Syrus?

SY. *(Intentionally ambiguous)* Bother! What a pity service

to friends at night isn't an equally venerable tradition!

quin tu otĭosŭs esto: ĕgo ĭlliųs sensum pulchre

                                           callĕo.

quom feruit maxŭme   tam plăcĭdum quăm͡ ŏuem

                        reddo. *CT.* quomŏdo?

535   *SY.* laudarĭer   te audit lŭbenter: făcĭo te ăpŭd

                               illum dĕum:

536   uirtutes narro. *CT.* me̯as? *SY.* tŭas:

           hŏmĭni ilĭco   lăcrŭmae cădunt

537   quăsĭ pŭĕro gaudĭo - em tĭbi autem!

                CT. quidnamst? *SY.* lŭpŭs in fabŭla.

538   *CT.* pătĕr est? *SY.* ipsus. *CT.* Sўrĕ quĭd ăgĭmus?

   SY. fŭgĕ mŏdo intro: ĕgŏ uidĕro. *CT.* si

539   quid rŏgabit, nusquam tu me: au-

(iv.2) distin? *SY.* pŏtĭn ut desĭnas? *DE,* ne ĕgo

540   hŏmŏ sum infelix: primum fratrem

     nusquam inuĕnĭo gentĭum;

   praetĕrĕa autem dum illum quaero, a uilla

                               mercennarĭum

542   uidi: is filĭum nĕgăt essĕ ruri:

                    nec quĭd ăgam scĭo.

---

533 es Σ*J*.   534 feruet Σ.   536 ia^{4+2+2}.   537 ia^{8}.   em *APC*:
hem *cett.*   538-40 *systema trochaicum xii metrorum cum synaphaea
et catalexi.*   538 adest γ.   ipsest *A*, ipsus est δ.   538/9
uidero/CT. si..ω.   539 rogitabit $D^{1}L$.   539/40 desinas/DE.   ne
ego...ω.   541-91 tr^{7}.   542 rure *Charisius.*

Why don't you just relax and enjoy yourself? I'm the

perfect expert in his tuning. When he's blowing

hottest, I can make him placid as a sheep.

CT. How?

SY. (535) He likes hearing you praised: I make you a saint

in his eyes: I list your fine qualities.

CT. Mine?

SY. Yours: the tears of joy roll down as if he were a child

(Catches sight of DEMEA entering from the country) -

Here, have these back *(Giving Ctesipho his wine-cup and*

garland).

CT. *(Puzzled, spilling wine)* What on earth...?

SY. *(Pointing)* We've conjured him up!

CT. *(Panic)* It's father!

SY. In person.

CT. What do we do now?

SY. Just get in there - I'll decide. *(Ctesipho in, more*

or less).

CT. Any questions, you never saw me. *(Lingering)* I say,

Syrus, did you hear what I said?

SY. Can't you ever stop? *(Ctesipho leaves door ajar)*.

DE. *(Halting, leaning on staff)* (540) I never have any

luck! First, I can't find Micio anywhere in the world;

second, while I was looking for him, I met a hired man

from the farm: he told me Ctesipho isn't there. I

don't know what to do next.

CT. Sўrĕ! SY. quĭd est? CT. men quaerit? SY. uerum.

          CT. pĕrĭi! SY. quin tu ănĭmo bŏno es.

DE. quĭd hŏc, mălum, infelicĭtatis?

               nĕquĕo sătis decernĕrê,

545 nĭsĭ me credo huic essĕ natum

                   rei, fĕrundis mĭsĕrĭis.

primus sentĭo   mălă nostră,

                 primus rescisco omnĭâ,

547 primus porro obnuntĭo, aegre

                 solus si quid fit fĕro.

SY. ridĕo hunc: primum ait se scire - is

                 solus nescit omnĭâ.

DE. nunc credo si fortĕ frater

              rĕdĭĕrit uiso. CT. Sўrê,

550 obsĕcro uĭdĕ ne ille huc prorsus

            se inrŭat. SY. ĕtĭam tăces?

ĕgŏ căuebo. CT. numquam hercle ĕgo hŏdĭe istuc

              committam tĭbĭ;

nam me iam in cellam ălĭquam cum illa

             concludam: id tutissĭmumst.

SY. agĕ tămên ĕgo. hŭnc amŏuebo.

---

543 SY. quid agis (ais *E*) γ. peri *A*.   548 CT. *A*. 549 credo
scripsi: redeo ω. 550 prorsus huc δ. 551 hodie ego *A Don*.
552 iam *om*. γ.

CT. *(From house)* Syrus!

SY. What?

CT. Is he...?

SY. Right!

CT. Death! *(Collapsing)*

SY. *(Holding him up)* Can't you just stop worrying?

DE. Damn! What is the meaning of all this bad luck? I
must have been fated from birth to bear distress;
there's no other way to explain it adequately. (546)
I'm the first to notice family trouble; I'm the first
to find it all out; on top of that I'm the first to
tell anyone; and whatever goes wrong, I'm the only one
who takes it to *be* wrong.

SY. *(Aside)* Good comedy, this! Claims he knows first, and
he the only one totally in the dark!

DE. Now I think I'll have a look on the off-chance Micio
has come back. *(Cleans himself during following exchange)*

CT. *(From doorway)* Syrus, (550) for Heaven's sake see he
doesn't crash straight in!

SY. Can't you keep quiet! The watch is my job!

CT. *(Drily)* I'm certainly not relying on *you* for that any
more. Yes, I'll lock myself up with her in one of the
storerooms – that's the safest.

SY. Move! I'll get rid of him all the same!

DE. sĕd ĕccum scĕlĕratum Sўrum.

SY. non hercle hic quĭdem durarĕ

quisquam, si sic fit, pŏtest.

555   scire ĕquĭdem uŏlo quot mihi sint dŏmĭni.

DE. quae haec est mĭsĕrĭa?

quĭd ĭlle gannit? quid uolt? quĭd ăis, bŏnĕ uĭr?

est frater dŏmi?

SY. quid, mălum, 'bŏnĕ uir' mihi narras?

ĕquĭdem pĕrĭi. DE. quid tĭbist?

SY. rŏgĭtas? Ctesĭpho me pugnis

mĭsĕrum ĕt ĭstam psaltrĭam |

usque occidit. DE. hem quid narras?

SY. em uĭde ŭt discidit lăbrum.

560   DE. quam ob rem? SY. me impulsore hanc emptam

esse ait. DE. non tu eum rus hinc mŏdô

produxe aibas? SY. factum; uerum

uenit post insanĭens:

nil pĕpercit. non pŭdŭissĕ uerbĕrare hŏmĭnem sĕnem!

quem ĕgŏ mŏdô pŭĕrum tantillum in mănĭbus

gestaui mĕis!

DE. laudo: Ctesĭpho, păᵗrissas:

---

554 hic qui uolt durare *Nonius 285*   555 *q. h. e. m. Demeae
dedi: Syro uulgo.* 556 quid agis *ɛE.* 559 em *APC*[1], hem *cett.*
560 ait esse *A:* esse *del. Marouzeau.*   hinc mihi δ, hinc γ.
561 aiebas ω. post *om. A.*

(Ctesipho petulantly bangs the door shut, Syrus staggers from it as if just now violently ejected; collapses, crawls)

DE. Ah! There's that blasted Syrus!

SY. *(Laying it on)* No-one can last out in *this* place if this is the way they carry on. (555) I want to know how many masters I've got.

DE. *(Aside)* What's *this* distress? What's he yelping? What does he mean? *(Poking Syrus)* Well, my fine fellow? Is my brother in?

SY. What the hell do you mean, 'fine fellow'? Here I am dying *(Does a 'dying Gaul')*.

DE. What's wrong with you?

SY. Stupid question! Ctesipho has just about murdered me and that *artiste* of yours with his bare fists! Show some sympathy!

DE. What on earth...?

SY. *(Rising)* Here, see how he's split my lip!

DE. (560) What for?

SY. He claims buying her was all *my* idea!

DE. Weren't you claiming just now you'd taken him to the farm?

SY. True... but he came back later; raving he was, and how! *(Recovering, and miming)* Whipping a poor old man! The cheek of it! To think only just now I was cradling him in my arms as a tiny tot!

DE. First class! Ctesipho, the father shows in you!

                                        abi, uirum   te iudico.

565   SY. laudas? ne ille continebit

                            posthac, si sapiet, manus.

       DE. fortiter! SY. perquam, quia miseram

                            mulierem et me seruolum

       qui referire non audebam,

                            uicit: hui, perfortiter!

       DE. non potuit melius! idem quod ego sentit -

                            te esse huic rei caput.

       sed estne frater intus? SY. non est.

                                    DE. ubi illum inueniam

                                            cogito.

570   SY. scio ubi sit: uerum hodie numquam

                            monstrabo. DE. hem? quid

                                    ais? SY. ita.

       DE. diminuetur tibi quidem   iam cerebrum.

                                    SY. at nomen nescio !

       illius hominis, sed locum   noui ubi sit.

                                    DE. dic ergo locum.

       SY. nostin porticum apud macellum hac deorsum?

                                    DE. quidni nouerim?

---

565 laudasne Σ.   566 qua A[1].   567 referi A.   568 non pote
melius. idem ille quod ego Bentley. senstit A, sensit Σ.
569 quaeram Σ. 570 quid agis CPG. 571 iam quidem δ.
573 hanc DLEp Don.

You've graduated to manhood!

SY. (565) First class? He'd better keep his hands off me in future, if he's any sense. *(Shadow-boxing)*.

DE. Bravo!

SY. Oh, yes! Overcoming a poor female and an honest working man who wasn't bold enough to hit back! *(Whistles and claps)* Bravissimo!

DE. The best he could have done! He can see the same as I do - that *you* are at the bottom of all this! But is my brother at home?

SY. No, he is not.

DE. *(To himself)* I wonder where I can find him?

SY. (570) I know where he is - but I'm never going to show you today.

DE. What?

SY. You heard.

DE. *(Brandishing his staff)* On your head be it!

SY. *(Taking evasive action)* What I mean is, I don't know the person's name, but I do know his address.

DE. So tell me the address.

SY. D'you know the arcade with the shops down the way? *(Pointing out of theatre)*

DE. Of course I do.

        SY. praetĕrito hanc recta plătĕa sursum:

                          ŭbi ĕo uenĕris,

575   cliuos dĕorsum uorsum est. hac te

                        praecĭpĭtato. postĕa

    est ăd hanc mănum săcellum,

                  ĭbi angĭportum proptĕr est.

    DE. quodnam? *SY.* illi ŭbi ĕtĭam căprĭficus

          magnast. *DE.* noui. *SY.* hac pergĭto.

    DE. id quĭdem angĭportum non est peruĭum.

                    SY. uerum herclĕ! uah,

    censen hŏmĭnem me esse? erraui; in portĭcum

                        rursum rĕdi.

580   sane hac multo propĭŭs ibĭs,

                et mĭnŏr est   erratĭo.

    scin Crătini hŭiŭs ditĭs aedes?

        DE. scĭo. *SY.* ŭbi ĕas   praetĕrĭĕrĭs,

    ad sĭnistram hac recta plătĕa,

              ŭbi ad Dianae uenĕrĭs,

    ito ad dextram; prĭŭs quam ad portam uĕnĭas,

                ăpŭd ipsum lăcum

    est pistrilla ĕt exaduorsum făbrĭca: ĭbist.

                DE. quĭd ĭbi facĭt?

---

574 hanc *scripsi:* hac ω. sursus *Bentley.* 575 uorsum *om. A.*
te *om. A.* 577 quonam *A.* illic ω. magnast. nosti(n)?
DE. noui δ*E.* 583 dexteram *DGE.* locum Σ *(praeter CP¹F¹).*
584 p. ei aduorsum *A.*

SY. *(With plenty of helpful gesticulation)* Go past it on

the main road up the hill. When you get to the top,

(575) there's a steep drop down right in front. Take

the quickest way down. After that there is a little

shrine on this side, and there's an alley next to it.

DE. What's it called exactly?

SY. Goatfig Lane - there's a big one   growing there.

DE. I know.

SY. Go on that way.

DE. That lane is a dead-end!

SY. *(Slapping forehead).* Yes, so it is! Silly me! You

wouldn't think I had any brains, would you? I wandered

off. Come back again to the arcade. (580) You'll

certainly get much closer this way, and there's less

wandering around. There's a rich man, Cratinus: he

lives near here - you know his house?

DE. Yes.

SY. When you've gone past it, left on to the main road this

way; when you get to the temple of Diana, turn right;

before you get to the city gate, there's a small mill

right beside the reservoir, and facing it, a workshop.

That's where he is.

DE. What's he doing there?

585   SY. lectŭlos †in sole ilignis

                                        pĕdĭbus făcĭundos dĕdît.

DE. ŭbĭ potetis uos: bĕnĕ sane.

                                        sed cesso ăd ĕum pergĕrê?|

SY. i sane: ĕgŏ te exercebo hŏdĭe ut dignŭs es,

                                                    sĭlĭcernĭum.|

Aeschĭnûs ŏdĭose cessat, prandĭum   corrumpĭtur;

Ctesĭpho autem ĭn ămorest totŭs.

                                        ĕgŏ iam prospĭcĭam mĭhi.

590   nam iam ăbibo atque unum quidquid,

                                        quod quĭdem ĕrit bellissimum,

carpam et cȳăthos sorbĭlans   paullatim hunc producam

                                                            dĭem.

(iv.3)

        MI. ĕgo ĭn hac re nil rĕpĕrĭo quam ob rem

                                        lauder tanto ŏpĕre, Hegĭo:

meum offĭcĭum făcĭo, quod peccatum a nobis

                                        ortumst corrĭgo.

nĭsĭ si me ĭn īllo credĭdisti esse hŏmĭnum

                                        nŭmĕro qui ĭtă pŭtant,

---

585 iligneis Σ. *an*   lectulos is oleagineis...?   586 DE.
ubi...SY. bene...DE. sed... $C^1P^1FD^1$, ubi...DE. bene...sed...
GLE. 'incerta persona', *Don.* recte sane *DGL*.   588 otiose δ.
589 est in amore γ.   590 adibo D^1LEF. quidque *DGL*.   *uel*
quĭdem ĕrĭt.   591 sorbillans Σ.   592-609 ia^8 *(at u. ad 602)*.

SY.   (585) He's placed an order for some couches to be made...

for out in the sun...with legs in holmoak.

DE.   For you people to loll about drinking on. Just the

thing! *(Starts to leave)* I must get to him, no more

delay.

SY.   *(as Demea crosses stage)* Just *move!* I'll keep you on

the double all day as you deserve, you old skeleton at

the feast! *(Pauses)* Aeschinus is annoyingly late, the

luncheon is spoiling, and as for Ctesipho, he's quite

lost in love. Time to look out for number one. (590)

Yes, what I'll do is go and sample each course in turn,

in the best possible taste of course, and fill in my

time with the odd little sip at the decanters.

(Exit into Micio's; enter MICIO and HEGIO from town)

MI.   I can't see in any of this why I should get so much

praise, Hegio, I'm only doing what I ought in making

good a wrong for which we're responsible. But maybe

you took me for one of that set of people who reckon

on the lines that

595   sibi fieri iniuriam ultro si quam fecere ipsi

                               expostules,

et ultro accusant. id quia non est a me factum,

                         agis gratias?

HE. ah minime: numquam te aliter atque es in animum

                              induxi meum.

sed quaeso ut una mecum ad matrem uirginis

                               eas, Micio,

atque istaec eadem quae mihi dixti tute dicas

                               mulieri,

600   suspicionem hanc propter fratrem eius esse et

                             illam psaltriam.

MI. si ita aequom censes aut si ita opus est facto,

                     eamus. *ME.* bene facis:

†nam et illi animum iam releuabis, quae dolore

                               ac miseria

tabescit, et tuo officio fueris functus. sed

                               si aliter putas,

---

597 te *om.* δ.   600 fratrem esse: eius esse illam *Bentley:*
eius se *A,* eius isse *J.*   601 si *alt. om. A. hunc uersum
interpolatum esse ut 602-9 omitterentur coni. Rieth.*   602
(?601) '*sane hi uersus melius desunt* (Schoell: *deesse possunt*
Wessner) *quos multa exemplaria non habent'*, Don.; *utrum ad
604 an ad 609 uelit, parum perspicuum.*   602 *laborat:* nam illi
animum releuabis *A. tr⁷ ut est in* Σ *(iam om. Lp), cf. 618.*
rell- *Bentley.*   603 *sic et Arusianus 474: at* fungor + *abl.
suspectum apud nostrum.*

(595) they are being done a gratuitous injury if

anyone remonstrates about a wrong they themselves have

done, and follow up with their own gratuitous accusations.

Are you thanking me for failing to do that?

HE. Certainly not: my conception of you has never been

anything but of the frank fellow you are. Well, do

you mind coming along with me to see the girl's mother,

Micio? You could tell the lady exactly what you've

told me, (600) that all this misunderstanding is on

account of his brother and that *artiste*.

DE. If you think it's right or if this is what needs to be

done, let us go.

HE. Very good of you; you will at once be taking a load off

Sostrata's mind - the strain and worry is beginning to

tell heavily on her - and you really will have done

everything you ought. But if you think otherwise,

ĕgŏmet narrabo quae mihi dixti. *MI.* immo ĕgo

ibo. *HE.* bĕnĕ făcîs.

605　　omnes quĭbŭs res sunt mĭnŭs secundae, mãgĕ sunt

nescĭŏquo mŏdo

suspicĭosi; ad contŭmelĭam omnĭa accĭpĭunt mãgis;

propter sŭam inpŏtentĭam　se semper credunt

claudĭer.

quapropter te ipsum purgare ipsi coram

placabĭlĭŭs est.

MI. et recte et uerum dicis. *HE.* sĕquĕrĕ me ergo

hac intro. *MI.* maxŭme.

(iv.4)

610　　　　*AE.* discrucior animi!

hoccin de inprouiso mali　　mihi obici tantum,

ut neque quid　　me faciam

nec quid agam　　certum siet;

membra metu　　debilia sunt;

animus timore obstipuit;

---

604 dixisti *G.*　　607 claudere *Don. in .comm.* neclegi ΣJ;
caluier *Faernus,* ludier *Bentley.*　　608 ipsis ΣJ.　　610–17
ita in A dispositi: <discrucior...<ut...<membra... (*fol. 110ᵘ*)
>pectore...>quo...>tanta...<Sostrata...>mihi...; *in P*:>
discrucior...<hocine...<ut...>membra...>animus...>pectore...>
quomodo...<tanta...<Sostrata... (< *in ecthesi,* > *in enthesi*);
inordinatius cett.　　610 *cʳ*, 610a *iaⁱ⁴ + cʳ.*　　611 certus siem
D¹G.　　611-3 *cho (1-3, 5, 8-10) cum ia²(4, 6-7) desinentes*
in 'di boni quid hoc' uel (uah *extra*

I shall tell her what you have said to me.

MI. No, I'll go.

HE. Very good of you. (605) Generally the less favourable people's circumstances, somehow the more likely they are to look twice, the more likely to take everything as an insult; because of their weak position, they feel themselves constantly under threat from outside. On that account it would be more genuinely acceptable to make your apology to the lady in person.

MI. A frank and accurate remark.

HE. Well, come in with me. This way.

MI. Of course. *(exeunt into Sostrata's. Enter AESCHINVS from town)*

AE. (610) The agony of my broken heart!

This unforeseen catastrophe,

This crushing blow,

So violent that I cannot sort

what I should feel or try to do.

I just don't know.

I've terror, paralysis, mental confusion.

613   pectore consistere nil   consili quit.   uah!

quo modo me ex hac   expediam turba?

tanta nunc suspicio de me incidit neque ea inmerito.

Sostrata credit mihi me psaltriam hanc

emisse; id anus

mihi indicium fecit.

618   năm ŭt hinc forte ăd obstĕtricem ĕrat missa,

ŭbĭ uĭdĭ, ilĭcoı

619   accedo, rŏgĭto Pamphĭlâ

quĭd ăgat, iam partŭs adsĭêt,

620   eŏn obstĕtricem accersat. illa exclamat, 'ăbi

ăbi iam Aeschĭnê,

sătĭs dĭu dedisti uerbă, săt ădhuc tŭă nos frus-

tratast fĭdes'.

'hem quĭd ĭstuc obsĕcro' inquam 'est?'. 'uălĕas,

hăbĕas ĭllam quae plăcet!'.

sensi ilĭco ĭd ĭllas suspĭcari, sed me rĕprĕhen-

di tămen

nequid de fratrĕ garrŭlae illi dicĕrem ac

fĭĕret pălam.

---

metrum, cf. Pl. Ps. 205?) in tr².   613 -ilii ω.   614-7
numeri incerti; 617 cʳ? u. comm. 618 *tr⁷*. nam id forte *A₄*
ad *AD¹G¹*: ea ad cett. ubi uidi *Don*: ubi eam uidi *A*, ubi uiɗ
eam Σ. 619 *ia⁴⁺⁴*. 620-4 *ia⁸*. 620 abi *(semel) A*.   621 uerḅ
nobis satis (sat *J*) Σ*J*.

Pull yourself together! Think, man, think! How do I

untangle myself from this confusion? I am the victim

of awful suspicion, suspicion I wholly deserve: (615)

Sostrata thinks that I bought the *artiste* in here for

myself - the old woman provided me the evidence for

that.

    For when she'd been sent off to the midwife, I chanced

to see her, and went straight across to ask how

Pamphila was doing, was the baby on its way, (620) was

that why she was fetching the midwife. She yelled at

me, 'Get away, Aeschinus, get away from us this instant!

You've lied to us long enough, your promises have misled

us far enough'. Dumbfounded! 'What do you mean?' I

asked her. 'For better, for worse with your fancy-

woman - goodbye'. I saw at once what they suspected.

But I held back from saying anything about Ctesipho to

that old gossip and having it all come out in the open.

625   quid nunc faciam? dicam fratris esse hanc?

                                        quod minimest opus

       usquam efferri. ac mitto: fieri potis est

                                        ut ne qua exeat:

       ipsum id metuo ut credant. tot concurrunt

                                        ueri similia: |

       egomet rapui ipse, egomet solui argentum, ad me

                                        abductast domum, |

       haec adeo mea culpa fateor fieri.

                                        non me hanc rem patri, |

630   utut erat gesta, indicasse! exorassem ut eam

                                        ducerem.

       cessatum usque adhuc est: iam porro, Aeschine,

                                        expergiscere!

       nunc hoc primumst: ad illas ibo ut purgem me:

                                        accedam ad fores.

       perii! horresco semper ubi pultare hasce

                                        occipio miser.

       heus heus Aeschinus   ego sum: aperite aliquis

                                        actutum ostium.

625-37 tr^7.   625 dicam om. A.   esse? id quod PC^1F^1.
626 ac Aδ (praeter G): age γG.   omitto DGL^2E.   629 fieri
fateor δ.   630 ut Σ.   631 Don., J: nunc iam δ, nunc cett.
632 hoc est primum γ.   me ut purgem δ.   633 miser D^1G:
fores A, fores miser cett.

(625) Now what shall I do? Explain that the girl really
is my brother's - just what mustn't be let loose all
over the place?... But suppose I do let it out: it's
possible it wouldn't go any further; but then, I'm
afraid they wouldn't grant me even that favour. All
that plausible convergent evidence: it was I that
carried the girl off, it was I that paid, it was my
house she was brought to. Besides it's all my own fault,
I can see that. Oh, how stupid I was not to tell my
father the whole story, (630) however sordid! I *would*
have got his blessing on our marriage.

(*Pauses*) Well, Aeschinus, so far you've done
nothing but put things off. (*Claps*) From now on,
Aeschinus, snap out of it! The first and most important
thing: I'll go to them and try to clear my name. Well,
there's the door. (*Shudders, draws breath*) Oh!
Facing up to knocking here always makes me a bundle of
nerves! (*Knocks and shouts more aggressively than he
needs to*) Hey! It's me, Aeschinus! Someone come and
open this door this minute. Hey!

635   prodit nescioquis: concedam huc.

(iv.5)   MI. ita uti dixi, Sostrata,

facite; ego Aeschinum conueniam, ut quomodo acta

                                        haec sunt sciat.

sed quis ostium hic pultauit?

                                AE. pater herclest: perii!

                                        MI. Aeschine!

quid huic hic negotist? tune has

                                pepulisti fores?

tacet. quor non ludo hunc aliquantisper?

                                        melius est

640   quandoquidem hoc numquam mihi ipse uoluit

                                        credere.

nil mihi respondes? AE. non equidem istas,

                                quod sciam.

MI. ita: nam mirabar quid hic negoti esset tibi.

erubuit: salua res est. AE. dic sodes, pater,

tibi uero quid istic est rei? MI. nil

                                        mihi quidem;

645   amicus quidam me a foro abduxit modo

huc aduocatum sibi. AE. quid? MI. ego dicam

                                        tibi:

habitant hic quaedam mulieres   pauperculae,

---

635 ut A𝛾p. dixti δE.   636 facito Σ.   haec acta δ.
sint A¹.   637 hoc Σ.   pulsauit Σ.   638-677 ia⁶.
638 AE. quid...negotist ω, at cf. 642.   640 dicere A.
641 instas δ C²P²F²E.   644 rei est 𝛾D².

(635) Someone is coming! I'll hide over here (*Scurrying away as MICIO enters, addressing Sostrata over his shoulder*)

MI. You and the others do as I say, Sostrata: I shall see Aeschinus and tell him what's been arranged. Who...?

AE. Oh, no: it's *father*! (*Trying to appear invisible*)

MI. (*Seeing him*) Aeschinus! (*Aside, with irony*) What business has *he* here? (*Aloud*) Was it you knocking at the door? (*Pause; Aeschinus squirms: Micio aside*) He's keeping his mouth shut. Why not play with him just a little? That would fit rather well, (640) given that he never chose to trust me with any of this. (*Tapping his shoulder; aloud*) No reply?

AE. D-door? Not that one, as far as I know.

MI. Of course not. You had me wondering what business you could have here. (*Aside*) He's blushing: all's well.

AE. Father, if you don't mind my asking, what is it that involves *you* in there?

MI. Me? Nothing to do with me. (645) A friend of mine brought me here from town to help him out.

AE. What about?

MI. Let me explain. (*Hand around shoulder, confidentially*) The occupants here are certain ladies in difficult
                                        circumstances,

ut opiner eas non nosse te - et certo scio,

neque enim diu huc migrarunt. *AE.* quid tum

                                 postea?

650   *MI.* uirgo est cum matre. *AE.* perge. *MI.* haec

                    uirgo orbast patre; |

hic meus amicus illi genere est proxumus;

huic leges cogunt nubere hanc. *AE.* perii!

                          MI. quid est?

AE. nil: recte: perge. *MI.* is uenit ut secum

                          auehat;

nam habitat Mileti. *AE.* hem uirginem ut

                    secum auehat?

655   *MI.* sic est. *AE.* Miletum usque obsecro?

             MI. ita. | *AE.* animo malest.

quid ipsae? quid aiunt? *MI.* quid illas censes?

                      nil enim.

commenta mater est   esse ex alio uiro

nescioquo puerum natum, neque eum nominat:

priorem esse illum, non oportere huic dari. |

660   *AE.* eho nonne haec iusta tibi uidentur postea?

MI. non. *AE.* obsecro,   'non'? an illam hinc

                  abducet, pater?

---

648 *Bentley:* ut opinor ω.   has γ.   649 commigrarunt Σ.
653 MI. recte. AE. perge GL^2E.   654 uehat *A*.
656 quid ipsae aiunt D^1GL.   istas Σ.   660 uidetur *A*.
uidentur poscere *Bothe*.

so I expect you don't know them - and I'm sure you
don't, as they've only moved here recently.

AE. Well then?

MI. (650) There's a girl along with her mother.

AE. Go on.

MI. The girl has lost her father; this friend of mine is
the closest male relative; the law requires her to
marry him.

AE. Oh, no! *(Breaking free)*

MI. What's the matter?

AE. Nothing. I'm all right. Go on.

MI. He's come to take her away with him; you see he lives
in Miletus.

AE. What? Take the girl away with him?

MI. (655) That's right.

AE. What, all the way to *Miletus*?

MI. Yes.

AE. *(Aside)* I don't feel well. *(Aloud)* What about them?
What do they say?

MI. What would you expect of them? Just nonsense! The
mother has worked out some story that there's a little
boy by some other man, but she won't name him; he was
first, she says, so the girl shouldn't be given to my
friend.

AE. (660) Well, doesn't that seem right in the circumstances?

MI. No.

AE. No? How can you possibly say that? Is he going to
take her away from Athens, father?

MI. quĭd ĭllam ni abducat?

                    AE. factum a uobis durĭtĕr

inmĭsĕrĭcordĭterque atque ĕtĭam, si est, păter,

dicendum măgĭs ăperte, inlibĕralĭter.

665   MI. quam ob rem? AE. rŏgas me? quĭd ĭlli tandem

                                            credĭtis

fŏre ănĭmi mĭsĕro quı †illa consueuit prĭor,

qui infelix haud scĭo ăn ĭllam mĭsĕre nunc ămet,

quom hanc sĭbĭ uĭdebit praesens praesenti erĭpi, ⌐

abduci ăb ŏcŭlis? făcĭnŭs indignum, păter!

670   MI. qua rătĭone istuc? quis despondit? quis dĕdit?

quoi quando nupsĭt? auctor his rebus quĭs est?

quor duxit ălĭenam? AE. an sĕdere ŏportŭit

dŏmĭ uirgĭnem   tam grandem dum cognatŭs hinc

illinc uĕnirĕt exspectantem? haec, mi păter,

675   te dicĕre aequom fŭĭt ĕt id defendĕre.

     MI. ridĭcŭlum! aduorsumne illum causam dicĕrem

---

666 A, Arusianus 460; cum illa Σ Don. in lemmate, 'legitur
et illam' in comm.; cum ēā Bentley, cŭm hac Grant.
prius γD². 667 quin felix ACF.. amat γD². 670 qui
despondit AD¹. 671 qui est CPF¹. 673 Don., Bentley:
huc (hic D¹) ω. 674 expectatum D¹. 676 ridicule (voc.)
Don. aduorsum me D¹. dicere D.

MI.· Why shouldn't he?

AE. You two have dealt harshly and unsympathetically and
even, father, if I have to say it more plainly,
squalidly.

MI. *(Feigning surprise)* (665) Why?

AE. What a question! For goodness' sake, what sort of
state do you think that poor fellow who was her first
love will be in - I daresay the ill-starred lad is
pining for her this minute - when he has to be there
face to face and see her cruelly dragged from his gaze?
That would be terrible, father!

MI. (670) How do you work that out? Who betrothed her? Who
gave her to him? Who is her husband? Since when?
The person responsible for all this - who is he? Why
did he take what was not his to take?

AE. Was a girl her perfect age meant to sit around at home
waiting for some relative to turn up out of the blue?
That (675) is what you should have argued, father,
and you should have prevented all *this*!

MI. Don't be absurd! You mean I should have argued against

the man

quoi uenĕram aduŏcatus? sed quĭd ĭsta, Aeschĭnê,

nostra? aut quid nobis cum illis? ăbĕamus.

quĭd est?

quid lăcrŭmas? *AE.* pătĕr obsĕcro ausculta.

MI. Aeschĭne, audiui omnĭa̦

680   et scĭo. nam te amo quo măgĕ quaĕ ăgis

curae sunt mĭhi.̦

AE. ĭtă uĕlim me promĕrentem ămes dum uiuas,

mi pătêr,

ut me hoc delictum admisisse in me id mihi

uehementer dŏlet,

et me tui pŭdet. *MI.* credo herclĕ,

nam ingĕnĭum   noui tŭom

libĕralĕ. sed uĕrĕor   ne indilĭgens

nĭmĭum sĭes.

685   in qua ciuĭtatĕ tandem te arbĭtrarĕ uiuĕrê?

uirgĭnem uĭtĭasti quam te

non ius fŭĕrat tangĕrê.

iam id peccatum primum magnum,

<   > ăt humanum tămen:

fecere ălĭi saepe ĭtem   bŏni. at postquam

ĭd ĕuenit, cĕdô

---

677 istic *A*: istaec *L Don.*   679-706 *tr*[7].   679 audi *A*.
681 o mi γρ.   686 ius non Σ.   687 <magnum> *add. Muretus,*
Bentley: <sane> magnum *Kauer* (*non A*), magnum, <indignum>
Bianco.   688 uenit *A*.

I came to help? *(Pause)* But what's all that got to do

with us, Aeschinus? *(Pause)* Or what have we got to do

with them? *(Pause)* Let's go. *(Aeschinus weeps)* What

is it? Why are you crying?

AE. Father , please, I've got something to...

DE. *(Embracing him)* Aeschinus, I've heard it: (680) I know

it all. My love for you only makes what matters to

you matter all the more to me.

AE. Father, all I want is truly to earn your lifelong love,

as truly as having let myself do this wicked thing

hurts me to the quick, fills me with shame for your

sake!

MI. *(Letting go)* Lord, I believe you, for I know you've

got a decent heart. But I am worried that you are so

extraordinarily thoughtless. (685) After all, what sort

of a society do you think you live in? You've seduced

a girl you had no right to approach. That's a great

wrong for a start, a great wrong, but at least

understandable: many others with a good background

have done it too. But after the event, tell me,

numquid circumspexti? aut numquid

                              tute prospexti tibi

690   quid fieret, qua fieret? si te mi ipsum

                                  puduit proloqui,

qua resciscerem? haec dum dubitas,

                              menses abierunt decem;

prodidisti et te et illam miseram et gnatum

                              quod quidem in te fuit.

quid? credebas dormienti haec

                              tibi confecturos deos,

et illam sine tua opera in cubiculum iri

                                  deductum domum?

695   nolim ceterarum rerum   te socordem eodem modo.

bono animo es: duces uxorem. AE. hem?

          MI. bono animo es   inquam. AE. pater,

obsecro, num ludis nunc tu me?

          MI. ego te? quam ob rem? AE. nescio:

quia tam misere hoc esse cupio

                              uerum, eo   uereor magis.

MI. abi domum ac deos conprecare ut uxorem

                              accersas: abi.

---

690 dicere Σ.   692 -isti te γD². 695 nollem D¹G.
696 uxorem hanc Σ.   est A.   697 δ: tu nunc me γ,
nunc ludis tu me *cum hiatu A. an* numnam tu ludis me?
uel sim., cf. Pl. M.G. 924?   698 ideo γ.

didn't you take any stock? Didn't you think ahead on
your own account (690) about ends and means? Granted
you were ashamed to tell me the truth yourself, but
how was I going to find out? While you were hesitating,
nine months have gone by; you have done your level
best to betray both yourself, that poor girl, and your
son. Well? Did you imagine that heaven would sort
it all out for you while you slept on, and she would
arrive as bride in your bedroom without any effort on
your part? (695) *(Sternly)* I shall not have you being
equally mindless in any other matters! *(Pauses; takes
his son's arm)* Don't worry; you're marrying her.

AE. What?

MI. Don't worry, I said.

AE. Father, please...you can't possibly be tricking me now?

MI. Me trick you? What for?

AE. I don't know...Because I so desperately want it to be
true, that's why I am over-anxious.

MI. Go in and ask heaven's blessing on the ceremony. Off
you go.

700   *AE*. quid, iam uxorem? *MI*. iam. *AE*. iam? *MI*. iam

               quantum potest. *AE*. di me, pater,

   omnes oderint ni mage te

                   quam oculos nunc ego amo meos.

   MI. quid? quam illam? *AE*. aeque. *MI*. perbenigne.

                    AE. quid, ille ubist Milesius?

   MI. periit, abiit, nauem escendit.

              sed quor cessas? *AE*. abi, pater,

   tu potius deos conprecare,

             nam tibi eos   certo scio,

705   quo uir melior multo es quam ego, obtemperaturos

                          magis.

   MI. ego eo intro ut quae opus sunt parentur:

              tu fac ut dixi, si sapis.

     AE. quid hoc est negoti? hoc est patrem esse,

             aut hoc est filium esse?

   si frater aut sodalis esset, qui mage morem

                    gereret?

   hic non amandus? hicine non gestandus in

                sinust? hem!

710   itaque adeo magnam mi inicit

              sua commoditate curam,

---

700 iamne uxorem ducam Σ.   701 ego *om. AL*.   702 quicquam
illam *A*.   703 abiit periit nauem ascendit γ, nauem
ascendit abiit periit δ. escendit *AC¹P¹*.   704 certe γ.
uel eos.   706 ego ibo δ.   707–11(?12) *ia⁷*.   709 amandus
est *Jδ*.   710 iniecit ω.

AE. (700) The ceremony? Now?

MI. Now.

AE. Now?

MI. Now, soon as may be.

AE. *(Embracing Micio)* Heaven can cut me off for good if I
don't love you more than my sight!

MI. What? More than her?

AE. The same.

MI. *(Ironically)* That's really kind!

AE. Hey - what about that Milesian?

MI. He's lost, he's left, he's boarded ship. Hurry up!

AE. You go, father, it's you who should ask heaven's
blessing, not I; I'm quite certain (705) you've got
more influence up there: you're a far better person
than I'll ever be.

MI. I'll go in to get the arrangements seen to. You'll do
as I said if you've any sense. *(exit Micio.)*

AE. What's going on? Is that what a father is supposed to
be, or is it what a son is supposed to be? If he were
my brother or best friend, how could he have humoured
me better? Isn't he loveable? Rock-a-bye daddy!
*(Mimes cradling a baby as he capers; stops suddenly;
hand over mouth, draws breath)* Oh dear! (710) By
fitting in with me like this he's filling me with dread

ne forte inprudens faciam quod nolit: sciens

cauebo.

sed cesso ire intro, ne morae

meis nuptiis egomet siem?

(iv. 6)

DE. defessus sum ambulando. ut, Syre, te cum tua

monstratione magnus perdat Iuppiter!

715   perreptaui usque ego oppidum; ad portam, ad lacum,

quo non? neque illi fabrica ulla erat nec

fratrem homo

uidisse se aibat quisquam. nunc uero domi

certum obsidere est usque donec redierit.

(iv. 7)

MI. ibo, illis dicam nullam esse in nobis moram.

720   *DE.* sed eccum ipsum. te iam dudum quaero, Micio.

MI. quidnam? *DE.* fero alia flagitia ad te ingentia

boni illius adulescentis. *MI.* ecce autem! *DE.* noua,

capitalia. *MI.* ohe iam. *DE.* ah nescis qui uir sit.

MI. scio.

DE. o stulte, tu de psaltria me somnias

725   agere: hoc peccatum in uirginemst ciuem. *MI.* scio.

---

711 inprudens forte γ.   712 *ia*$^{4+2+2}$.   sim *Guyet (ia*^{7}).
713-854 *ia*^{6}.   716 neque fabrica illic γ, neque illic
fabrica δ: nec fabrica illi *Bentley*.   fratrem domo *A*.
717 *an* domum?   723 eho *A, cf. 769.*   ah *om. A.*   siet δ.
724 ah stulte ΣJ.

in case I do anything inadvertently to hurt his feelings

through not thinking. I'll conscientiously watch my

step. Quick, home! The groom mustn't be late for the

bride! *(Exit into Micio's; enter DEMEA from town)*.

DE. I'm worn out with walking. God damn you, Syrus, and your

signposting to boot! (715) I've trudged all over town

- to the City-Gate, to the reservoir, where haven't I

been? There was no workshop there, and not a soul

could say he had seen my brother. Well, my plan now

is to sit on his doorstep however long he takes to get

back. *(Settling down painfully; enter MICIO from behind*

him, speaking back)

MI. I'll go and tell them there's no delay on our part.

DE. *(Getting up awkwardly)* (720) Ah, here he is! I've been

after you for ages, Micio.

MI. What is it this time?

DE. I bring more terrible, shocking news of that fine

young man to lay before you...

MI. *(Aside)* Here we go again!

DE. ...fresh crimes, putting his neck at risk!

MI. Whoa there.

DE. Ah, you don't know his mettle!

MI. I do.

DE. You poor fool, you imagine I mean the *artiste*: (725)

this is a wrong against a girl of standing!

MI. I know.

DE. oho scis et patere? *MI.* quidni patiar?

DE. dic mihi,

non clamas? non insanis? non... *MI.* malim quidem...

DE. puer natust. *MI.* di bene uortant. *DE.* uirgo

nil habet.

MI. audiui. *DE.* et ducenda indotatast.

MI. scilicet.

730　*DE.* quid nunc futurumst? *MI.* id enim quod res

ipsa fert:

illinc huc transferetur uirgo. *DE.* o Iuppiter,

istocin pacto oportet... *MI.* quid faciam amplius?

DE. quid facias? si non ipsa re tibi istuc dolet,

simulare certe est hominis. *MI.* quin iam uirginem

735　despondi, res conpositast, fiunt nuptiae,

dempsi metum omnem. haec mage sunt hominis.

DE. ceterum

placet tibi factum, Micio? *MI.* non, si queam

mutare. nunc quom non queo, animo aequo fero.|

---

726 eho Σ, *Don.; cf. Pl. Ps. 988.*　　727 *Marouzeau:*
MI. non. malim quidem *uulgo ('alii uolunt Micionem dicere
malim quidem, alii Demeam', Don.).*　　728 natus *A*, n. est γ*J*,
est n. δ.　　733 facias rogitas Σ.　　738 id mutare *A*.
aequo animo fero Σ.

DE. What on earth? You *know*, and you accept it?

MI. Why shouldn't I accept it?

DE. Tell me, doesn't it make you want to scream? To go
       wild? To...

MI. I certainly would prefer...

DE. A boy is born!

MI. God bless him!

DE. The girl has nothing...

MI. Yes, I heard.

DE. ...and must come without a penny to her name!

MI. That's logic.

DE. (730) What will happen next?

MI. Why, what the situation suggests: she'll be brought
       across from there to here.

DE. Good God, can *that* be the proper way...?

MI. What more should I do?

DE. Do? do? If you really don't cringe at the idea in
       its own right, it would at least be reasonable to
       pretend!

MI. Well look, (735) I've betrothed the girl to him, the
       unpleasantness is patched up, the ceremony is going
       ahead, and I've removed everyone's dreads. That is
       still more reasonable.

DE. But what about what went before? Are you happy about
       that, Micio?

MI. No, not if I were in a position to change it. As it
       is, since I'm not, I have to take it philosophically.

ĭtă uitast hŏmĭnum quăsĭ quom ludas tessĕris:

740   si illud quod maxŭme ŏpŭs est iactu non cădĭt,

illud quod cĕcĭdit forte, ĭd arte ut corrĭgas.

DE. corrector! nemp¹ tŭa artĕ uiginti mĭnae

pro psaltrĭa   pĕrĭĕrĕ; quae quantum pŏtest

ălĭquo abĭcĭundast, si non prĕtĭo, at gratĭis.

745   MI. nĕque est nĕque illam sane stŭdĕo uendĕrê.

DE. quĭd ĭgĭtur făcĭes? MI. dŏmi ĕrit. DE. pro

diuom fĭdem!

mĕrĕtrix et materfămĭlĭas   una in dŏmo?

MI. quor non? DE. sanum te credĭs esse?

MI. ĕquĭdem arbĭtror.

DE. ĭtă mĕ di ament   ut uĭdĕo ĕgô   tŭam

ĭneptĭam.

750   facturum credo ŭt hăbĕas quicum cantĭtes.

MI. quor non? DE. et nŏuă nupta ĕădem haec

discet? MI. scilĭcet.

DE. tu intĕr ĕas restim ductans saltabis?

MI. prŏbe.

---

744 at Jp, om. A, uel (at uel G) Σ. gratis ω. 746 facias
γD²G.   deum Jδ.   747 erit una ΣJ.   748 sanumne
γD²L.   749 di bene ament A.   tuam ego γJ.
751 haec eadem δ.

Human life is like a game of dice. 740   If what you

particularly need doesn't fall on your throw you must

use skill to make the best of what has happened to

fall.

DE. You, making the best! So it was thanks to your skill

that two thousand have been thrown away on that *artiste*!

And she must be got rid of as soon as may be to the

first taker, if not for a price, well then, for nothing!

MI. (745) *(Seeming to weigh this up carefully)* Certainly

not for nothing; and I'm not particularly keen on selling

her anyway.

DE. So what are you going to do?

MI. I'll keep her.

DE. Saints alive! A mistress and a respectable wife under

one roof?

MI. Why not? *(Pause)*.

DE. Do you believe you're sane?

MI. *(Apparently puzzled)* I certainly *think* so.

DE. By the love of Heaven, I can see how far out of line

you are - (750) I do believe you're aiming to get

yourself a partner for a duet!

MI. Why not?

DE. And the blushing bride will learn the same tune?

MI. Of course.

DE. You'll caper between them tugging the rope?

MI. With grace!

DE. prŏbe? MI. et tu nobiscum una, si ŏpus sit.

             DE. ej mĭhi,

non te haec pŭdent? MI. iam uero ŏmittĕ, Demĕâ,

755 tŭam istanc iracundĭam atque ĭta ut dĕcet

  hĭlărum ac lŭbentem fac te gnati in nuptĭis.

  ĕgo hos conuĕnĭo, post huc rĕdĕo. DE. o Iuppĭtêr,

  hancin uitam! hoscin mores! hanc dementĭam!

  uxor sĭnĕ dotĕ uĕnĭĕt; intus psaltrĭast;

760 dŏmŭs sumptŭosa; ădŭlescens luxu perdĭtus;

  sĕnex delirans. ipsă si cŭpĭat Sălus,

  seruarĕ prorsus non pŏtest hanc famĭlĭam.

(v. 1)

  SY. ĕdĕpol, Sўriscĕ, te curasti mollĭter

  lautequĕ munŭs admĭnistrasti tŭom:

765 abĭ. sed postquam intus sum omnĭum rerum sătur,

  prodeambŭlare huc lŭbĭtumst. DE. illud sis uĭde

  exemplum discĭplinae! SY. ecce autem hic ădest

  sĕnĕx noster. quid fit? quid tu es tristĭs?

            DE. o scĕlûs...

---

753 probe *om.* γGL. 755 istam Aδ. 756 hilarem δF.
in nati γDL. in *om.* AG. 757 conueniam ΣJ. 763 *an*
me? 765 abi *om.* A. rerum omnium δ. 766 libuit A.
767 disciplinai *Lindsay-Kauer in app. crit.*

DE. Disgrace, you mean.

MI. And you'll make up the foursome, if required.

DE. It's too much! Aren't you ashamed of all this?

MI. *(Taking Demea's arm)* (755) For once at least, Demea,
       set that bad temper of yours aside and make yourself
       good-humoured and friendly on the occasion of your
       son's wedding. I'm seeing the family here; back
       presently. *(Exit into Sostrata's)*

DE. Good God! What a way of life! What immorality! What
       lunacy! A wife arriving without a penny, an *artiste*
       installed, (760) a staff that soaks up money, the son
       and heir ruined by soft living, the master off his head.
       If Hercules himself wanted to save this establishment,
       he couldn't manage it. *(Enter SYRVS from Micio's,
       garlanded, and unsteady; he mimics the voice of an
       upper-class twit)*

SY. 'Syrus my dear boy! You've really pampered yourself
       and the standard of service was really super! (765)
       That'll do!' Well, since I'm full *chez moi (Pats
       stomach)* of everything *(Burps)* I thought it would be
       nice to have a stroll in the open. *(Urinates against
       the wall of the house)*

DE. Just look at that model of good training!

SY. *(Over shoulder)* Here he is again, our dear old gentleman.
       All right? What's the matter then?

DE. Damn and...

SY. ohe iam! tu uerba fundis hic   sapientia?

770   DE. tun si meus esses... SY. dis quidem esses,

                                          Demea,

ac tuam rem constabilisses. DE. ...exemplo

                                          omnibus

curarem ut esses. SY. quam ob rem? quid feci?

                                          DE. rogas?

in ipsa turba atque in peccato maxumo

quod uix sedatum satis est, potatis, scelus,

775   .quasi bene re gesta. SY. sane nollem huc exitum.

(v. 2)

DROMO heus Syre, rogat   te Ctesipho ut redeas.

                                          SY. abi.

DE. quid Ctesiphonem hic narrat? SY. nil.

                               DE. eho carnufex,

est Ctesipho intus? SY. non est. DE. quor hic

                                          nominat?

SY. est alius quidam, parasitaster paullulus -

780   nostin? DE. iam scibo.

───────────────────────────────────

769 eho γD^2.   fundes δ. 'utrum sapientia uerba an tu,
Sapientia?', Don., cf. 394.   771 exemplo Bentley:
exempla A, -plum Σ. exempla...essent Marouzeau. 774 J:
potis A, potasti Σ, potastis Don.   775 $D^1 G$: hunc cett.
776 heus heus δ.   780 scio A.

SY. *(Finishing, and turning round)* Whoa! What, spouting
wisdom, here?

DE. (770) I can tell you, if you were my servant...

SY. You'd be a rich man, Demea, and you'd have consolidated
your economy.

DE. ...I'd see you were a lesson to all!

SY. What for? What have I done?

DE. Done? done? Confusion rampant, and monstrous
immorality that's barely been brought under a modicum
of control, and you people are at the bottle, damn it,
(775) as if you were celebrating a triumph!

SA. *(Aside)* Coming out here wasn't such a good idea!
*(As he says this Micio's door opens, DROMO puts his
head out)*

DROMO Hey, Syrus! Ctesipho's asking you to come back!

SY. Go away!

DE. What's this talk of Ctesipho?

SY. Nothing.

DE. Wait a minute you butcher's hack - is *Ctesipho* in the
house?

SY. No, he's not!

DE. Why did he say his name?

SY. It's somebody else, a small-time would-be hanger-on -
know him?

DE. (780) I'll soon find out! *(Making to enter: Syrus tries
to stop him)*

SY. quid agis? quo abis? DE. mitte me!

SY. nolo inquam. DE. non manum abstines,

mastigia?

an tibi iam mauis cerebrum dispergam hic?

SY. abit:

edepol comissatorem haud sane commodum,

praesertim Ctesiphoni! quid ego nunc agam,

785   nisi dum haec silescunt turbae interea in angulum

aliquo abeam atque edormiscam hoc uilli? sic agam.

(v. 3)

MI. parata a nobis sunt ita ut dixi, Sostrata,

ubi uis - quisnam a me pepulit tam grauiter fores?

DE. ei mihi! quid faciam? quid agam? quid clamem

aut querar?

790   o caelum, o terra, o maria Neptuni! DE. em tibi!

resciuit omnem rem: id nunc clamat: ilicet,

paratae lites: succurrendumst. DE. eccum adest

communis corruptela nostrum liberum.

MI. tandem reprime iracundiam atque ad te redi.

---

781 SY. *om. A.*   782 iam *om.* γ. dispergi Σ.   786 *EF²G*:
uillis *A,* uini *cett.*   787 dixti *D²LEF².*   789 quid agam
om. γ.   791 clamitat *L (cf. 60).* scilicet γ*GL²,* licet
Dp.

SY. (780) What are you doing? Where are you going?

DE. Let go!

SY. No! You mustn't, you mustn't!

DE. *(Making Micio's door, breaking loose)* Get your hands
off, you vandal! *(Waving staff)* Or do you want me to
spatter your brains on the doorstep? *(Exit)*

SY. He's gone. Deary me, not really a very desirable
gatecrasher, especially not from Ctesipho's point of
view! The only thing for me to do while this storm
blows itself out (785) is hide in some corner and snooze
off that nice little drop of wine. Yes, that's what
I'll do. *(Sneaks into Micio's. Enter MICIO from*
Sostrata's as at 719)

MI. Everything's ready on our side as I said, Sostrata,
whenever you like... *(Din from Micio's, DEMEA enters)*
Who thunders at my portal so?

DE. Disaster! Panic! Woe! I'm lost for words!
(790) O sky, o earth, o Neptune's seas!

MI.   That's it;
He's learnt the truth; that's why the noise; all's up;
Fresh quarrels. Time to send in aid.

DE.   'Tis he -
The impartial ruination of our brood!

MI. Oh come off it. Control yourself. Get back to your
senses.

795   *DE.* rĕpressi rĕdĭi, mitto mălĕdicta omnĭâ.

        rem ipsam pŭtemus. dictum hoc inter nos fûĭt —

        ex te ădĕo est ortum — ne tu curares mĕum

        neue ĕgŏ tŭom?   responde! *MI.* factumst, non nĕgo.

        DE. quor nunc ăpud te potat?   quor rĕcĭpis mĕum?

800   quor ĕmĭs ămicam, Micĭo?   numqui mĭnus

        mĭhi ĭdem ius aequomst essĕ quod mecumst tĭbi?

        quando ĕgŏ tŭom   non curo, ne cura mĕum.

        MI. non aequom dicis. *DE.* non? *MI.* nam uĕtŭs

                                         uerbum hoc quĭdemst,

        communĭa esse ămicorum inter se omnĭâ.

805   *DE.* făcete! nunc demum istaec nata oratĭost?

        MI. ausculta paucis, nĭsĭ mŏlestumst, Demêâ.

        principĭo, si id te mordet, sumptum filĭi

        quem făcĭunt, quaeso hoc făcĭto tecum cogĭtes.

        tu illos dŭo olim pro re tollebas tŭa,

810   quod satĭs pŭtabas tŭă bŏna ambobus fŏrê, ¦
                                                    ¦
        et me tum uxorem credĭdisti scilĭcet

        ducturum. eandem illam ratĭonem antiquam optĭne:

        conserua, quaerĕ, parcĕ, fac quam plurŭmum

---

796 inter nos hoc γ.   797 ortumst γ, exortumst δ.
800 numquid ΣJ.   801 quid m. *Ap*, quam m. *D¹F*.   803 DE.
del. Don.   804 se *om. A.*   808 facito hoc δ, facito
haec γ*D²*.   809 duo *Ap*: duos *J, cett.* olim duos δ.
tolerabas *AδF²*.

DE. (795) I am in control, I am myself. No more hard words
from me: let's reckon the facts. There was an agreement
between us - and it was all your idea - that you wouldn't
concern yourself with my son, nor I concern myself with
yours? Well?

MI. True, I'm not denying it.

DE. Why is he tippling in your house this minute? Why are
you harbouring my son? (800) Why are you buying him a
mistress, Micio? How can you justify not respecting
my rights exactly as I do yours? Since I don't concern
myself with your son, you'll kindly not concern yourself
with mine.

MI. You're not being fair.

DE. I'm *not*?

MI. Well, there's the old saying, 'Friends say not mine and
thine but ours'.

DE. (805) Very glib! A fine time to start talking like
that!

MI. *(taking his arm gently)* Demea, if you don't mind, hear
me out. I won't be long. First about the expense our
sons are causing, if that's what really hurts you.
Please think this over carefully. You were ready to
take the two on in accordance with your long-term
prospects (810) because you reckoned your property.
would be enough for both, and you then naturally
expected I would get married. Hold on to that old
policy! Scrimp, earn, save every penny, to see that
you leave behind as much as you possibly can for them,

illis rĕlinquas, glorĭam   tu istanc tĭbi.

815   mĕă, quae praeter spem euenere, utantur sînê.

de summa nil decedet; quŏd hĭnc accessĕrît,

id de lŭcro   pŭtato esse omne. haec si uŏles

in ănĭmo uere cogĭtarĕ, Demĕâ,

et mihi et tĭbi ĕt ĭllis dempsĕris   mŏlestĭam.

820   DE. mitto rĕm: consuetudĭnem amborum... MI. mănĕ;

scĭo; istuc ibam. multa ĭn hŏmĭnĕ, Demĕâ,

signa insunt, ex quĭbŭs coniectură făcĭlĕ fĭt,

duo quŏm ĭdem făcĭunt saepe ut possis dicĕrê, ¦

'hoc lĭcĕt inpunĕ făcĕre huic, illi non lĭcet',

825   non quo dissĭmĭlis res sit sed quo is qui făcit.

quăe ergo ĭn ĭllis essĕ uĭdĕo, ut confidam fŏrê ¦

ĭta ŭt uŏlŭmus? uĭdĕo săpĕre, intellĕgĕre, in lŏco

uĕreri, inter se ămarĕ. scire est libĕrum ¦

ingĕnĭum atque ănĭmum: quouis illos tu dĭe

830   redducas. ăt ĕnim mĕtŭas ne ab re sint tămên

ŏmissĭores paullo. o noster Demĕâ, ¦

ăd omnĭa ălĭa aetatĕ săpĭmus rectĭus;

solum unum hoc uĭtĭum adfert sĕnectus hŏmĭnĭbŭs:

814 Bentley: tu istam optine Aδ, istanc (-am) tibi optine γ;
cf. Hec. 461.   816 decedit A.   817 omnia Σ.   820
ipsorum Σ. 824 hoc Aγ: huic δ. 825 quod...quod γ, quod...quo δ.
826 scripsi: quae ego inesse illis A, quae ego illis inesse
Don., quae ego in illis esse Σ; quae ego inesse in illis
edd. recc. uulgo.   quae relatiuum accipiunt.   827 uideo
eos sapere Σ.   828 scire et A.   833 senectus adfert γ.

and for yourself, the esteem which goes with that.(815)

As for *my* wealth, it came to me against expectation;

let them use it. Nothing will disappear from the total

you envisaged. In future, reckon whatever will have

come from me as clear surplus. If in time you're

honestly willing to think this over, Demea, you will

at one stroke eliminate all embarrassment to yourself,

to me, and to the boys.

DE. (820) Never mind our property: it's the way both of

them are behaving...

MI. Wait, I know: I was coming to that. There are many

signs in a person, Demea, from which, in the case of

two people doing the same thing often one can

easily infer,'this one can get away with that, but

not the other'; (825) not because the deed is different,

but the doer. Well, what signs do I see in them to

make me so certain that they will turn out just as we

wish them to? I see that they have sense, discrimination,

respect where it matters, and mutual affection. It's

possible to tell inherited decency of spirit (830):

one could call them to heel any day of the week. But

yes, there's still the worrying objection that they're

rather too slack over money. My dear brother, our true

appreciation of things in general varies with our age;

there is only one real failing that old age brings to

us all – we older people are more

adtentiores sumus ad rem omnes quam sat est;

835   quod illos sat aetas acuet. *DE.* ne nimium modo

bonae tuae istae nos rationes, Micio,|

et tuos iste animus aequos subuortat. *MI.* tace;

non fiet. mitte iam istaec; da te hodie mihi;|

exporge frontem. *DE.* scilicet ita tempu' fert:

840   faciundumst. ceterum ego rus cras   cum filio

cum primo luci ibo hinc. *MI.* de nocte censeo:|

hodie modo hilarum te face. *DE.* et istam psaltriam|

una illuc mecum hinc abstraham. *MI.* pugnaueris;

eg pacto prorsum illi adligaris filium.

845   modo facito ut illam serues. *DE.* ego istuc uidero;|

atque ibi fauillae plena fumi ac pollinis

coquendo sit faxo et molendo; praeter haec

meridie ipso faciam ut stipulam colligat:

tam excoctam reddam atque atram quam carbost.

                                       MI. placet:

850   nunc mihi uidere sapere. atque equidem filium

tum etiam si nolit, cogam ut cum illa una cubet.

DE. derides? fortunatus qui isto animo sies.

---

837 -ant Σ.   840 ego *om.* Σ. cras *om.* γ.   841 primo
luce *J*, prima luce Σ. immo (ego) de Σ.   842 *Lp*: fac te
A, te fac *cett.*   844 illic *ΣJ*.   846 *ADPC*: atque illi
(illa) *cett.*   atque/illi *Bentley, cf. 375.*   850 DE.
atque *AγL*.   851 tuum...cogas δ*E*². 852 MI. derides.
DE. fortunatus *A*: *an* MI. erudies. DE...?

preoccupied with money than it's proper we should be.
(835) Time will duly sharpen them in that.

DE. I only hope these all too noble principles, this so-
called philosophical outlook of yours doesn't end in
our ruin!

MI. Hush: it won't. Forget all that for now; put yourself
in my hands for today; get rid of that frown.

DE. I can see things now lead that way: (840) there's no
alternative. But I'm off to the farm with my son at
the crack of dawn!

MI. While it's still night I'd say; just put on a happy
face for today.

DE. And I'll drag that *artiste* all the way with me!

MI. You'll win hands down! At that rate you will tie
Ctesipho to the farm for good. (845) But be sure to
keep your eye on *her*.

DE. No problem there: I'll see she gets covered in ash,
smoke, and flour from milling and baking, and besides
that I'll have her gathering stubble at high noon:
I'll roast her black as coal.

MI. Good idea; (850) now you seem to me showing the right
spirit. And then for good measure let me force your
son into bed with her even if he can't stand the
prospect!

DE. You can scoff: life's easy for you with that attitude.

ĕgŏ sentĭo...*MI.* ah pergĭsnĕ? *DE.* iam iam desĭno.⌐

MI. i ergo intro, et quoi reist, eĭ rei hunc

                          sumamus dĭem.

(v. 4)

855   *DE.* numquam ĭtă quisquam bĕnĕ subducta

                         rătĭone ad uitam fŭit,

quin res aetas usus sempĕr ălĭquid adportet nŏui,⌐

ălĭquid mŏnĕat, ŭt ĭllă quae te

                     scissĕ credas nescĭas,

et quae tĭbĭ pŭtaris prima, ĭn expĕrĭundo ut

                        rĕpŭdĭes.

quod nunc mi euenit; nam ĕgŏ uitam duram

                   quam uixi usque ădhuc

860   prŏpĕ iam excurso spătĭo ŏmitto. id quam ob

                     rem? re ipsa reppĕri

făcĭlĭtatĕ nil esse hŏmĭni mĕlĭus

                     nĕquĕ clementĭa.⌐

ĭd ĕssĕ uerum ex me atque ex fratrĕ

                 quoiuis făcĭlest noscĕrê.⌐

ill' suam sempĕr egit uitam ĭn otĭo, in conuiuĭis;

---

854 DE. i... *Kauer.*   quod res est *A*: cui rei opus est
δ*E.*   hilarem (-um *J*) hunc δ*EF*[2]. 855–81 *tr*[7]. 857 scire γ.
858 putares δ.   ut *om.* γ.   860 iam decurso (*om.*
prope) *Eugraphius*   decurso iam (*om.* prope?) *Priscianus.*
mitto *CFE.*   863 gessit δ.

What *I* think is...

MI. Oh, not again!

DE. I'm on the point of finishing.

MI. Well, come indoors, and let's spend today as it was
meant to be spent. *(Exit Micio)*

DE. (855) *(Lingering)* No-one has ever had his way of
life so precisely worked out that circumstance, time,
experience is not always producing something fresh,
always teaching a lesson, so that we unlearn what we
believe we knew, and reject on testing it what we had
reckoned fundamental.

And such is my case now.

Yes, my race is almost run, but I now drop the austere
life (860) that I have always lived up to now. Why
do that? I have learnt from the facts that there is
nothing better for a person than affability and mildness.

Anyone can easily tell that from my brother and me.
His life has been one long merry holiday;

clemens plăcĭdus, nulli laedĕre os,

                   adridere omnĭbus.

865   sĭbĭ uixit, sĭbĭ sumptum fecĭt;

               omnes bĕnĕ dicunt, ămant.

ĕgo ĭlle ăgrestis saeuos tristis

               parcus trŭcŭlentus tĕnax

duxi uxorem: quam ĭbĭ mĭsĕrĭam uidi! nati filĭi:

ălĭă cura. heia autem, dum stŭdĕo ĭllis ut

               quam plurĭmum

făcĕrem, contriui in quaerendo

            uitam atque aetatem mĕam.

870   nunc exacta aetate hoc fructi

             pro lăbore ăb ĕis fĕro -

ŏdĭum: ille alter sĭnĕ lăborĕ

              pătrĭă pŏtĭtur commŏda.

illum ămant,   me fŭgĭtant; illi

             credunt consĭlĭa omnĭa,

illum dilĭgunt, ăpŭd illum sunt ambo, ĕgŏ

             desertŭ' sum;

illum ut uiuat optant, meam autem mortem

             exspectant scilĭcet.

875   ĭta ĕos mĕo lăbore eductos maxŭmo hic fecit sŭos

---

868 heia Aδ: porro γ.   875 meo *om. FF.*   edicatos *A:*
edoctos *C¹D.*

always mild, calm, never lashing out at anyone,
smiling at everyone.

(865) He has lived for himself, he has spent on himself;
people admire him, people like him. It was I, the very
model of the peasant, wild, dour, mean, aggressive,
tight-fisted that took on marriage - and what distress
I found in that! The arrival of sons: yet more worry.

(Signs) So: putting all my energy into making as much
as I could for them, I have quite worn my life and
time away. (870) Now, my time quite spent, this is the
return I get from them for my struggles - their
loathing.

It's that opposite of mine who wins the comforts of a
father without any effort. They think he's special,
they avoid me; they confide everything in him, they
are at his side, both of them; I am left alone; they
pray for his preservation, and it's clear they look
forward to my death.

(875) So at paltry expense he has taken over the
children whom I struggled desperately to raise.

paullo sumptu: mĭsĕrĭam omnem ĕgŏ căpĭo, hic

pŏtĭtur gaudĭâ. |

ăge ăgĕ, nuncĭam expĕrĭamur

contra ecquĭd ĕgŏ possĭem

blande dicĕre aut bĕnigne

făcĕrĕ quando hoc prouŏcat.

ĕgŏ quŏque a mĕis me ămari et magni pendi

postŭlo;

880   si id fit dando atque obsĕquendo,

non postĕrĭores fĕram.

deerĭt: id mea mĭnĭme re fert,

qui sum natu maxŭmûs.

(v.5)

SY. heus Demĕa, orat frater ne ăbĕas longĭus.

DE. quĭs hŏmo? o Sўrĕ noster, salue: quid fit?

quĭd ăgĭtur?

SY. recte. DE. optŭmest. iam nunc haec trĭă

primum addĭdi

885   praeter naturam: 'o noster, quid fit? quĭd

ăgĭtur?'.

seruom haud inlibĕralem praebes te et tĭbi

lŭbens bĕnĕ faxim. SY. gratĭam hăbĕo.

DE. atqui, Sўrê, |

---

876 potitur commoda A.   877 iam om. γG.   porro contra
Ap.   possim DLJ.   878 huc D¹G: eo γD²L.   879 magni
fieri A.   882-933 ia^6.   882 rogat Σ.   883 homo est
δEJ.

All I get is the anguish, he monopolizes the joys.

Well, all right then: let's now try in response to see
if I can say anything nice, act kindly, now that he
challenges me to it. I too have a claim to the love
and admiration of my own children; (880) if that is
what you get by giving things and falling in line,
I shan't take second prize. Ruin? That's none of my
concern - I am the oldest. *(Enter SYRVS from Demea's
House)*

SY. Excuse me, Demea, your brother asks you not to go off
too far.

DE. Who's that? Ah, our own dear Syrus; hello. All right?
How are things?

SY. (884) Er - oh fine.

DE. Delighted to hear it! *(Aside)* That's three new phrases
straight off that I didn't have in me before - 'Our own
dear Syrus', 'All right?', 'How are things?'. *(Aloud)*
Your conduct as a servant does you no small credit and
I'd like to see you right.

SY. *(Ironically)* Much obliged!

DE. No, I really mean it, Syrus -

hoc uerumst ĕt ĭpsa re expĕrĭerĕ prŏpĕdĭem. |

(v.6)

GE. ĕra, ĕgo huc ăd hos prouiso quam mox uirgĭnem |

890 accersant. sĕd ĕccum Demĕam.　　saluos sĭes.

DE. o...qui uŏcarĕ?　GE. Gĕtă.　DE. Gĕta, hŏmĭnem

　　　　　　　　　　　　　　　maxŭmi

prĕti te esse hŏdĭe iudĭcaui ănĭmo mĕo.

nam is mĭhi prŏfectost seruos spectatus sătis

quoĭ dŏmĭnus curaest, ĭta ŭti tĭbĭ sensi, Gĕtâ, |

895 et tĭbi ŏb ĕam rem si quĭd usus uenĕrit

lŭbens bĕnĕ faxim. mĕdĭtor esse adfabĭlîs,

et bĕnĕ procedit. GE. bŏnŭs es quom haec existŭmas.

DE. paullatim plebem primŭlum　　făcĭo mĕam. |

(v.7)

AE. occidunt mĕquĭdem dum nĭmĭs sanctas nuptĭas

900 stŭdĕnt făcĕre: ĭn adpărando consumunt dĭem.

DE. quĭd ăgĭtŭr Aeschĭne?　AE. ehem

　　　　　　　　　　　　păter mi, tu hic ĕras?

DE. tŭŏs herclĕ uero ĕt ănĭmo et natura păter

---

889 hinc C^2D^2LE.　　ad uos A.　　prouisam γL.　　892 esse
te γ.　　iudicaui hodie δ.　　893 est profecto Σ.　　894 ut
Σ.　　898 facito P^1F.　　meum A.　　899 mĕquĭdēm *anapaestus;*
uel mē quĭdēm *dactylus* (qu. *ad* occidunt); me equidem A.
900 totum consumunt Σ.　　901 tun Σ.

I'm serious, and you'll get practical proof any
time now. *(Enter GETA from Sostrata's)*

GE. Madam, I'm going out to see how soon (890) they'll be
fetching the girl. Ah, there's Demea. My best
respects to you, sir.

DE. Oh...what's your name?

GE. Geta.

DE. Yes of course, Geta. Yes, Geta: my verdict on you
today is that you are an extremely valuable fellow.
For the worker who really has made the grade in my
opinion is the one who cares about his master exactly
as I have seen you care, er.....Geta, (895) and in
reward, if the opportunity arises, I'd like to see you
right. *(Aside)* The out-going style – it's going well!

GE. Thank you for thinking that! You're a real gentleman!

DE. *(Aside)* I'm making my modest start by winning the
masses. *(Enter AESCHINUS from Micio's, dressed for
the wedding)*

AE. They're killing me, the groom, in their enthusiasm
for an elaborate formal service! They're taking all
day to get ready!

DE. (901) How are things, Aeschinus?

AE. Er...father! I didn't know you were here!

DE. *(Embracing him)* Yes indeed, your own true father, in

heart and soul,

qui te amat plus quam hosce ŏcŭlos. sed quor

non dŏmum
. . .
uxorem accersis? *AE.* cŭpĭo; uerum hoc mihi mŏraest
905   tĭbicĭna ĕt hȳmĕnaeum qui cantent. *DE.* ĕho

uin tu huic sĕni auscultarĕ? *AE.* quid? *DE.* missa

haec fāce,
. . .
hȳmĕnaeum turbas lampădas   tĭbicĭnas,

atque hanc ĭn horto macĕrĭam   iŭbĕ dirŭi,

quantum pŏtest: hac transfĕr, unam fac dŏmum:
910   transduce et matrem et fămĭlĭam omnem ad nos.

AE. plăcet,

păter lĕpĭdissĭme. *DE.* euge, iam 'lĕpĭdus' uŏcor!

fratri aedes fĭent peruĭae,   turbam dŏmum
. . .
adducet, sumptu amittet mʋlta - quid mĕa?

ĕgŏ lĕpĭdŭs ĭnĕo gratĭam.   iŭbĕ nuncĭam
915   dinŭmĕret illĕ Băbȳlo uĭginti mĭnas!

Sȳrĕ, cessas ire ac făcĕrĕ? *SY.* quĭd ăgo?

DE. dirŭĕ.

tu illas ăbi et transducĕ. *GE.* di tĭbĭ, Demĕa,

---

904 uxorem quaeso accersis γ; uxorem quaeso *Marouzeau.*
morast *A.*   905 cantet *DG*, canat γ.   906 istaec *Aδ.*
907 turbam hymenaeum γ.   turbam γ*D.*   lampedes *A.*
909 potes *P²GL.*   910 traduc *A.*   912 fratris *ΣJ.*
913 adducet *om. A*; adducet/ sumptu *J*, adducet et sumptu *G*,
adducet et sumptum *cett.*   915 *hinc deest A.*   illi
p *Don.*   916 ago γ *(ego F¹) Lp*: ego *cett.*   917 et γ: ac δ.

who loves you more than his own sight. But why aren't
you fetching your bride home?

AE. I'm eager to; but the reasons for the wretched delay are
(905) the musician and the choir for the wedding-hymn.

DE. Listen! Would you take a suggestion from an old man?

AE. What?

DE. Forget all that stuff, wedding-hymns, crowds, torches,
music. Have the garden-wall broken down as quick as
possible. Carry her over that way, make it one house,
(910) and bring her mother and the whole lot over
to us!

AE. I like it! Father, you're wonderful!

DE. (*Aside*) Great! Now I'm Mr Wonderful! My brother's
house will be an open street, he'll have the throng
at his house, he'll lose lots in the cost; what does
that matter to me? I'm Mr Wonderful and I'm coming
into favour! Just let (915) that pasha pay out two
thousand now! (*Aloud*) Syrus, hurry up and get on
with it!

SY. What am I supposed to be doing?

DE. Excavations, man! Geta, you go and take the ladies
across.

GE. God bless you, Demea.

bĕnĕ făcĭant, quom te uĭdĕo nostrae fămĭlĭae

tam ex ănĭmo factum uellĕ. *DE.* dignos arbĭtror.

920   quid tŭ ais? *AE.* sic ŏpinor. *DE.* multo rectĭust

quam illam pŭerpĕram hac nunc duci per uĭam |

aegrotam. *AE.* nil ĕnĭm mĕlĭus uidi, mi păter.

DE. sic sŏlĕo. sĕd ĕccum Micĭo egrĕdĭtur fŏras.

(v.8)

MI. iŭbĕt fratĕr? ŭbi ĭs est? tu iŭbes

                       hoc, Demĕâ? |

925   *DE.* ĕgŏ uero iŭbĕo ĕt hac re et ălĭis omnĭbus

quam maxŭme unam făcĕrĕ nos   hanc fămĭlĭam,

cŏlĕre adiŭuare adiungĕre. *AE.* ĭtă quaeso, pătêr.

MI. ha ! ălĭter censĕo. *DE.* immo hercle ĭtă nobis

                       dĕcet:

primum huius uxorist matĕr. *MI.* est: quid

                       postĕa?

930   *DE.* prŏba et mŏdesta. *MI.* ĭta aiunt. *DE.* natu

                       grandĭor.

---

920 agis *C.*   921 hanc δ*F.*   922 uidi melius *C.*   924
tu *Don.*: tun(e) Σ.   929 uxorist *Arusianus 494:* -is est
Σ.   est *alterum om.* γ*G.*

I can see that you really and sincerely mean to help
our family.

DE. I think you've all earned that.(920) What do you say,
Aeschinus?

AE. It sounds perfect!

DE. It's much better than having the girl with the baby
brought round here through the street. She can hardly
be feeling very well!

AE. *(Who plainly hasn't thought of that)* Father! I never
heard a better idea!

DE. Just one of my usual. But there's Micio coming out.
(Enter Micio speaking back to Syrus indoors)

MI. Demea said so? Where is he? *(Seeing him, gesturing)*
Demea, did you say so?

DE. (925) Yes, I did, so that by this and every other
conceivable means we make this household one
with our own, looking after it, helping it, tending
it.

AE. How right he is, father!

MI. *(Taken aback)* I can't quarrel with that.

DE. *(More lively)* Good heavens, it's up to us! First,
there's his new mother-in-law...

MI. There is; so what?

DE. (930)...a respectable, sensible lady...

MI. So they say.

DE. ...getting on a bit.

MI. scĭŏ.   DE. părĕrĕ iamdĭu 'haec pĕr annos non

                                                    pŏtest;

nec qui eam respĭcĭat quisquam est: solast.

                                    MI. quam hic rem ăgît?

DE. hanc te aequomst ducĕre, et te ŏpĕram ut

                                        fĭat dărê.

MI. me ducĕre autem?   DE. te.   MI. me?   DE. te inquam

                        MI. ĭneptis.   DE. si tu sis hŏmo, |

935   hic făcĭat.   AE. mi păter!   MI. quid tu autem huic,

                        ăsĭne, auscultas?   DE. nil ăgis:

fĭerĭ ălĭter non pŏtest.   MI. deliras.   AE. sĭnĕ te

                        exorem, mi pătêr.

MI. insanis: aufĕr.   DE. ăgĕ da uĕnĭam filĭo.

                        MI. sătĭn sanŭs es?

ĕgŏ nŏuŏs mărĭtŭs anno demum quinto et sexagesĭmo

fĭam atque ănum decrĕpĭtam ducam?   idne estĭs

                        auctores mĭhi?

---

932 recipiat GEF². 934-45 iα⁸. 935 autem om. γ.
937 aufer ex Don.: om. Σ. quaeso filio γD²p.

MI. I know.

DE. Her age means she's long past having children;
there's no-one to look after her: she's alone.

MI. *(Aside)* What's his game?

DE. It's only right that you, Demea, should marry her,
and that you, Aeschinus, should encourage the union!

MI   What, me *marry*?

DE. Yes.

MI. *Me?*

DE. Yes, you.

MI. This is in bad taste!

DE. *(To Aeschinus)* If you were to use your brain, (935)
he'd do it.

AE. Father...!

MI. And why are *you* letting him bend your ear, you
brainless ass?

DE. You're wasting your time; there's no possible alternative.

MI. You're off your head!

AE. *(Kneeling, grasping his father's knees as a suppliant)*
Please let me have what I ask, father.

MI. You're mad! Let go!

DE. Come on, do your son a favour.

MI. Are you quite sane? Me become a bridegroom at last
at sixty-four, marrying a broken down old woman?
Is that what you seriously suggest?

940   *AE.* fac: promisi ego illis. *MI.* promisti autem? de

                          te largitor, puer.

    DE. age, quid si quid te maius oret? *MI.* quasi non

                        hoc sit maxumum!

    DE. da ueniam. *AE.* ne grauare. *DE.* fac, promitte.

                      MI. non omittitis?

    AE. non, nisi te exorem. *MI.* uis est haec quidem!

                  DE. age prolixe, Micio.

    MI. etsi hoc mihi prauom ineptum absurdum atque

                     alienum a uita mea

945   uidetur, si uos tanto opere istuc uoltis -

                 fiat. *AE.* bene facis.

    DE. merito te amo.   uerum... *MI.* quid ergo?

               ducam: hoc confit quod uolo!

    DE. quid nunc, quod restat, Hegio?

    est his cognatus proxumus,

---

940 promisisti Σ.   941 hoc non γ.   943 DE. non...
exorem *G*.   945-8 *notae* AE. bene...amo. DE. uerum...decet
Σ, *ut taceat omnino Micio, nisi quod* 947 MI. quid? DE.
nunc... *D[1]*, MI. quid...restat? DE. Hegio *P[1]*.   946 *ia[8]*,
947 *ia[4+4]*   946 DE. merito *C*, (...tuo te amo) *Bentley.* amo t
MI. quid ergo? ducam *scripsi*: quid ego (ego quid δ) dicam
Σ.   quid ego dicam? hoc confit quod uolo *Don. ad And. 167*,
CGL 5.57: hoc cum fit (hoc fit *G*) Σ; hoc <quom> confit
Kauer, edd. recc., at ...quid ego dicam... *laborat a rhythmo,*
cf. Drexler PA ii 184.

AE. (940) Do it: I've promised them.

MI. Oh, you have, have you? From now on squander at your
own expense, sonny boy!

DE. Come on, what if he were to ask you for something
really important?

MI. As if this weren't the most important he could!

DE. Do him the favour. *(Grasping one arm)*.

AE. Don't be grumpy. *(Grasping the other)*.

DE. Do it! Promise!

MI. *(Struggling)* Let go of me, won't you?

AE. No, only if you let me have my way!

MI. You're murdering me!

DE. Be lavish, Micio!

MI. Though it seems to me immoral, tasteless, and stupid
and at odds with my whole outlook, (945) if you both
want it so badly - very well.

AE. Thank you! *(Hugs him, lets go)*.

DE. Well done! I'm very pleased with you. *(Pause while
Micio straightens himself out)* But...

MI. *(Testily)* Well, what? I'll marry her: that is the
sum-total of what I'm willing to do!

DE. What about the remainder? Hegio and his future?
What will he do now? *(Pauses)* He is their nearest

kin.

adfinis nobis, pauper: bĕnĕ nos ălĭquid făcĕre

           illi dĕcet.

MI. quid făcĕre? *DE.* ăgellist hic sub urbĕ

      paullum quod lŏcĭtas fŏras.

950 huic demus quo frŭatur. *MI.* paullum ĭd autemst?

          DE. si multumst, tămen

făcĭundumst: pro pătre huic est, bŏnŭs est,

      nostĕr est: recte dătur.

postremo non mĕum illud uerbum făcĭo quod tu, Micĭo,

bĕne et săpĭenter dixti dudum? 'uĭtĭum commune

          omnĭumst

quod nĭmĭum ad rem ɪn sĕnecta adtenti sŭmŭs'. hanc

       măcŭlam nos dĕc̃et

955 effŭgĕre. *AE.* et dictumst uere et re ipsa fĭĕri

       ŏportet, mi păter.

  MI. quĭd istic? dăbĭtur quandŏquĭdem hic

       uolt. *DE.* gaudĕo:

948-955 *ia*[8]. 949 sub urbe est his agelli δ. foras
P[1]*C*[1]: foris *cett.* 950 paululum Σ. etsi δ. multum sit
γ. tamen *om.* γ. 952 nunc meum *Palmerius, Bentley.*
953 est omnium *DL*: est *om.* G. 955 et *(prius) om.* γ.
ipsa re γ. AE. mi pater *Umpfenbach ex 956*: MI. gaudeo
DL, uacant cett. et *Micioni Grant.* 956-7 *ia*[6]. 956
MI. quɪd...γG. istuc Σ. quidem quando γ. uolt.
AE. mi pater Σ. (AE. mi pater *om. F*[1]).

a connection of ours, and poor; it's up to us to be
helpful to him.

MI. *How* helpful?

DE. There's a little patch of land just outside town that
you rent out. (950) Let's give him the benefit of
that.

MI. So that's little, is it?

DE. An ell or an acre, we still must do it: he has been
a second father to the girl, he's respectable, he's
one of us: right on target, eh? After all, Micio,
shouldn't I be taking to heart that very sensible
observation you made just now? 'The real failing
common to all of us in old age is that we become too
preoccupied with money'? It's up to us (955) to steer
clear of *that* black mark.

AE. A noble sentiment, and one to put into practice, father!

MI. *(Groans)* Oh well. The gift is to be granted since
Aeschinus wishes it so.

DE. I'm very pleased.

nunc tu germanu's pariter animo et corpore.

suo sibi gladio hunc iugulo.

(v.9)

SY. factumst quod iussisti, Demea.

DE. frugi homo's. ergo edepol hodie

mea quidem   sententia

960   iudico   Syrum fieri esse aequom

liberum. MI. istunc liberum?

quodnam ob factum? DE. multa. SY. o noster

Demea, edepol uir bonu's.

ego istos uobis usque a pueris

curaui ambo sedulo.

docui monui bene praecepi

semper quae potui omnia.

DE. res apparet: et quidem porro haec,

opsonare cum fide,

965   scortum adducere, adparare de die   conuiuium.

non mediocris hominis haec sunt

officia SY. o lepidum caput!

DE. postremo hodie in psaltria hac emunda hic

adiutor fuit.

---

957 om. $P^1C^1F^1$.   MI. nunc... G.   nunc tu germanus D:
tu mihi es (es, es mihi) germanus cett.   et animo γD^2.
957/8 corpore/gaudeo (-io G) suo Σ, corr. Umpfenbach.
958 ia^8 (tr^7 suo...?).   959-97 tr^7.   960 liberum
aequom δ.   961 bonus es δE.   967 istac γ.

(Embraces Micio) Now you're one with me in body *and* spirit. *(Aside)* I'm cutting his throat with his own razor. *(Enter SYRVS from Micio's)*

SY. Your instructions have been carried out, Demea.

DE. Useful fellow! Well then, in my view, (960) the verdict on Syrus today is that it's really only right he should be a free man.

MI. Him? Free? What on earth for?

DE. All sorts of reasons.

SY. My dear, dear Demea, you really are a gentleman! I did my honest best to concern myself with both of those lads of yours from boyhood. I taught them, I told them what to watch, I always gave all the good instruction I could.

DE. We see the result! And you taught these extra subjects – Advanced Menu-planning, (965) Introductions to Tarts, and Dawn-to-dusk Symposiacs. Not the services of any ordinary fellow!

SY. Demea! How wonderful can anyone be?

DE. And to cap it all, today he was their backer in purchasing the *artiste* in here;

hic curauit: prodesse aequomst:

　　　　　　　　　　　　　　alii meliores erunt.

denique hic uolt fieri. *MI.* uin tu hoc fieri?

　　　　　　　　　　　　AE. cupio. *MI.* si quidem hoc

970　　tu uis. Syre, eho accede huc ad me:

　　　　　　　　　　　　liber esto. *SY.* bene facis.

omnibu' gratiam habeo et seorsum

　　　　　　　　　　　　tibi praeterea, Demea.

DE. gaudeo. *AE.* et ego. *SY.* credo. utinam hoc

　　　　　　　　　　perpetuom fiat gaudium,

Phrygiam ut uxorem meam una mecum uideam liberam!

DE. optumam quidem mulierem. *SY.* et quidem

　　　　　　　　　　　　tuo nepoti huius filio

975　　hodie prima mammam dedit haec.

　　　　　　　　　　　　DE. hercle uero serio

siquidem prima dedit, haud dubiumst

　　　　　　　　　　　　quin emitti aequom siet.

MI. ob eam rem? *DE.* ob eam; postremo a me

　　　　　　　　　　　　argentum quantist sumito.

SY. di tibi, Demea, omnes semper

---

968 erant *G¹*.　969/70 tu uis/Syre *PLF*.　970 hoc uoltis
D¹G¹.　eho Syre δ.　975 primam *CDLEF*.

he saw to it all. It's only right to treat him well
to encourage the rest of the staff. And the decisive
factor is - Aeschinus wants it.

MI. Do you want it?

AE. Oh, yes!

MI. (970) Well, if you really do..., Syrus, hey, come over
here. *(Gives him more than a symbolic slap on the face)*
Henceforth be thou free.

SY. *(Reeling)* Thank you! I'm obliged to you all and especially
to you, Demea, over and above!

DE. I'm very pleased. *(Shaking hands)*

AE. And so am I. *(The same)*

SY. I know you mean it: thanks. How nice it would be if
this fleeting moment of joy could be made to last for
ever by my seeing Phrygia here beside me, a free lady
and my wife!

DE. A most worthy lady!

SY. Yes, and it was she that (975) gave his baby, your
grandson, his first feed today!

DE. Saints alive! Well, I mean to say - if she was the
first to feed him, there's no question - it's only
right that she should be free.

MI. For that?

DE. For that: and to cut any argument, you can get the
money she's worth from me later.

omnĭa optata offĕrant.

MI. Sy̆rĕ, processisti hŏdĭe pulchre.

DE. sĭquĭdem porro, Micĭo,

980   tu tuọm offĭcĭum fácĭes atque huic

ălĭquid paullum prae mănu

dĕdĕrĭs unde utatur; reddet

tĭbĭ cĭto. MI. istoc uilĭus..!

AE. frugi hŏmost. SY. reddam herclĕ, da mŏdo.

AE. ăgĕ păter! MI. post consŭlam.

DE. făcĭĕt. SY. o uĭr optŭme! AE. o păter mi

festiuissŭmê!

MI. quĭd ĭstuc? quae res tam rĕpentĕ

mores mutauit tŭos?

985   quod prolŭbĭum? quae istaec sŭbĭtast

largĭtas? DE. dicam tĭbi.|

ŭt ĭd ostendĕrem, quod te isti

făcĭlem et festiuom pŭtant,

id non fĭĕri ex uera uita

nĕque ădĕo ex aequo et bŏno,

sĕd ĕx adsentando indulgendo et largĭendo, Micĭo.

---

979 SY. *Lindsay-Kauer in app.*   980 tu *om. G.*   paululum
γG.   982 *DE. frugi homost Lindsay-Kauer.*   983 o mi
pater γ.   985 proluuium C^2δ, *Serv. auct. Aen. iii.*
217, Nonius 373. Cf. Caecilius com. fr. 91 R³ = 80 W.

SY. Demea, may heaven ever grant you all the things you've
ever wanted!

MI. Syrus, you've had luck at your side today.

DE. (980) Yes, if you do what you ought and give him a
little something in hand to draw on. He'll soon repay
you.

MI. Don't look a gifthorse in the mouth!

AE. He's a useful fellow.

SY. Lord, I'll repay, just give me! *(Holding out his hand)*

AE. Come on, father!

MI. I'll think about it later.

DE. He'll do it.

SY. Demea, you're a hero! *(Shaking his hand)*

AE. *(To Demea)* Father, you're fantastic! *(Embracing him)*

MI. Demea, what does all this mean? What attack has brought
this change in you? (985) What sudden wanton whim,
what squander-lust?

DE. Let me explain. My purpose was to show you that if
certain people see you as an adaptable spirit of
jollity, that does not come from the evident rightness
of the way you live, nor from a sense of just proportion
in you, but, from your fawning on them, Micio, and from
your pandering to them, and from your squandering on
them.

nunc ădĕo si ŏb ĕam rem uobis

                  mĕă uita inuisa, Aeschĭne, est,

990   quĭă non iusta iniustă prorsŭs

                            omnĭa omnino obsĕquor,

missos făcĭo. effundĭte ĕmĭte făcĭtĕ

                                  quod uobis lŭbet.

sed si id uoltis potĭus, quae uos

                            proptĕr ădŭlescentĭam

mĭnŭs uĭdetis, măgĭs inpense

                            cŭpĭtis, consŭlĭtis părum,┆

haec rĕprĕhendĕre et corrĭɡĕrĕ

                            me ĕt ŏbsĕcundare in lŏco,┆

995   eccĕ me   qui id făcĭam uobis.

                  AE. tĭbĭ, păter,   permittĭmus:

plus scis quĭd ŏpus factost. sed de fratrĕ

                            quid fīet? DE. sĭno:┆

hăbĕat: ĭn ĭstac finem făcĭat.

                  AE. istuc recte. OMNES plaudĭtê!

---

990 iusta *CP¹*: ista *cett.*   sequor δ.   991 missos *Grant:*
missa Σ (*propter 990* ista).   992 id *om.* δ.   994 secundare
Don.   995 quid f. *P¹*δ. 996 quod *Becker.* facto sit δ.
997 in ista γ*D²*.   AE. γ*G: nulla nota D*, MI. *Ip, Don.*
an CETERI?   Ω plaudite Σ (*nulla nota D*).   calliopius
(-io *D¹G¹*) recensui Σ.

(Turning to Aeschinus) Well now, Aeschinus. If the reason my outlook on life is repellent to you boys is this, (990) that I do not simply go along indiscriminately with anything you do, right or wrong, I wash my hands of you both. Pour money down the drain, buy what you like, do what you like. But if instead you want me to catch and correct things which you are unwary of because you are too young, want too intensely, and think over too little, and if you want me to back you up on occasion, (995) here I am to do that for you.

AE. We surrender to you completely, father: you know better than we what is appropriate. But my brother - what's his fate to be?

DE. Yes; he may keep her; but he's to draw the line with her.

AE. The right decision, that.

ALL FOUR Spectators, that's your cue!

228

Notes to the Translation

<u>PRODUCTION NOTICE</u> (p. 73)

Apparently authentic but corrupt; for a separate tradition
(*Brothers* the second play) see p. 6. Actors Hatilius
(*alias* Atilius), Ambivius, Minucius (*app. crit.* p. 72),
see Garton (1972) 61-5. Flaccus was Terence's regular
musician; a slave's job. 'Tyrian double-pipes': a reed-
instrument with that family's characteristic *timbre*; drone
and chanter? Or did one pipe extend the range? See *OCD*
Music 10 (ii), Grove (6) *s.v. aulos*

<u>SUMMARY</u>. Sulpicius Apollinaris *fl. c.* 150 A.D. His summaries
feature in both branches of the Mss. tradition. As summaries
they are pretty useless, failing to distinguish background
and action and concentrating on the former at the cost of
the latter. In the case of *Brothers* he fails to indicate
the real theme: from the summary one might think that the
'Brothers' of the title were the younger, not the older
ones. It is of interest that Apollinaris thought Demea
was only '*somewhat harsh*' (*subduro*, 4), not plain '*harsh*',
and his wording at 5 f. is relevant to the text at 280.

<u>DRAMATIS PERSONAE</u>. Not listed in the Mss. In the 4th c.
B.C. at Athens most of the 'masks of the action' were perhaps
recognizable by name (e.g. Getas, Syros, Demeas); this would
explain why in Menander Moschion is never old, Chremes never
young, Parmenon never free, etc., and why there is so little
variety and so much conventional repetition of names in New
Comedy. Type-masks were however certainly used in the 3rd
c. B.C. by the travelling Artists of Dionysus so that when
Roman drama got going stereotyped names appeared a mere
stuffy convention against which Plautus reacted strongly by
choosing his own more or less fantastical Greek names.
Caecilius and Terence reacted in turn, not by simply keeping
the names in their models, which they too only did sometimes,
but by ringing the changes on Greek names which do or might
occur in New Comedy. See *CHCL* ii 103 ff.

The connotations of the names:

MICIO 'paullus', 'homuncio'; 'Tiny'
DEMEA 'plebeius', 'tribulis'; 'Folkman'
HEGIO 'dux'; 'Leader'
AESCHINUS 'pudens'; 'Considerate', 'Respectful'
CANTHARA 'winebowl', 'beetle'
SANNIO 'Buffoon' (or worse)
SYRVS, GETA, 'Syrian, Thracian', with connotations respectivel
   of guile ('Solly', 'Ali') and rough simplicity ('Mac',
   'Boris')

CTESI-PHO, first element 'res', 'substance, wealth', second
'clarus', 'conspicuous, famous'
SO-STRATA, first element 'tueri', 'keep safe' second,
'exercitus', 'army'
PAM-PHILA, 'amata, amanda omnibus', 'beloved of all'

Of the named extras, *Storax* (26) is a slave-name like
Libanus 'Frankincense' (Plautus *Asinaria*) denoting a fragrant
resin, *Parmeno* (168) means 'steadfast', and *Dromo* (376)
'runner'.

THE PROLOGUE. 'Prologus' in Terence was not as in Plautus
a genial quasi-character, part of the entertainment, but a
spokesman who would not feature at all if Terence had not
been involved in a running dispute with 'hostile critics'
and 'rivals' (line 2), i.e., Luscius Lanuvinus; Garton (1972)
41-72, 236 f. See above, pp. 3-4.

The previous year (161 B.C.) Luscius had attacked Terence
for incorporating in *Eunuchus* characters allegedly taken
from a Latin source, the *Colax* of 'Plautus and Naevius'.
The reply (*Eun.* prologue) was that Terence had gone straight
to the Greek source the *Kolax* of Menander, did not know
the Latin version, and that in any case the types of the
theatre were surely common property anyway. Here in
Brothers Ambivius and Terence are clearly most concerned
to avoid repetition of the charge of plagiarism from a Latin
source.

For the scene in question (155-96) see pp. 43-5.

* * *

26-40 MICIO'S ENTRANCE. The opening lines elegantly establish
several things with originality, assurance, and economy.
It is dawn (26) and chilly (38); the speaker is wealthy,
for sending staff to act as escorts late at night is like
sending James with the Rolls to fetch young Nigel.
Evidently he went to bed last night expecting them to be
late, but not this late; he has got up expecting to find
them at home, and is alarmed at their absence. Storax must
be one of the escort. We expect to see them and the missing
son turn up from 'town' in due course. The evaluation and
paradox *'It's quite true what they say... the boy isn't even
my own son'* (28-40) show Micio as a worried father and as
the master, not the victim of his emotions. This 'private
view' of a worried Micio is denied to his brother Demea
throughout, but is important in establishing Micio's good
faith and humanity in our eyes right away.

So dramatic time, situation, an implied sequel, and ethos are being established at once and in an unusual way. For Micio's entrance is not to be confused, as it usually has been, with the conventional doorstep-address directed back to someone indoors as a means of linking scenes (e.g., as at 209).

This is pure Menander faithfully rendered, evidently a famous scene, for Plautus had used the ideas here characterizing *senex lepidus* worried about an absent son (37 f.) in a large-scale elaboration of his own at *Miles gloriosus* 718 ff. Though corrupt, the text there is a nice illustration of the essential differences between the styles of Plautus and Terence.

29 *or linger there*: even if *aut* = *uel*, this is padding; *ut ibi sic cesses* would mean 'so as to be as late as this', much more to the point.

33 *gambling*: Havet's *aleari* is spot-on for sense but ill-attested, which matters in Terence. The intolerable *tete amari* would give lit. 'she thinks you love someone or *you* are loved by someone'.

* * *

40-7 <u>THE BROTHERS' WAYS OF LIFE</u>. Given that there was a prologue in the original at 154/5 (see pp. 36-40) and that Varro observed substantive differences between the beginnings of Menander's and Terence's plays (see p. 263), the suspicion arises that Terence is here anticipating material deployed in the prologue by Menander. Two aspects of the content support this.

(i) It is relevant that Aeschinus is an adopted nephew and Micio a bachelor, but anything else biographical or ethical is off the dramatic point. Demea's outlook only becomes relevant when he is introduced at 59 ff. Terence is making Micio say too much and too little. Too much, because the theme relevant before and after 40-7 is Micio's love for Aeschinus and it is only after he has reviewed his relationship with the boy that Demea's different point of view becomes *à propos*; too little, because in 40-7 Micio raises without answering the questions why Demea ever let Micio adopt a son of his and an elder son at that when still a baby.

(ii) Terence is pigeonholing *senex lepidus* and *senex durus* in a philosophical opposition. But Menander appears to have represented in Micio and Demea not the conflict of

two comparably systematic philosophies, but of two
personalities, one intellectual and representing not a
particular school of philosophy but the rational outlook
necessary for *any* philosophy, and one unintellectual,
representing the unexamined life (see p. 22, 49 ff.).

It is not a difficulty that Donatus quotes the Greek original
of the line alluding to Micio's bachelorhood (43 f., see
p. 263), because that is one of the two essential points
needed to make the transition from 40 to 48, and it may
well be that the original point of the Greek citation was
to illustrate how Terence here *differed* from Menander;
see p. 39, and the *scenario*, p. 58.

* * *

48-58 <u>MICIO'S PARTICULAR POLICY</u>. Still concentrating on
Aeschinus, Micio in effect declares:

(i) 'I am a hedonist, and my happiness is my love
for Aeschinus' (49)

(ii) 'I systematically avoid interference and practice
generosity towards him because I want him to reciprocate my
feelings freely and frankly as that will ensure my
happiness'.

(iii) 'Such frankness is best cultivated by exactly the
opposite means to those used by most fathers in dealing
with their sons'.

(iv) 'Since frankness is a basic social virtue, my
self-interest and the true moral education of Aeschinus
are both best served by my policy'.

These arguments are potentially more disturbing to
traditional Roman ways of thinking than they would seem in
an Athenian context, where enlightened self-interest frankly
recognized would count as a positive sign of self-knowledge,
not as Macchiavellian, and where *'the letter of a father's
legal rights'* (52) denoted something very different from
what is involved in Roman *patria potestas* (see p. 25).
But *senex lepidus* must have his day, and Terence does not
mean us to be alienated by these un-Roman sentiments.

In presenting an unashamed hedonist, Menander was not
of course labelling his Micio specifically as an Epicurean,
even if we assume that the second *Brothers* was a late work
composed well after 307/6 B.C., when Epicurus set up his
'society of friends' at Athens; there were hedonists before

Epicurus, e.g. DEMOCRITUS, ARISTIPPIIS OF CYRENE (see *OCD*), and the kind of argument advanced by Micio would not have seemed paradoxical to an Athenian audience even well before Menander's time.

57 *rising generation...generosity*: the sentiment is Menandrian (*Sam*. 16 ff., fr. 609 K.-Th.) but there is a play on words in the Latin which will not work in Greek: *liberi* 'children' and 'free people', *liberalitate* 'generosity'.

59-67 DEMEA'S ATTITUDE. The mimicry here affords the opportunity to raise a laugh, and neatly prepares Demea's entrance at 81 ff.; his demeanour ironically confirms Micio's caricature.

64-6 *grotesque*...: the repetitions of *nimium* ('excessive') suggest that both brothers have their theories of what is *satis* ('just right'), i.e., of the mean.

66 f. *power...might...friendship*; this second rhetorical climax (cf. 57 f.) seems to ask to be taken out of context and put in the anthology, and has obvious political applications; cf. p. 20 f.

* * *

68-77 MICIO'S GENERAL THEORY. In 48-58, the particular case; in 59-67, Demea's particular reaction; each paragraph rounded off with highly effective rhetorical generalization.

Micio now returns to the first (57 f.) and amplifies it in splendidly earnest manner. In the Latin, disyllabic line-ends are bunched here and give a much more formal character to the verse than in 26-40, where they have been avoided except at one important rhythmical punctuation-point (34).

Micio's argument is antithetical: (a) 69 ff., repression has no lasting effect, (b) 72 ff. liberality does. This is logically faulty, for the subject considered under (a) is someone with a *bad* native disposition and under (b) a person with a *good* native disposition.

There are two other categories to take into account. What happens when (c) you repress a person with a *good* disposition, and (d) when you are kind to a person with a *bad*?

Micio reckons that Demea risks alienating Ctesipho and merely postponing what is excusable in the young but not in the grown-up person (107-110); that is case (c) (for

both boys have basically good dispostions, 826 ff.). But
Terence suppresses explicit distinction though it is
implicit and necessary for (a), so that Micio appears to
be arguing that repression is *never* right and liberality
is *always*, case (d) included, liberality towards a *bad*
disposition. Whether Terence was aware of the illogicality
of the rhetorical argument is a moot point; the audience,
surely not.

Micio later emphasizes that there are good and bad
natural dispositions (820 ff.) and accepts that it would
be wrong to allow the latter liberties appropriate to the
former. Bad dispositions have to be repressed for their
own and everyone's sake. Aristotle, not to say the man
in the Athenian street, thought the same, cf. on 829;
pp. 22, 53.

Thus in this passage Micio is given a simpler, more
extreme and more comprehensive opinion than he held in
Menander; for what is said in 820 ff. is certainly
Menandrian.

Micio's didactic zeal in 68-77 seems such that he
has forgotten all about Aeschinus. Here he appears not
so much a character in a worrying situation as a man on
a soapbox.

In Menander's play there was no need to consider the
general question, whether liberality is a right policy
towards all and sundry; Micio and Demea are only concerned
with Aeschinus and Ctesipho. There would therefore have
been no point in making Micio expatiate on liberality as
always the better policy.

A probable inference would be that 68-77 is Terentian
rhetoric, generalizing on the theme of enlightened
paternalism, and written not just with fathers and sons
in mind but also the stronger and the weaker in politics.
Its immediate purpose is to elicit our wholehearted
applause; but the misrepresentation of the Menandrian
Micio creates space for Stoic rectitude to castigate the
Terentian at the end for an indiscriminate advocacy of
liberality (986 ff.).

* * *

81-97 <u>DEMEA'S ARRIVAL</u>. It is now 'full market time',
people are up and about; Demea comes from his farm not
far from town (524).

Donatus (p. 263) implies that in Menander Demea returned
a greeting; Terence makes him the brusquer by omitting it
(cf. 266). But in general in 26-854 Terence appears to
have been unusually scrupulous in following the substance,
pacing, and metrical form of Menander's character.

84 f. *no respect*: those aware that *Aeschinus* meant *pudens*
'respectful', 'considerate' might notice a play here and
at 244, 643. It is possible that Terence has for once kept
Menander's character-name; but Αἰσχίνης is not yet directly
attested in New Comedy. Cf. Men. fr. 528 K.-Th. for the
sentiment.   \

87 *brewed...something...special*: taking *dis-signauit*
literally as 'sealed as separate (from the ordinary)', which
sounds like a vintner's technical term.

91-3 *disgraceful...talk of the town*. Menander was neatly
establishing two leading traits straightaway - Demea's
volatility and his awe of what people will say.

* * *

98-110 <u>MICIO'S RESPONSE</u>. Micio begins provocatively by
telling his elder (881) brother that he the younger has
seen more of life (98 f.), takes the initiative with a
salvo of denials (100-3), and then instead of deploying
such 'reasonable' arguments as 'we don't know the
circumstances', 'it's hearsay', etc., attacks with two
arguments *ad hominem* quite startlingly irrelevant and
meant as such to divert the simple Demea's attention.

The first (103 ff. *If neither you nor I did all that...*)
is irrelevant: Demea has not cited his own youthful
continence but Ctesipho's; the other (107 ff. *And if you
really understood*) diverts attention from Aeschinus to
Ctesipho.

This is what Micio later refers to as *standing up to him*
(144); a tactic, not a way of condoning Aeschinus' behaviour.

107 *if you really understood*: lit. 'if you were a man',
ironically picked up in 111 *Good God, 'Understanding'
indeed...*' where *tu homo* is in itself an impatient form
of address, 'you fool'. The 'full' sense of ἄνθρωπος
'man' is well known in Menander (*Sam.* 17, cf. fr. 484
K.-Th. 'What a graceful thing is a man, if he be a man';
Dysk. 6; *CHCL* ii. 122 f.); the thinking is that men differ
absolutely from animals by the possession of reason, and
that man differs from man by the extent that he uses it.
It has seemed right to bring this out here and elsewhere
by substituting expressions in English which explicitly
refer to reasoning-powers (cf. 143, 146, 579, 734, 736).

111-128 <u>MICIO'S POSITION</u>. He now insists in the simplest
words and slow, end-stopped verse (contrast 88-97) that
Aeschinus' behaviour is none of Demea's business; defines
exactly how far he will let the boy go; insinuates the
theme of parental expense (a trump-card with which he is
going *to frighten him off*, 144); and ends with a challenge –
an irritating claim to moral and intellectual superiority.

121 *replaced*: lit. 'repaired', but that sounds mean to the
modern ear.

* * *

129-40 <u>ULTIMATUM AND RETREAT</u>. Micio feigns anger and
threatens to return Aeschinus to Demea's jurisdiction.
This would require Demea's agreement in Athenian or in Roman
law; but Micio is really threatening to embarrass Demea:
'My brother thinks I am making a terrible job of bringing
up the son he gave me to adopt. Very well, let him try'.
If Demea refuses, people will call him a hypocrite; if he
accepts, he will be involved in heavy expense (cf. 88 ff.,
117 ff.). Demea is forced to retreat, mockingly quoting
phrases from his brother (139, cf. 117-21), and emphasizing
'him' in 140; he sticks to the gun he was firing at 97.

129-37 *It concerns me...*: translating the text in the
transmitted order with its division of parts we have:

'*DE*. It concerns me. *MI*. And it concerns me. But,
Demea, let us each concern ourselves an equal amount: you
with your boy, I with mine. For concerning yourself with
both is virtually to demand back the one you gave. *DE*.
Ah, Micio! (133) *MI*. That's how it seems to me. *DE*.
Very well; if that's what you want, let him stew in his
own juice, the wastrel; it's none of my business. (135)
Now if (......) another word hereafter... *MI*. Getting
angry again, Demea? *DE*. Yes! Don't you believe (......)?
Asking back the one that I gave? Am I doing that? It's
hard: I'm not an outsider; if I do try to block you... all
right, that's it, I've done.'

Demea's contributions here are muddled: remonstrance,
sudden acceptance of the terms, an angry threat of something
entirely obscure, an ambiguously broken question (does
Demea mean '*...believe what I say?*' or '*...believe that I
am serious?*'?), re-assessment, reluctant acquiescence.
In particular, the second-last item beginning '*Asking back
the one I gave?*' ought to pick up Micio's challenge '*...
to demand back the son you gave me!*' directly, and precede,
not follow the acceptance of the terms in the words '*very
well...*'. It will not do to say that Demea is simply being

incoherent. We have to tell the actor how to bring his
part off, and Terence is normally very precise in marking
the progression of feeling when someone is upset (cf.
e.g. 323 ff., 447 ff., 543, 610 ff., 726 ff. for various
examples that work well). And the threat absolutely
requires a strong statement by Micio, not Demea (135).

The transposition and redistribution solve these problems
and have the advantage of making Micio appear to abandon his
air of calm detachment: Demea's immediate reaction is ironic
satisfaction that he has at last needled Micio into anger.
This outburst will need explanation, and that comes in Micio's
next soliloquy: he is feigning anger to 'frighten Demea off'
(144).

* * *

141-154 <u>MICIO'S REFLECTION</u>. Both brothers must be sent to
town, but separately, Demea to hear more bad news (355),
Micio to be found by Aeschinus and learn the truth about
the escapade (384 ff.). The monologue sets this up and
allows Micio to reveal what he really thinks; Thais' speech
at *Eun.* 197 ff. is technically similar.

143 *For this is his style of reasonability*: lit., 'for
he is a man in this way', but more than just 'the fellow
is like this', cf. 145 *his reaction is barely that of a
creature that thinks*, lit. 'even so he scarcely takes it
like a human being'; see on 107. Micio is likening his
brother to a ferocious dog: you have to stand up to it and
frighten it off without letting it 'smell fear' and get
all the more excited. *Cave canem*: we have seen Micio
'stand up' to Demea by arguing as he does at 100 ff. and
112 ff.; he has 'frightened him off' in 130 ff. Syrus
knows another less frank way of dealing with Demea's
volatility, cf. 534 f.; and note on 389.

150 f. *he spoke of wanting to marry and settle down*: in
Menander, this will have been immediately picked up and
explained in the prologue-narrative which came after Micio's
departure at 154. In Terence, the Roman audience is almost
bound to have forgotten by the time that the themes of
Aeschinus' liaison with Pamphila and of his shame are
successively broached (330 ff., 471 ff., 610 ff.); see
pp. 35-8. Meanwhile, the allusion may mislead us into
thinking that the girl abducted from Sannio's is really
a citizen, for Aeschinus is apparently taking her for
himself, and if he is thinking of marrying and settling
down, then his beloved must really be a citizen. See on
193 ff.

* * *

155-196 <u>THE SCENE FROM DIPHILUS</u>. Two major departures from Menander, the dropping of his prologue and the substitution of this material from Diphilus for Menander's continuation; see pp. 34-41, 43-5.

Unless a pause is made at 154/5, Sannio *et al.* ought to enter from the 'wrong' side to avoid meeting Micio; and it is not clear enough from the script in what order the characters should enter (Rosivach (1973)).

Once everyone is 'on', the best guide to the staging Terence intended is the musical structure of the recitative.

He begins with trochaic 'systems', rhythmically continuous runs or sequences of so many pairs of feet (measures) of which the last is cut short and has a characteristic cadence-rhythm (see Appendix III, IV).

Systems end here with the phrases ...*risk another going over today'* (159), ... *as ever there was in the trade* (161), ...*I'll have the law on you* (163),...*harm you've done me* (164; in this context, a single line is a minimal system), ...*this dreadful service* (166).

Then, after three trochaic lines in which Sannio makes his break (167-9), the rest of the scene is composed in iambic octonarii 'by the line' with one major punctuation in the rhythm coinciding with a change of theme at 184-6.

Iambic octonarii, sung verse differing from the spoken iambic senarius only in length (4:3), were much favoured by Terence, especially in this play; the species which is really two short lines is elegantly deployed by Terence to mark changes of theme or direction (260, 313, 343, 536, 619, 947 in addition to 184/6) or wherever for any reason Terence wishes us to be particularly aware of the iambic rhythm (254 ff.).

155 *Help...* lit. 'I call on you, fellow citizens, lend aid to one distressed and innocent, rally to one defenceless'.

161 *girls and punters*, lit. 'I am the pimp', tantamount to saying 'I am the comic villain, dedicated to lucre and to lying'. Here and at 187 ff. (*that's a good one...*) Terence seems to have in mind offering us someone a little more subtle than the usual *leno* of the traditional *palliata*, but he does not succeed, for at the same time he simply expects us to be for Aeschinus and against Sannio simply as Lover and Pimp respectively. The result is an awkward compromise, and since Sannio has nowhere to go

but down, and represents no threat after 175 when the girl
is sent indoors, the role as spun out by Terence is a poor
one and not easy for the actor to sustain.

191 *two filthy thousand*: lit. 'twenty *minae* (= 2,000
drachmae), may the business turn ill for you'. In Roman
Comedy these girls conventionally cost between 20 and 60
minae. The price here is meant to sound expensive but
by no means incredible in the light of some extravagant
prices paid in Terence's Rome, see on 370.

193 ff. *nor do I hold...for I claim her at law as free*:
There is a 'loose end' here which has been much discussed
in connection with the grafting of Diphilus' scene into
Menander. In the sequel there is no question of the status
of the girl; she is a slave. Since 'it is inconceivable
that in New Comedy a young man should offer to pay for a
girl he seriously believes to be a freeborn citizen'
(Martin), the generally favoured explanation is that the
young man in Diphilus must have been bluffing, and that
that is also what Terence means us to understand:
Aeschinus is threatening to frame Sannio with false evidence.

But whatever the situation in Diphilus (and there is no
point in speculation about that) Terence is not in fact
posing the alternatives '*sell* me the girl or face
prosecution for depriving a citizeness of her rights', real
or imaginary.

One essential condition for a valid sale in Roman law
was that there should be no duress; if there were, the
contract was void (Watson (1971) 130-6). There is a
captious point to Sannio's question (192 f.) *What if I
choose not to sell her? You'll make me?.* Aeschinus avoids
falling into that trap (*Oh no, no, no*) and counters with
an equally captious argument: a freeborn person is a *res
extra commercium,* 'a thing outside trading'. Being a
citizeness, the girl cannot be the subject of buying and
selling in due form (*emptio venditio*); so Sannio will not
have the chance to raise the objection of duress. The
money being offered is not a legal price but *ex gratia*
compensation for what he himself paid for her, and we have
no reason to suppose that Aeschinus does not intend to do
the proper thing and find her parents, etc.

All we spectators know at this stage is that Aeschinus
has expressed a wish to marry (151) and we must assume
that it is he who is in love with Sannio's girl; so when
he says she is freeborn, we have to believe what he says.
At this stage it must seem perfectly probable that the
play is going to run along these lines familiar in all

of Terence's earlier works and involve a recognition.
Besides, if Terence expected us to infer against the available
evidence that he is bluffing about the girl's status, he should
have made Aeschinus express himself differently: not 'I
claim her at law as free', but 'I shall cook up evidence to
claim her...'

The literal meaning of the ancient legal formula is 'I
grasp her with my hand in suit of liberty' (193-4).

The allusion to the girl's free birth is no doubt
occasioned by what Terence found in Diphilus, but has a
very Roman point in its captious play on what is a lawful
sale.

It is a moot point whether Terence has simply overlooked
the fact that the theme of her free birth is inconsistent
with the sequel, or not bothered, or wanted to imply that
'tomorrow' there will be another whole comedyful of events
leading to Ctesipho's marrying the girl.

* * *

197-208 SANNIO'S MONOLOGUE. In Menander, this is where
Sannio came in, more or less aggressively, complaining of
his treatment (cf. Menander *Kolax* 120-32), intending to
bang on Micio's door and perhaps alluding to his plans to
be off to Cyprus (cf. 224). One enigmatic fragment
apparently from Menander's speech is preserved by Donatus
(see p. 263). In Terence, the point of Sannio's speech
is really only to separate Aeschinus' departure (196)
and Syrus' entrance (209); the dramatic pace falters, as
Sannio has nothing much worth the saying and it is pretty
poor stuff. It is odd that Sannio completely ignores the
dilemma posed by Aeschinus (196), bluff or otherwise, and
only considers another way he might be done out of his
money. Naturally enough, the speech cannot correspond
either to the substance of Diphilus or of Menander and
Terence is probably extemporizing; as elsewhere, his own
recipe for humour is simple inversion and heavy irony:
we should accordingly probably read *'kindnesses'* in
199 rather than *'unkindnesses'*, v. app. crit.

* * *

209-252 SYRUS AND SANNIO. A programmatic scene; 'Figaro'
is introduced undertaking to do the difficult and does it
(209 f./247 ff.). Terence is again following Menander's
substance but not his metrical form nor in every detail
his dramaturgy (228-35).

Syrus' part is excellent, one of the best in Roman drama.
He is an elderly (562) Levantine, in charge of a large staff,
and an expert chef. That Micio employs a *cordon bleu*
specialist is another sign of his wealth; it was usual to
hire cooks for special occasions. Syrus is on to a good
number and has been with Micio for years (563). Intellectually
he is a downstairs counterpart to the *signore*; he understands
and plays on the psychology of the less intelligent
opposition (Sannio, Demea), and he has his own parody of a
theory of education (420 ff., 962 ff.). Terence presents
him as 'mastermind' in the tradition of Plautus; but his
virtuosity lies not in his controlling events, but in the
swiftness of his reactions (as here, 366 ff., 537 ff.).
Things happen which even he cannot control (776), and, like
Micio, he can make mistakes for all his brains (517). All
this is Menandrian, and next to Demea's, Syrus' role is the
most faithfully reproduced as regards what he does and says
in 26-854.

But Terence seems responsible for the substantial
extension of Syrus' role into the last scenes of the play
(882 ff., 958 ff.), cf. p. 43 – and for having him rather
than Geta rewarded with freedom for his 'services'. This
is excellent Saturnalian farce, Plautine in spirit, and
the best and most positive aspect of Terence's handling of
the end of the play. In Menander, his final exit was less
glorious (786).

209-10 *Quiet*... Sannio's monologue is in trochaic recitative
'by the line' with word-end prominent at the eighth place
in most lines; Syrus' entrance 209 f. should probably be
a system of trochaic measures ending not with catalexis
(cf. on 155 ff.) but a transitional colon – x – x –
leading back to iambic octonarii (from ...*that you have had*...
..: but the text and that analysis is uncertain.

219 *futures*: lit. 'hope', a technical term in financial
parlance, *spes OLD* 3 d, e; 4.

* * *

228-35 <u>SANNIO'S REACTION</u>. Terence neatly modulates to
spoken verse: Sannio's first words *Damnation*! *Just see*...
are the last in recitative. The technique, however, is
Roman rather than Menandrian. Remarks mutually 'aside'
(228 *SA. I've had it*... *SY He's afraid*...) evoke the
Plautine tradition (*Am.* 262-301), and Menander avoids
elaborate asides amounting to monologues (228-35) when
others present have nothing particular to do. What Sannio
says here sounds like material transferred from the
Menandrian entrance-speech replaced by 197 ff. For a
technically similar case, cf. 911-915.

* * *

252-264 <u>THE ARRIVAL OF CTESIPHO</u>. The off-hand revelation
that Ctesipho loves the girl, not Aeschinus, is a surprise
of dubious merit resulting from Terence's dropping the
prologue; it is obscure in Terence where Ctesipho has been
and what he has been doing and he is supposed not to have
taken part in the raid (cf. 355 ff. 402); his entrance at
this point entails a fourth actor playing Aeschinus' part
in the sequel; Sannio's presence during the exchanges
between Ctesipho and the others is awkward, for he has
nothing to contribute except an anxious presence which,
however, must not be played up visually as it would only
be distracting; the background to Ctesipho's affair is
left very vague. Terence has postponed Ctesipho's entry,
and in Menander he will have entered before Sannio and have
been ensconced in Micio's safely with his beloved, cf.
p. 29, p. 38.

Ctesipho's role is entirely in recitative as befits the
extravagant lover in Roman Comedy; here, iambic octonarii,
of very contrasting species (254-6, 257-9, 260, then four
lines each with a contrasting inner structure).

264 *The door*: the young men's relationship with doors is
a comic theme (281, 539, 543, 643 f.).

* * *

265-287 <u>AESCHINUS' ARRIVAL, SETTLEMENT WITH SANNIO</u>. Terence
is aiming at the strongest possible contrast between
Aeschinus and his brother, again with the idea of surprising
us in the sequel. At this point, we are to think highly
of him and of Micio, to smile at Ctesipho, and regard Demea
as a silly old fool; our expectations of the traditional
typology are being fully satisfied. See p. 29f.

* * *

288-510 <u>MENANDER'S SECOND ACT</u>: Less drastically re-arranged
by Terence than the first, but differing in metrical form,
in the exploitation of sentimental themes, and involving
obscurities of presentation consequent on the dropping of
Menander's prologue. On Sostrata and Canthara, see p. 46-7;
on Hegio, p. 36-8.

288-91 *Nanny...Geta is out*: these lines add up to a trochaic
system of 16 measures, and 292-294 *either to send... cure
of my troubles* to another of 12 measures.

* * *

299-326 <u>GETA'S BAD NEWS</u>. Geta is the downstairs counterpart
of Demea - old, honest, loyal, reliable (480 f.), emotional,

not very bright; in the original it is probable that he,
not Syrus was rewarded with freedom at the end (cf. 891-6,
p. 61, p. 20-1) by an act of generosity on Demea's part.

In New Comedy the running slave (Men. *Dysk.* 81 ff.) was
conventionally used to communicate news to eavesdroppers;
he normally spoke iambic trimeters, and the listener(s),
prompted to intervene, would attract his attention without
much fuss (*P. Hib.* 5 fr. *a*, 8 lines; but cf. Men. *Mis.*
284 ff.).

At Rome this manoeuvre became a musical 'routine' in
its own right (*HT.* 37); there is a running slave in every
other play of Plautus, and on average he takes 35 lines
to acknowledge anyone's presence. He never appears merely
speaking iambic senarii. When the news is bad, there is
parody of the sentiments and language of Roman Tragedy.

This is Terence's most confidently Plautine essay in
the *genre* (cf. *An.* 338-45, *Ph.* 179-99, 841-54). On the
style of Terence's Latin here cf. Denzler (1968) 68, 112.
It is in excellent contrast with the styles of 26 ff. and
of 155 ff.; Terence is aiming for the maximum variety of
presentation.

The lines 299-303 '*Yes, you're quite right...loss of
face*' add up to a trochaic system of twenty measures
bridging the entrance of Geta with the preceding dialogue;
or we can analyse them as lines, v. app. crit. In either
case 304 *violence...treachery* stands in quite strong
relief, a trochaic septenarius with four resolutions and
a striking run of nine light syllables from *genera*, an
excellent contrast with 303. The metre then settles to
iambic octonarii definitely by the line; these are
'punctuated' at 313 *I'd reckon...my way* (bipartite
octonarius, cf. on 155-96) and 317 *to spatter...brains*
(iambic quaternarius), followed by two more excellent
trochaic lines (*as for his nibs...mortar 'em flat*), after
which the reversion to iambic octonarii at 320 *But I'd
better hurry up...* is comical. The switches of rhythm
here are clearly related to the violence and extravagance
of Geta's mood, and the translator felt that he could not
let Geta come on in English without *some* hint of this.
Hence the 'verse'.

* * *

330-4 <u>SOSTRATA'S REACTION</u>. Whereas the grand manner
affected by Geta is comic parody, Sostrata is made to evoke

it as a 'serious' character for pathos (cf. 855 ff.). This way of depicting genuine emotion belongs properly to the dramatic conventions of Tragedy and does not ring true in Comedy. On the image of Aeschinus *setting the baby on his father's lap*, see p. 35.

* * *

335-50 <u>GETA'S ADVICE, SOSTRATA'S PLAN</u> Geta's initiative and orderly argumentation seem out of character for one just now so comically distraught. Perhaps in Menander Sostrata was represented as recovering from the terrible news for herself (*'well, tears won't get us anywhere'*), argued along the same lines as Geta in Terence, and then (342) rejected capitulation as unworthy (*'No, no, no! Things couldn't be worse...'*); see p. 46, p. 60.

347 *the ring he lost*: not 'the ring he *sent*' (so A and most recent editors). This would be an unofficial engagement ring, and a Roman allusion, for giving engagement rings was a Roman custom (whence ours), not a Greek (Pliny *Nat.* 33. 4, *Dig.* 24. 1. 36). A Greek jury would naturally interpret a ring 'sent' by Aeschinus as just the sort of gift which Sostrata goes on to describe as *beneath either her or me* (349). Why 'sent', not 'gave', and why has Mother got it and not Pamphila? For the point of '*lost*', see p. 35.

350 *I only hope*...sc., you're right; but the line is corrupt and the exact meaning of *ut melius dicas* unclear. If *cedo* is right (Bentley), 'I yield', maybe Canthara is commenting 'Don't say that word!', as of ill omen.

* * *

355-434 <u>DEMEA AND SYRUS</u>. Classic high comedy in spoken verse; Terence at his very best, and very close to Menander.

365 *In its proper light*: vague enough not to convey anything to Demea; Micio is delighted (366) because the truth has allayed his worries about Aeschinus (141 ff.) and vindicated his estimate of him. All the more reason for a generosity which seems to Demea sheer folly (367). It is unfair to Micio to represent his harbouring of Ctesipho as a breaking of his agreement with Demea not to interfere with his affairs (Tränkle 1972); it was not his initiative, and what is the alternative? (Pöschl 1975).

370 *fifty for expenses*: lit. 'half a *mina*', fifty drachmas. In Menander's time, a drachma was enough to keep a working man fed for two days (Sandbach on Menander *Epitrepontes* 136, 140). In Terence's Rome the value of 300 drachmae

would get you a good ploughman - or a barrel of exotic fish-
preserve (Walbank on Pol. 31. 25. 2-8); Polybius also
mentions as scandalous a price of one talent (6,000 drachmae)
for a catamite and Diodorus Siculus reports a price from
Terence's time of four talents (24,000 drachmae) for a good
chef (37. 3. 5) - i.e., for someone like Syrus. Cato is
said 'never to have paid more than 1,500 drachmae for a
slave' (Plut. *Cat. maj.* 4), which means that was no
extravagant price.

386 ff. *There's real smack...* punning; *sapere* 'have sense',
'smack of', 'be pungent'.

388 *What? Is that artiste...* The abrupt change of subject
requires motivation; hence the stage-direction. A *psaltria*
lit. 'girl who plays a stringed instrument' seems to have
been more highly regarded than a *tibicina* 'girl who plays
the pipes', see Sandbach on *Epitr.* fr. 1; but the Greek
loanword is even more contemptuous on Demea's lips than its
native Latin metrical equivalent and synonym *fidicina* would
have been.

389 *Take a look inside*: a cheeky risk. Knowing his man
(390) Syrus leads him on by doing what his more honourable
master had refused to do in dealing with his brother - play
the yes-man (145 f.).

394 *small*: lit. 'however big you are'. In New Comedy
smallness seems to have gone with testiness in old men, cf.
Men. *Sik.* 353. *Sharpness*: cf. on 386 ff.

398 f. *I just want him to be...* Superbly ironical!

399 *The father's wish...* lit. 'As each wishes his own to
be, so he is', a deliberately muddled variation on the theme
'each likes his own'; what Syrus ought to say is, '...so
let him be', expressing a wish.

402 *I was the one who...* In Menander, Demea seems to have
supposed that Ctesipho was spending the night at Micio's
cf. 355 f., 531.

406 *happened to drop in*: Demea fails to notice that this
is incompatible with Syrus' confident claim that Ctesipho
is on the farm; cf. on 561.

411 *Hope springs eternal!*: *spero* deserves prominence both
because Demea is so addicted to triadic utterance and
because Syrus is unwittingly relieving Demea of genuine
anxiety that Ctesipho is being spoilt by Aeschinus, cf.
355 ff. *Sires of yore*: *suom* for *suorum* (cf. 793 *liberum*
for *liberorum*) already rang old-fashioned in Terence's time.

411-2 *I don't believe this...Yuck*: *hui* (common) is perhaps
a whistle, *phy* (rare) a snort.

413 *His own special apprenticeship*: lit. 'he had at home
whence he might learn'; *domi habere* both literal and in
its common idiomatic meaning 'have available', 'have on
tap'.

414 *One does one's honest best*... explicit ironical echoes
of Micio at 50–54, showing that that passage is certainly
Menandrian; and, indirectly, of Plato *Protagoras* 325 d;
Demea's 'method' is to go on applying an approach which
might suit young children as yet incapable of appreciating
general principles at an age when the subject ought to be
asking, 'Yes, but what is it that is common to and behind
your praise of ABC and blame of XYZ?'. Demea does not in
fact have a criterion of right and wrong derived from
principles, only an excessive awe of what most people think,
leading him near to hypocrisy (734). Most people think
that the bluff peasant is the best kind of citizen (Xenophon
Oeconomicus 5. 3, 5. 5, 5. 13, Cato *Agr. praef.*,
approximately contemporary with *Brothers*) and Demea's
life-style in Menander (not Terence) was represented not
as the natural expression of 'himself', but the wholesale
adoption of a ready-made suit of attitudes and behaviour
the wearing of which, though on the whole creditable, has
not been comfortable. Demea has his own role-model and
guru in Hegio, the idealized peasant farmer, of whom
precious few still walk the earth (or ever did, if the
truth be told). It is ironic that Demea's hard work has
lifted him out of the very class he admires. Cf. Plautus
Trin. 276 ff. for a similar exponent of precept (that play
is from Philemon).

424 *not as good of course*: lit. 'as far as I am able',
quod = quoad.

425 *more salt...crisper...lacks flavour*: *parum* goes in
common with all three expressions; parody of a doctrine
of the mean, of course.

427 *kitchen-wise*: lit. 'in accordance with my pungency/
wisdom', cf. on 386, 394.

428 *as if into a mirror*: the distant original version of
the well-known Renaissance theory of the utility of the
drama as a 'mirror of life' (cf. Hamlet's advice to the
Players, *Hamlet* iii.2) seems to have been ironically
alluded to here by Menander; New Comedy acquired status
and 'importance' because it could be admired as paradigmatic
like Tragedy. If this theory were current in his own day
(and it certainly was not long after), he evidently did
not take it too seriously. cf. p. 8.

* * *

435-46 DEMEA'S SOLILOQUY. Pure Menander; contrast the
mannered and distorted Menander of Demea's second major
soliloquy, 855 ff. The essence dramaturgically is merely
'I'm off to find Ctesipho – ah, here comes my old friend
Hegio', but Menander takes the opportunity to add detail
and perspective subtly altering our appreciation of Demea.
There is a touching simplicity in his allusion to his
treaty with Micio (435 ff.), and he evidently really loves
Ctesipho. His contemplation of Hegio's character (439-45)
shows us a Demea capable of friendship, admiration, and
enjoyment of life as well as indicating his loneliness;
in Hegio we see the mirror into which Demea has looked for
his own pattern. He is the 'genuine article', the pure
and self-sufficient peasant of the good old days, the
working farmer 'whose kind alone sustain the land' (Eur.
Orestes 920). Demea does not exclaim 'how few of *us* are
left' (444) but expresses a conservationist's pleasure
at finding a rare specimen in danger of extinction; for
Demea is, in fact, really rather well off. See p. 39, 50.

* * *

447-86 HEGIO'S NEWS. Terence follows Menander in metre,
pace, and substance, but presents the following scenes
against a vaguer and more sentimental background than in
Menander. He suppresses Hegio's role as 'master' (κύριος)
to Sostrata and to Pamphila and with it his prior knowledge
of the pregnancy and his having been a necessary partner
to the arrangement between Sostrata and Aeschinus; see
p. 36-8. Aeschinus' original offence is glossed over, and
the effects are to place emphasis on Hegio's goodness as
a virtual outsider and on Geta's merits as the *only* 'man
of the house'. Terence has done well here and in the
sequel by following Menander in making Demea say no more
than the minimum: he is shocked and embarrassed, and the
contrast of his mood in 435 ff. and in his dialogue here
is excellent.

471-7 *When he found out the truth*...Menander could afford
to be allusive here, because we know what he is talking
about from the prologue (cf. on 347). Terence is rushing
past an important element in the background without giving
it perspective. Terence neatly dissociates Hegio from
any part in the arrangement between Sostrata and Aeschinus
by using impersonal constructions; some of the forceful
brevity achieved, itself a trait of Menander and typical
of a certain laconic style of narrative very much at home
in Latin (cf. 40 ff. and Cicero in his racier correspondence)
can be matched in the translation by nouns.

* * *

486-8 *Mother in Heaven*: lit. 'Juno who bringest (children) to light', originally 'Guardian-spirit (*iuno* feminine equivalent to *genius*) *Lucina*', the name interpreted by popular etymology (*lux*); the goddess invoked in Menander will have been Artemis, cf. Evanthius on Andria 473 where there is the same theatrical ploy, as also at *Aulularia* 692, this too probably a Menandrian play.

* * *

489-510 HEGIO'S DECLARATION AND OUTLOOK   Hegio's powerful rhetoric is like that of Syriskos at Men. *Epitrepontes* 302 ff. taking the part of the babe there in dispute. By recalling how he and Simulus survived 'the heaviest of hard times' (486), typically generic in Terence, Hegio is made to insinuate a theme which probably dominated the end of Menander's play more clearly than it does in Terence: *'friends say not mine and thine but ours'* (804). Legally at Athens and Rome Demea and Micio count as the heads of separate families on a par with each other, but (500 ff.) the representative of the good old days takes it for granted that a clan shares and shares alike, nor does he accept that Demea is a genuine peasant like himself any longer: wealth and prominence in society bring corresponding responsibilities.

511-16 HEGIO'S SPEECH. The obvious beginning of Menander's third act; there ought to be an *entr'acte* at 510/11 to allow time for the conversation indoors between Hegio and Sostrata (cf. Men. *Samia* 420/1, *Misoumenos* 275/6), cf. p. 41. If performance in Terence is strictly continuous, Demea's exit-speech is barely adequate for this; similar problems are frequent in Plautus' scripts (e.g. *Menaechmi* 881/2) but perhaps less troublesome, since Plautus was less concerned with a specious realism than Terence. Here Terence certainly intended the main articulation to come *after* Hegio's speech with the change from spoken to chanted verse.

In itself the speech is necessary and 'right': Hegio must be sent to town to meet Micio so that Micio may explain to Hegio the true meaning of the abduction and himself learn all about Pamphila and that Aeschinus has not been as frank with him as he supposed; all this is supposed to have been sorted out when the two return from town at 592 ff. and enter Sostrata's - a lot, and important.

Donatus states that the speech was omitted in 'some standard copies', i.e., Hegio's role was represented as over at 506; the omission appears to have been deliberate. But if so, it implies a version of Terence's play in which

Micio must have been represented as coming back *alone* at
592 ff. and having learnt the facts about Pamphila and
about Aeschinus' prevarication in some other way; or by
then meeting Hegio, in other words, something quite
different from the scene as we have it; and that scene
itself is problematic, see *ad loc.*

* * *

517-39 SYRUS AND CTESIPHO. Recitative: a trochaic system
ends on '...*I hope he gets so tired*' (519), then iambic
octonarii by the line to '...*enjoying myself as I'd started
to*' (522), then two more systems ending '...*further off*'
(524), '...*any minute*' (526). The conversation from
'He'll stick to the question...' (527) to *'we've conjured
him up*' (537) is in iambic octonarii the rhythms of which
are manipulated to stand in strong contrast with the
break-neck speed of the *finale*, what appears to be a
trochaic system running from *'It's father!...* (538) to
'...*I can't find Micio anywhere in the world*' (541),
arranged so that Demea becomes the unwitting participant
in a *trio*; a nice musical anticipation of the thematic
point Syrus makes at 548, *'Good Comedy this! Claims he
knows first, and he the only one totally in the dark!*'

529 *Dependants*: so Demea is quite an important personage,
no mere peasant; cf. 541-2 (he is an employer of labour)
and 806-19.

530 *Which haven't I answered*: i.e., 'I've used all those
excuses up', rather than 'which I haven't answered', i.e.,
'he'll be able to check that I haven't been busy that way'.

534 *tuning: sensus, callere,* and *feruere* sound like a
musician's language.

537 *conjured him up: lit.* 'the wolf in the story'; 'speak
of the devil'.

* * *

541-91 SYRUS' SECOND ENCOUNTER WITH DEMEA: a superb scene
in which Terence is probably keeping close not only to the
substance and pacing of Menander's original but also to its
metrical form; he too favoured trochaic recitative in such
situations (*Pk.* 267-353, *Sam.* 670-737). Terence's virtuosity
in the pacing and texture of the rhythms of his trochaic
septenarii is brilliant, a facet of his writing that cannot
survive prose translation.

561 *Weren't you claiming...* Putting Syrus in a tight corner;
logic would suggest that Demea has not *seen* Syrus stagger

from Micio's door, for that should prompt the dreaded
· question 'is Ctesipho in there?' (cf. 778), but it is
funnier if he has.

592-609 <u>MICIO AND HEGIO</u>. The sequel to 511-16. There
appear to be longer and shorter versions transmitted,
neither, however, compatible with the omission of 511-16
in some Mss. as reported by Donatus.

The shorter version stops with Hegio's remark *'very good
of you'* (601), and is dramatically better than the longer,
in which there are a number of odd technical weaknesses –
the scansion of line 602, the un-Terentian use of *fungor*
+ abl. (for acc.) in 603, the gratuitous hiatus in 604.
There are also what seem lapses of taste. The pathetic
condition of Sostrata is unhappily dwelt on in 602 f.,
lit. 'she is beginning to rot with pain and grief' (the
translation tones this down); there is no thought of
Pamphila or the baby; the gentlemanly politeness seems
overdone; Hegio's platitudes (604-8) ring false, for he
should concern himself with the particular rather than
the general. See p. 266.

The shorter version is not very much better. Micio's
opening words 592-6 *'I can't see why...'* seem awkwardly
didactic and pompous. One misses a clear indication that
there has been mutual enlightenment; for while Micio has
cleared up Hegio's misunderstanding, the dramatist too
glibly skips over the important points that Micio too
has taken on board unpleasant surprises about Aeschinus,
one concerning the facts of Pamphila's case and the other
about Aeschinus' frankness. Too much is put into a single
line (600) *'...all this misunderstanding is on account of
his brother and that artiste'*, and too little in the rest.

Further complications are the omission of 511-16 in some
MSS. and Donatus' further information that 602 *'you will
at once be taking a load off Sostrata's mind...'* "and
the following" (what exactly he means is disputable) were
also omitted in "many copies" and "may indeed be omitted".

There is no simple solution to all this; but it seems
clear that in Menander Hegio went to town as in Terence
(511-6), met Hegio, and that they returned in a scene
equivalent to 592-609. But there is suspicion that
Terence has cut something out: and that might well include
Micio's asking Hegio's formal permission to marry Sostrata.
See pp. 48, 56-7, 61-2.

* * *

610-35 <u>AESCHINUS' LAMENT AND RESOLVE</u>. Lyric verse for
his emotions (610-7), mixed trochaic and iambic lines for

his narrative (618-24), trochaic lines for his deliberation
(625 ff.). On the lyric, cf. Questa (1984) 399-415; but
even if we knew more than we do about the structure of
Plautine lyric, particularly those involving Aeolic cola
and verses, there is too little Terentian lyric for us to
be at all confident about basic points of prosody that
might differ from those of his iambo-trochaic verse. The
layout of the song in the Mss. is at best an ambiguous and
doubtful guide to its inner structure, and it is not clear
that we should be looking for 'lines' at all in the same
sense as in iambo-trochaic verse.

For what it is worth the song begins and ends with what
can be interpreted as *cola reiziana* (x - x - x), and we
have mixed choriambs and iambic metra, first self-contained
(611 f.), then bridged together; it is nowhere necessary
to postulate hiatus or a light syllable in a notionally
long place; but it is unclear whether *uah* (613) is meant
to be in or out of the metre.

618 *For when she had been sent to the midwife*...cf. p. 47

622 *'For better for worse*...' Canthara uses a formula of
divorce, cf. Plautus *Amphitruo* 928 *ualeas, tibi habeas res
tuas, reddas meas*; literally, Canthara says 'farewell, take
- her who pleases you'.

* * *

636-78 <u>MICIO'S DECEPTION</u>. Terence links Micio's entrance
to the preceding trochaic recitative, switching to spoken
verse just after Micio call *'Aeschinus!'* (637) so that
Micio's comment aside *'What business has he here?'* initiates
the iambic senarii, cf. the transition at 227/8. In Menander
it is probable that the whole of 610 ff. was in iambic
trimeters and that there was no change of metre here; the
scene is certainly closely translated.

It is held by some (Johnson (1968), Grant (1975 b)) that
Micio's behaviour here is cruel. This seems unfair. He
is surely affording Aeschinus the chance to own up, rather
than making accusations directly.

639 *Why not play with him a little*... If in Menander Micio
had just fixed his marriage with Sostrata, there was more
deception here undertaken than appears in Terence - a
pleasant surprise for Aeschinus in due course. See pp. 56-7.

643 *He's blushing: all's well*: the kind of 'sign' later
alluded to by Micio, 822 ff. For a Menandrian parallel,
cf. p. 267.

648 *Moved here recently:* fresh information; Menander was making a virtue of the necessity that the two families should live next door by drawing attention to it. Micio ironically assumes that a 'blade' like Aeschinus could not possibly know humble people like these.

652 *The law:* cf. p. 43-4. *Ph.* 125 f., MacDowell (1978) 95-8. The neat point is lost in Terence that there really is someone indoors with the right to the option claimed by the 'visitor from Miletus' - Hegio himself, Pamphila's guardian.

654 *Miletus:* casually dropped at the end; Miletus was on the coast of what is now Turkey.

663-4 *harshly...unsympathetically...squalidly:* the opposites of what Aeschinus respects and expects in Micio; and they ironically describe his own behaviour towards Pamphila.

665 ff. *What a question...that poor fellow:* Aeschinus ought not to believe in him - an ingenuous slip.

673 *Her perfect age:* again, Aeschinus ought not to have any idea how old she is; lit. 'so ripe', 'full-grown', 'Sweet sixteen' is meant, cf. *Eun.* 318.

* * *

679-706 RECONCILIATION. There is an effective modulation from spoken verse to recitative in trochaic septenarii as Aeschinus breaks down, starting with *'Why are you crying...'*. It is likely that there was a similar modulation in Menander too.

The son's readiness to confess, his penitence, Micio's expression of his love, and his fatherly lecture represent real communication and the vindication of Micio's policy towards Aeschinus. However, cf. below on 707 ff.

683 *Lord:* even this mild expletive is striking on Micio's lips. Terence has followed Menander in making Demea far more addicted to expletives and ejaculations than Micio (c.60 to 12 in parts of roughly equal length) and as much given to triadic rhetoric; but in Micio's case, such interjections are reserved for specially emotional moments such as this; cf. 38 *uah 'It's quite daft'*.

691 *nine months:* lit. 'ten months have gone', cf. 475; the names of ten, the length of nine.

692 *poor girl:* Menander used a racier expression, 'stuck out on a limb' (see p. 263) to describe her state; a

typical example of Terence's tendency to dilute the specific
qualities of Menander's diction.

695 *I won't have you being equally mindless...*: as stern
and firm as anyone could wish.

697 *Me trick you? What for?*: cf. on 639.

700 *now...now...now...now*: cf. *me...me...you* at 934; the
staccato is expressive of astonishment. In Latin, strong
monosyllables were more prominent and rarer than they are
in English.

703 *He's lost, he's gone, he's boarded ship*: the rhetorical
figure 'hysteron-proteron', reversing logical order, seems
for some reason that escapes us to have appealed to Terence
as an elegance especially appropriate for Micio; he
expresses himself that way in the Latin at 30 and 55 too.

* * *

707-12 <u>AESCHINUS' VERDICT ON MICIO</u>. Joy as unconfined as
the panic with which Aeschinus arrived at 610 ff.; so no
doubt in Menander too, but with differences of nuance.

Terence gives Aeschinus a brief dance of delight in
iambic septenarii; these jaunty lines are the only ones in
that metre in the play, much more freely used in Terence's
earlier work. Menander probably had either trochaic
recitative or spoken trimeters here.

If either dramatist wished to endorse Micio as a man
for all seasons and a true father, this was the place for
it; we should hear Aeschinus recognizing in Micio a wise
and good *man* whom he intends to emulate.

Terence stops definitely short of this. He gives
Aeschinus two typological paradoxes. The first plays on
the inversion of roles of father and son apparent in Micio's
attitude. The father is doing what one expects in a brother
or a friend of one's own age, as Aeschinus has for Ctesipho;
if Micio is a son, that makes Aeschinus a father; things
are all upside down and mildly absurd ('*rockaby daddy*', 709).
The second assumes as obvious that any father-figure operates
psychologically by creating repressive fears in the child.
Filling someone with dread not to do something is the very
paternal weapon that Micio thinks wrong and ineffective;
paradoxically, Aeschinus is 'filled with dread' by his
father's very 'humouring him' (708, *morem gereret*) and
'fitting in with him' (710, *commoditate*). This motivation
for resolving not to do anything to hurt his father
inadvertently is on a lower plane than what the apparently
genuine communication established at 679 ff. would lead one
to expect.

The paradoxes played with here are Roman, and Terence, without here condemning Micio, is deliberately creating space for us to smile patronizingly at Aeschinus. This is necessary preparation for the *dénouement* in which Micio's approach is represented as irresponsible and indiscriminate pandering and Aeschinus' attitude is that of a spoilt baby.

And yet, 'Terence *almost* seems to approve of such a father' (Donatus on 707). The ambiguity is Terence's; he witholds unequivocal approval of Micio's approach by implicitly attributing to Aeschinus the Roman prejudice that there really *is* no other true fatherliness than the kind affirmed at the end of the play by Demea.

It is simple and natural to suppose that Menander made his young man deal in personalities, not stereotypes, as the corollary to 679 ff.; for in Menander, there was no reversal of our sympathies at the end of the play: see pp. 53 ff.

* * *

713-854: <u>MENANDER'S FOURTH ACT</u>: here Terence again renders Menander very closely in substance and form, but as usual, diluting his specific quality.

Demea is on stage with one short break (or two?; 783-8, ?854/5) from now until the end of the play. The victim first of comic deception by Micio (720-63), then of cheek from the tipsy Syrus (764-75), then of an unpleasant surprise (776-84), Demea shows the ability to control his temper for the first time at 795; and, after listening to Micio's earnest persuasions (804-35), agrees without enthusiasm to be affable for the wedding of Aeschinus and to allow Ctesipho to keep his girl; then, his 'conversion' and 'revenge', see pp. 56-62.

731 *from here to there*: In Greek and Roman weddings the bride would normally be conducted along the street from her parents' to her husband's house; in Greek weddings, she would be accompanied by the groom and 'best man', in Roman the groom would be waiting at his house. But ours will be an unusual wedding, cf. 906 ff.

739 f. *dice*: the game Micio has in mind will have been more like poker-dice or a card-game like Whist or Bridge than simple 'shooting'.

752 *tugging the rope*: evidently some sort of folk-dance that went with a wedding; the 'rope-dance' alluded to by Livy at 27.13.14 can only be relevant in that Juno there is the goddess honoured, but not as goddess of marriage, which is what counts here.

762 *Hercules*: lit. 'Salvation herself'; the Latin appears to
to be proverbial (Pl. *Capt.* 529, *Most.* 351).

788 *Who thunders at my portal so*: *pepulit* (rather than
pulsauit fores) was a consciously 'theatrical' way of
putting it (cf. Donatus on 638), introducing a sudden
excursion to tragic style, equally suddenly deflated (794).
Cf. Men. *Sam.* 324-7 for a similarly managed effect in
Menander.

800 f. *How can you justify*...lit. 'Surely there isn't any
way (*numqui*) in which it is unfair that I should have the
same right along with you as you have along with me?',
clumsy, but not inappropriately.

803 *You aren't being fair.* Donatus holds this against
Micio: 'because he has put himself in the wrong, Micio
plays the whole thing in a facetious, fawning manner, since
he knows that he cannot defend himself on grounds of justice'
But this depends on retrospective interpretation of the end
of the play. All that Micio has done is respond in a
crisis with the necessary money (364-9); the girl's presence
in his house is *fait accompli*; the earliest opportunity
that Micio has to tell Demea only comes at 745, but to tell
him straightaway would have been fanning the flames of his
temper (cf. 144-6); so he has used guile to puzzle and
shock his brother into relative calm instead. This is
parallel to the way in which Micio dealt with Demea in the
opening scene. In his speech 806-830 Micio is clearly not
'thinking on his feet'; he is being far too coherent for
that.

804 *Friends say not 'mine and thine' but 'ours'* Lit. 'all
things of friends are in common'; in Greek, κοινὰ τὰ τῶν
φίλων 'in common (are) the things of friends'; cf. p. 264
for its occurrence here in Menander.

Erasmus gave the proverb pride of place in his *Adagia*
(1508) and quotes the numerous Latin writers who used it;
cf. also Otto (1890) s.v. *amicus* I.

Donatus says that it was Pythagorean; but it could apply
as a motto for any Utopian society where friendship was
emphasized, as in, say, the Stoic Zeno's *Republic* (cf.
Baldry (1959) 3-15) or in Epicurus' community.

* * *

806-19. MICIO'S REPLY (A), THE MONEY. Obscure in Terence
because he has dropped the prologue; it only comes out
clearly now that though we know both brothers were originally
poor (103 f.) Demea is in fact wealthy thanks to his own

hard graft and that Micio's wealth is some sort of windfall; Demea has fulfilled a long-term plan to make enough
to leave a tidy inheritance for two boys, and this is to
his great credit; Micio draws a distinction between true
patrimony such as that and his own good luck. The legal
situation is that Ctesipho is to get all Demea's property
and Aeschinus all of Micio's; in Athenian law, unlike
Roman, a father with a male heir (natural or adopted)
could not devise his property otherwise by will (MacDowell
(1978) 101, Crook (1967) 121). Micio's proposal could
not be made 'official' in Athenian law, and it looks as
though Menander was criticizing the inflexibility of
Athenian inheritance law here (cf. MacDowell (1978) 97 f.
for the case of heiresses). The arrangement must depend
entirely on the good will of the four people involved;
to Romans, it would simply appear that the two
patresfamilias could change their wills appropriately.
Menander's Micio was proposing that the two brothers
should henceforth practice the sort of 'communism'
advocated in Zeno's *Republic* (see on 804). Micio's
proposal entails that Aeschinus will get, or go through,
less than he otherwise would, but that Ctesipho will get
more, and in the sequel (855 ff.) Demea interprets that
as a crafty bid for Ctesipho's respect and affection as
well as Aeschinus', and maliciously decides to apply the
family's new motto in ways which he thinks Micio cannot
have meant.

* * *

820-35 <u>MICIO'S REPLY (B), THE BOYS' CHARACTERS</u>. Reading
ergo in line 826 clears up a source of difficulty to
commentators since Donatus' time; he comments on the
speech as a whole at 821 'extremely obscure in substance
and expression', reading *ego* in 826 and taking *quae* as
a relative rather than interrogative pronoun. That, of
course, is illogical; as if *any* signs observed would be
good ones. See Grant (1976) for another view.

829 *inherited decency*: what is born in one, *ingenium*;
he is talking of breeding. Aristotle *EN* 10. 9 (1179 b 3):
'(If exhortation were all that were needed to persuade the
young to aim at virtue, there would be no problem); but in
fact, exhortation will only inspire such young people as
are naturally liberal and make the well-born and truly
beauty-loving character tenacious of virtue. But it is
no use for turning most people in the direction of the
noble, for it is not born in them to obey shame but fear,
and they refrain from base deeds not because of the
intrinsic disgrace, but because of punishments'. Here
Aristotle is only stating what everyone knew, that there
are bad dispositions as well as good, and here Micio is
made to acknowledge this more squarely than Terence makes
out in 68 ff.

835 *duly*: Micio is a kind of behaviourist: self-knowlege
and awareness of human behaviour-patterns is our best way
of avoiding extremes. The old man who recognizes in himself
the tendency to be miserly has already begun to make the
appropriate correction. *all too noble*: Demea typically
worries about what cannot be controlled, the long-term
future, at the same time as he capitulates.

837 *Forget all that now.* Micio has won four points from
Demea: his agreement to 'share and share alike'; as a
corollary of that, his readiness to let Ctesipho keep the
slave-girl – but at Micio's expense; his acceptance that
both their boys are of good character but passing through
a phase; the need for him to be affable at least for today,
the theme prematurely broached by Micio at 754 f. But he
has not won a fifth, his brother's good will; the opposite,
as soon appears.

850-4 The division of parts and the exact tone is problematic,
and though it is obvious that in Menander Demea will have
gone indoors with Micio as the text suggests he should, we
must either postulate a musical interlude in Terence as in
Menander after 854, or make Demea ignore Micio's invitation
and linger. Neither solution is clearly right, but either
is better than making Demea go in and immediately return
or have Demea speak line 854 (Kauer).

855 ff. MENANDER'S LAST ACT: DEMEA'S MONOLOGUE, 855-81:
The writing here, though vigorous, is bad; elaborately
rhetorical in a way singularly ill-adapted to the portrayal
of private thoughts. Contrast any of the other soliloquies
in the play even Sannio's at 197 ff., and especially Demea's
at 435 ff. The paragraphs of the translation correspond
to:

    (i) General proposition (855-8)
   (ii) Application to self (859)
  (iii) Paradoxical abjuration (859-60)
   (iv) Rhetorical question (*to whom?*) (860)
    (v) Reason (861)
   (vi) Proofs direct and from the contrary (862-74)
  (vii) Summary of result (875-6)
 (viii) Proposed action, two reasons, envisaged consequences
                                     (877-81)

Menander will either have been less painfully forensic, or
will have let Demea address us directly. Terence is
altering, not inventing this speech; and he is changing
its form from iambic trimeters to trochaic recitative (for
the original of line 866, cf. p. 264).

855-61 *No-one has ever had his way of life so*... The real
and unacceptable change in character here is not in the
proposal that Demea henceforth will drop his old 'life'
and try another, for that is a matter of strategy (or
tactics); it is in Demea's suddenly acquiring a wise
head and consequent moral weight. See p. 55.

862-76 *Anyone can easily tell that from*... The commendation
of affability and mildness is bitterly ironical; while the
actor who has rehearsed can easily communicate that directly,
the reader must go through at least twice to pick that up.
Demea's review begins in what sounds an objective spirit
(*his life has been...yet more worry*, 862-68), but the
consequent evaluations are strikingly distorted in half
a dozen ways (870-6).

877-81 *Well all right then*... *now that he challenges me*...
The 'challenge' is Micio's proposal at 804 ff. But 'friends
say not mine and thine but ours', Demea feels, amounts to
'I take all, you lose'. Demea is being pathetically
represented as willing to abandon the principles in which
he still really believes in a sentimental bid to win back
what matters more than mere philosophy, the love of his
children, which Micio has artfully and wrongly alienated;
and it will be a long haul.

This is in startlingly bad dramatic taste.

The simple and sufficient motive for his ploy, the desire
for revenge, has been put in the background as neither
pathetic nor 'philosophical'. But that is surely what
prompted Menander's Demea to adopt Micio's motto and
attempt to turn it on him by giving away what Micio could
not possibly want to give away - his bachelor status.

882-8, 889-98, DEMEA'S REHEARSALS. Spoken verse. Here
Terence duplicates the comic theme of Demea's rehearsal of
affability by resurrecting Syrus and neatly integrating
him into the action (916, 958); the idea of making Demea
Syrus' commender and benefactor is excellent as farce, but
can scarcely be Menander's, as it twice entails the
presence of four actors, cf. p. 42, p. 240.

899 ff. AESCHINUS' ENTRANCE. From Aeschinus' point of
view in Menander, Demea's 'conversion' had already begun
with the relieving news that Demea, however reluctant
and embarrassed, has agreed to let Ctesipho keep his
beloved; that was communicated during the Menandrian act-
break at 854/5. Terence postpones that revelation to the
very end (996/7).

The first stage of Demea's plan is to unite Micio's and
Sostrata's houses; in Menander, Syrus was not present, only
Geta. Both households have to be informed about Demea's
'helpful' suggestion; so Geta had to be sent home as in
Terence and Aeschinus despatched to give the order to breach
the wall. Consequently what in Terence is an over-lengthy
'aside' (911-15 *'Great! Now I'm Mr. Wonderful...*) will
have been a brief soliloquy between Aeschinus' departure
and his return with Micio; cf. on 228-35. The good point
that *'the bride can't be feeling very well'* (920-2)
obviously belonged with the making of the suggestion *before*
Aeschinus' departure.

What Terence first presents as the first shot in a long
battle with Micio to win the boys' affection proves to be
no contest: he is already *pater mi* to Aeschinus on
entering at 902, an affectionate expression, not 'dad',
but nearer that than 'sir'; cf. 911, 922. In the sequel
Aeschinus addresses Micio as 'father' at 927, 935, 936,
956, 982; in the last scene, the accolade is transferred
to Demea at the climax (983, 995).

924-33: <u>MICIO'S ARRIVAL</u>: following Menander, in whom
however Aeschinus accompanied Micio as he entered.

931 *long past having children*: i.e., marrying her will
not affect what the boys are to inherit.

933 *It's only right*: introducing a theme-word (*aequom*)
ironic in the sequel, cf. 960, 968, 976, 987.

* * *

934-46 <u>THE PROPOSAL</u>: the metre changes from spoken iambic
senarii to chanted iambic octonarii as Micio is stunned
by the proposal (*'What, me marry?'*, 934); for the highly
effective monosyllables, cf. on 700. As usual in this
play iambic octonarii coincide with Terence's departing
very substantially from Menander. For the significance
of Donatus' information that in Menander Micio did not
complain, see p. 56.

In what follows, Donatus refers to 'Terence' in his
commentary in a way that implies 'not Menander', see
Sandbach (1978) 123-45. Modern study of the dramatic
Brothers was first stimulated by Lessing's
misinterpretation of Donatus' comment on 938 (see p. 264)
in *Hamburgische Dramaturgie* pieces 99-100 (April 1768);
he though Donatus meant there *was* no wedding in Menander,
and that the whole idea was Terence's, cf. Rieth (1964)
1-11.

938 *at sixty-four*: lit. 'in my sixty-fifth year'.

940 *I've promised them*: nonsense, of course. The presentation of Aeschinus here and subsequently as 'brainless ass' depends upon the rejection of Micio's ideas as humbug and on the space created by Terence at 707-11.

943 *You're murdering me*: lit. 'this is sheer assault', Caesar's second-last words (Suet. *Iul.* 82).

946 *Well, what? I'll marry her...*: lit. 'this completes what I am willing to do' or 'what I am willing to do stops here' (*hoc* = *huc*, adv.); either way, there is a financial metaphor; *confio* is passive to *conficio*, 'settle, conclude (an account)'.

* * *

947-58 <u>THE THEME OF HEGIO</u>: for this in Menander, cf. p. 36, p. 57, p. 62.

947 *What about the remainder...?* Here and in what follows Demea as *lepidus senex* embarks on some word-play; he picks up Micio's financial metaphor by saying lit. 'What (will) Hegio (do) now for the rest of his time?', but expresses this in words which could equally mean lit. 'what (will) that which remains (on the account, namely) Hegio (do) now?' (*subject*). The change of theme is marked by the bipartite octonarius, cf. on 155-96.

950 *An ell or an acre* lit. 'if it is much' and also 'if it is a nuisance'; cf. *OLD multus* 7.

951 *Right on target, eh?*: lit. 'it is given rightly' and also 'a palpable hit'.

954 *It's up to us*, cf. 948, of a piece with the ironic repetitions of *aequom*, cf. on 933.

956 *Oh well...* The music stops, and Micio gives in speaking an extremely ungainly iambic senarius strongly contrasting with the elegant rhythm of the spoken line with which Demea replies (*Now you're one with me...*). The music begins again as he comments aside ('*I'm cutting his throat*; but it is ambiguous whether this is the last iambic octonarius, or the first trochaic septenarius of the finale.

* * *

958-983: THE MANUMISSION OF SYRUS: wholly Terentian,
transferring the theme of manumission from Geta to Syrus,
and systematically ironic. The manumission is a thoroughly
Roman one: Syrus and Phrygia are becoming citizens and can
marry (973); at Athens, manumitted slaves were in the same
legal position as resident aliens, and had no civil rights
as such.

962 *I did my honest best*: Terence farcically casting Syrus
as Educator; cf. 50, 413. *Both...from boyhood*: scarcely
fitting the background.

964 *advanced menu-planning*... lit. 'and indeed further,
these things, purchasing reliably (*cum fide* not 'on credit'
but 'getting the best quality available as instructed',
cf. 372, 420), picking up girls, and arranging banquets
starting at daybreak'. *Dawn to dusk* is a wild exaggeration
of what has happened today; in Athenian life, the
ἀριστόδειπνον 'banquet that starts as lunch and ends as
dinner' was dissolute enough.

979 *Syrus, you've had luck at your side today*: lit.: 'You
set forth (from home this morning) propitiously' (*pulchre*
here a technical term in augury); Roman superstition about
threshold-crossing, not just 'you've done well'.

981 *Don't look a gifthorse...*: misunderstood by Donatus
and commentators as '(I shan't give anything) more
worthless than that', i.e., a bit of fluff or the like;
but that ought to be *hoc* (abl. of comparison) carius,
'dearer than this'. Understand lit. '(he will be free)
by that much the more meanly, (but he will nonetheless be
free)'. Micio is quoting the proverb explained by
Suetonius quoted in Charisius p. 260 Barwick s.v. *isto
uilius*: 'A patron who asked guests to dinner would reply,
if an item were specified for him to serve which he could
not serve, "(you will dine) *isto uilius*, by that much the
more meanly, *nihilominus* (ASG: hominis *cod.*) *erit cena*"',
'but it will nonetheless be a dinner', i.e., be grateful
for what you get. Patrons like that lack the liberality
to which they pretend.

985-997 THE VERDICT: highly rhetorical and antithetical
like 855 ff. and, in this reader's opinion, Terence at
his worst. Martin (1976) on 992 seeks to find ethical
and psychological coherence in the Demea of the last act
by speaking of 'a genuine change of heart' in Demea at
855 ff.; when he puts it into practice, "he finds
(899 ff.) a still better way of securing popularity,
namely by being generous at his brother's expense. In
924 ff. this new idea is pushed to extremes, until the

process is halted by Micio's questions at 984-5. By now
Demea has realised that the extreme he has gone to after
his change of heart is as ridiculous as was his earlier
duritas. He has seen that the true mean lies between
those two extremes...At the end of the play *both* brothers
have come to realise the need to alter their ways. In
this way concord can be established between them".

But is it adequate to describe what happens at 855 ff. in
Demea as a 'change of heart'? Are we right to postulate
subsequent changes of motive in him about which nothing
is hinted in the text? Where does Demea indicate to
Micio that he has learnt anything true from him at all,
or declare that he has really modified his principles?
Where does Micio admit to being wrong as charged, and what
in his earlier behaviour justifies them? See pp. 49-57.

This play ends not with the British compromise that many
readers would like, but with black and white. Micio is
roundly condemned (986-8); the boys are told that they
can take Demea or leave him (989-91); Demea asserts his own
unmodified claims as a judge of what is just right,
excessive, and defective (992-4).

985 *What sudden wanton whim...*: apparently a specific
quotation from Caecilius (see app. crit.), but the point
if any escapes us.

986 *certain people*: cf. 15, 43 for the expression; he means
us, of course, theatrical admirers of *senex lepidus*.

994 *back you up on occasion*: Demea has his own 'theory' of
the mean and this owes nothing to Micio; cf. 64-6.

996 *But my brother*: see on 899 ff.; already settled in
Menander.

997 *The right decision, that*: Demea's dominion begins with
an instance of 'backing the boys up on occasion' (994) and
as such it is Aeschinus who should express approval. If
one makes Micio say '*the right decision, that*', one is
desperately seeking to leave Micio with *some* authority;
but he has been robbed of *all* that in 986-8, and it will
still be left ambiguous whether Micio is supposed to sound
wholehearted in his approval (so that he really is a toady)
or to be qualifying his approval by emphasizing '*that*'.
The last word of a scene so heavily dependant on clear,
broad antitheses is no place for sublety. But a sort of
compromise *is* perhaps possible: Syrus, Aeschinus, and Micio
might all say *istuc recte*, and all four, *plaudite*.

262

Appendix I: The Quality of the Transmission

Terence's *stemma* is essentially as follows:

(2nd-3rd c. A.D.?)

(5th c.)

(?)

(9th-11th c.)

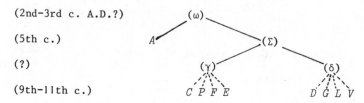

For details of the Mss., see p. 70 and Reeve (1983), Grant
(1986). In principle *A* and Σ where ascertainable are of
equal authority for establishing ω, itself a text of uneven
quality and from its orthography and idiosyncrasies not
even near a Republican date in origin, let alone Terence's
time.

The modern vulgate is represented by Lindsay-Kauer
(1926), Marouzeau (1949), and Martin (1976). They differ
in detail but share tacit assumptions that ω, while not
infallible, represents a uniformly good line of descent,
that where it is unacceptable, the ancient side-transmission
(Donatus etc.) will frequently provide the solution, and
that Renaissance and modern conjecture has comparatively
little to contribute to the diagnosis of error in ω. The
present editor's perspective of ω is less sanguine. He
marks the text corrupt at 29, 33, 60, 121/2, 316, 350,
527, 585, 602, 666, 687; he adopts readings from side-
transmission at 92, 167, 206, 264, 389, 522, 618, 673,
946; Renaissance and modern conjectures are adopted at
67, 83, 105, 131 ff., 199 f., 224, 235, 236, 278, 297,
313, 322, 499 f., 549, 573 f., 648, 771, 814, 826, 946 f.,
991; and the text of ω further appears to him more or less
suspicious at 37, 44, 53, 73, 127, 166, 210, 232, 256,
261, 306, 439, 568, 697, 716, 717, 727, 763, 852.

No two readers of Terence are likely to agree exactly as
to the detection of error in ω, let alone as to its
correction; only the broad point can be made here that
any self-consistent diagnosis will imply that ω was a
text significantly poorer in the *earlier* part of the play -
23 (+ 11?) mistakes in the first 400 lines, 18 + (8?) in
the latter 600 on these figures.

There are questions of punctuation at 42-5, 141, 153, 411,
443, 769 and of assignation at 83, 172, 216, 323 f., 336,
343, 532, 555, 586, 727, 850 ff., 945 ff., 955, 997; these
are (and always have been) matters of interpretation
rather than of textual deterioration.

Appendix II: Traces of the Greek Original

(i) Latin sources

i. 1-2: Donatus *Life of Terence* 3 nam Adelphorum principium
Varro etiam praefert principio Menandri, 'for Varro even
prefers the beginning of Terence's *Brothers* to that of
Menander's'.

43 f.: Donatus *ad loc.* FORTVNATVM ISTI PVTANT: utique uxorem
non ducere; dicit autem Romanis id uideri quos spectatores
habet. Menander (fr. 3 K.-Th.)

τωμαν·καριαημύγινεκα ορλ.αμβανω

μακάριον Dziatzko, γυναῖκ' οὐ λαμβάνω(ν) Bentley

An enviable status, according to certain people: not marrying
a wife at all: he means that is what the Romans he has as his
spectators think. Menander has '...blessing...I do not take
(? not taking) a wife'.

81: Donatus *ad loc.* HEM...QVAERITO: melius quam Menander,
quod hic illum ad iurgium promptiorem quam resalutantem
facit, '*Ah - it's you...the one I'm after*: better than
Menander because Terence makes Demea readier with a complaint
than a return of greeting.'.

199: Donatus *ad loc.* MISERO MIHI: secundum illud Menandri
(fr. 4 K.-Th.)

†αιγοστηποιων/τοιγοερποτατον γρῶνον οἰκέτην λαβών

'*Poor old head*: following the remark of Menander '...doing
(*line-end*)...hottest(?), bringing a dumb servant!'.(cf.
Gaiser (1964) 157 n. 21)

275: Donatus *ad loc.*: PAENE E PATRIA... Menander mori illum
uoluisse fingit, Terentius profugere, '*Leaving Athens*:
Menander has him determined to die, Terence, to flee'.

351: Donatus *ad loc.*: ATQVE HEGIONI: apud Menandrum Sostratae
frater inducitur, '*And tell Hegio*...: in Menander Hegio is
introduced as Sostrata's brother (? cousin)'.

693: Schol. Bemb. *ad loc.* (Mountford 1934) DORMIENTI: Menandri
u.rsus est in illo loco que i... γυμνοτέραν [πα]ττάλου *(sic
Headlam: -ον cod.)*, 'WHILE YOU SLEPT: Menander's line in that
place is... "(her) more exposed than a peg"' (fr. 9 K.-Th.).

938: Donatus *ad loc.*: NOVOS MARITVS...apud Menandrum senex de
nuptiis non grauatur (*cf.* *942*): ergo Terentius εὑρετικῶς,
'Bridegroom...: in Menander the old man does not complain about
the marriage; so Terence (is writing) out of his head'.

981, 983, 992, 993: Donatus refers here to 'Terentius' by name
in a way that suggests substantive difference between his
ending and Menander's, cf. Sandbach (1978).

(ii) Greek sources clearly assignable

804: Friends say not mine and thine...: *Schol. ad Plat. Phaedr.*
279 e (fr. 10 K.-Th.) κοινὰ τὰ τῶν φίλων· ἐπὶ τῶν εὐμεταδότων
(other examples), καὶ Μένανδρος ἐν ᾿Αδελφοῖς β´, 'in common the
things of friends: (a proverb used) of those who readily share:
(other examples), and Menander in his *Second Brothers*'.

A precious fragment, confirming that Menander wrote two play
called *Brothers* (the first must be the model underlying Plautus'
Stichus, see its production notice), and giving the theme of
the whole ending of Menander's play. (cf. *P. Oxy.* 2462 ἀδελφοί

866: It was I the very model of the...: *Photius s.v.*
σκυθρός· αὐθέκαστος, αὐστηρός· Μένανδρος (fr. 11 K.-Th.)

　　　　ἐγὼ δ᾿ ἄγροικος ἐργάτης σκυθρὸς πικρὸς
　　　　φειδωλὸς...,

'scowler means plainspeaking, rugged: Menander:

"While I, the peasant, workman, scowler, bitter pill,
skinflint..."'.

Not assigned to *Brothers* by name, but from a context of
comparison and review by one proposing to change his ways, and
generally agreed to belong here.

*(iii) Greek sources naming Menander's Brothers but not
unambiguously placeable in Terence*

N.b. Any of these in principle could come from either of
Menander's plays called *Brothers;* the relation of Plautus'
Stichus to the *First Brothers* was very distant.

Fr. 5 K.-Th. *(Ammonius 134 Nickau)* διέφθαρται καὶ διέφθορε
διαφέρουσι...Μένανδρος ᾿Αδελφοῖς·

　　　　εἰ δ᾿ ἔστιν οὕτως (-ος *cod.*) τὴν κόρην διεφθορώς,

'Has been ruined' and 'Has ruined' are different... Menander
in the *Brothers*, 'But if he is in the position of having thus
ruined the girl...'

Demea's reaction to Hegio's news about Aeschinus?   478, 505?

Fr. 6 K.-Th. (Stobaeus 3. 10. 24) Μένανδρος Ἀδελφοῖς·

ἔργον εὑρεῖν συγγενῆ
πένητός ἐστιν· οὐδὲ εἷς γὰρ ὁμολογεῖ
αὐτῷ προσήκειν τὸν βοηθείας τινὸς
δεόμενον, αἰτεῖσθαι γὰρ ἅμα τι προσδοκᾷ,

'It is a job to find a poor person's kinsman: for no-one admits
a person needing some help is his kin, as he immediately expects
to be asked for something...'.

The poor person should be Sostrata, the kinsman Hegio;
Meineke identified the fragment with Geta's observation at 353
'Yes, certainly no-one else is going to want to know us', but
it could perhaps fit Hegio responding to Geta's appeal 458-9,
or even Micio or Demea in the last scene on helping Hegio.

Fr. 7 K.-Th. (Stobaeus 4. 2. 3 et alibi) Μένανδρος Ἀδελφοῖς

οὐ παντελῶς δεῖ τοῖς πονηροῖς ἐπιτρεπεῖν
ἀλλ' ἀντιτάττεσθ'· εἰ δὲ μη, τἄνω κάτω
ἡμῶν ὁ βίος λήσει μεταστραφεὶς ὅλος,

'Menander, *Brothers*: 'It is completely wrong to give way to bad
men; we must stand up to them; if we do not, our whole
civilization will be changed from top to bottom and disappear'.'

Perhaps Sostrata at 341?   cf. p. 60.

Fr. 12 K.-Th. (Stobaeus 2. 8. 8) Μένανδρος Ἀδελφοῖς·

τί πολλὰ τηρεῖν πολλὰ δεῖ δεδοικότα;,

'Menander, *Brothers*: 'Why should one suffer the great fears of
guarding great wealth?'.'

The sentiment fits Demea after he has decided to 'help'
Micio get rid of his money; 881? 947 ff.?

Fr. 13 K.-Th. (Justin Martyr De monarchia p. 152 Otto)

θεός ἐστι τοῖς χρηστοῖς ἀεὶ
ὁ νοῦς γὰρ †οἱ σοφώτατοι (ὦ *Bentley*)

'The same (Menander) in *Brothers*: 'For to the good, Mind is ever a divinity, ye (*Bentley*) that are wisest'.'

If Bentley's correction be correct this would come from the prologue, and would make 'Mind' the speaker. But the fragment could be manipulated to fit the conversation of Demea and Syrus (iii.3).

(iv) Doubtfully assigned

Fr. 8 K.-Th. (Stobaeus 4. 32. 30) Μενάνδρου·

ᵛ - πρὸς ἅπαντα δειλὸν ὁ πένης ἐστὶ γὰρ
καὶ πάντας αὐτοῦ καταφρονεῖν ὑπολαμβάνει

ὁ γὰρ μετρίως πράττων περισκέλεστερον
ἅπαντα τἀνιαρά, Λαμπρία, φέρει.

'For the poor man is a wretched thing in the face of everything and assumes that everyone despises him... for the person who is doing so-so (*or* is fairly well-off) takes all grievous trouble too hard (*or* harder, *i.e.*, more to heart, *or* (?) more resolutely), Lamprias'.

Transmitted as a single passage, but probably two separate quotations (Cobet). Either or both together are supposed to correspond to *Ad.* 605-7, but this is doubtful. If the second couplet says something different from the first, but goes with it, it is inapposite; if it merely says the same in different words, it is a separate fragment and certainly not from *Brothers*. Nor is it right to generalize in the *masculine* singular in a context where Hegio is thinking about a poor old *lady*; and there is some doubt about the passage as a whole in Terence (*v.* app. to 602-8).

In view of these doubts it is hazardous to claim Lamprias as the name of Micio in Menander, an idea which is not independently supported by the awkward equation Mīcio - *mĭcare* 'flash' - Lamprias 'Lantern'.

(v) Still more doubtfully assigned

Webster (1950) 86 inferred the identity of Menander's

Brothers and his *Homopatrioi* interpreted as 'Having the same Father', on the strength of the similarity between 643 *erubuit: salua res est* 'he's blushed: all's well' and fr. 301 <ἄ>πας ἐρυθριῶν χρηστὸς εἶναί μοι δοκεῖ, 'any who blushes seems good to me'. But apart from the improbability that the alternative titles should refer to different pairs of characters in the play, this is merely a parallel (cf. e.g. 527 K.-Th.); and Terence is surely reproducing an epigrammatic, not a gnomic utterance in Menander. With this we have moved into the broad field of parallels, of the kind represented by (e.g.) 57 f. and fr. 609 K.-Th.; 72 f. and fr. 605 K.-Th.

Appendix III: Metre and dramatic form

1. *Speech, Recitative, Song*. The traditional sequence of
episodes in a Roman drama was

$$...S(C)RS(C)R...$$

S meaning 'spoken verse' (iambic senarii), C polymetric
song (*canticum mutatis modis*), R 'recitative' in the longer
iambic and trochaic metres. C and R were both accompanied
by the musician; how obtrusively is not known. Plays would
normally start with S or C, not R, and end with R, not S
or C; but the audience could not know whether or how much
polymetric song there was going to be in a play, or how
long passages of S, C, or R would be.

In *Brothers* there is only one instance of C (610-7).
For us that is the last echo of a metrical diversity much
more prominent in the work of Plautus and apparently
Caecilius than in Terence; but it remained important after
Terence's time in the work of at least Afranius (see p. 4).

In keeping mainly to iambic and trochaic metres, Terence
is superficially more like Menander than other Roman
dramatists; and he varied the texture of his writing in
a more subtly Menandrian manner than others, 'loose' here,
'strict' there. This seems to have disturbed contemporary
audiences; and it would have pained the considerable artist
in Terence that the fact that he wrote verse at all or as
he did was disputed in later antiquity, forgotten in the
mediaeval period, and only imperfectly understood in the
Renaissance and even modern times.

But far more of Menander was in the Greek equivalent
of spoken iambic senarii, and far less in recitative;
Terence writes this in several brands, but Menander kept
mainly to the Greek equivalent of trochaic septenarii and
only rarely used anything else (iambic septenarii, *Dyskolos*
880 ff.).

Refining a technique already known in Plautus and Ennius'
tragedies, Terence not only writes recitative 'by the line',
but also uses trochaic 'systems'. It is in the nature of
Latin trochaic verse that the rhythm wants to 'run' or
'roll' on (this is the literal meaning of 'trochaic'), and
the poet has to apply the 'brake' more positively than in
writing iambic verse. In a system, that brake is not
applied hard until we arrive at a definite cadence-rhythm
and fresh start involving the disruption of the simple
pattern of alternation basic to both iambic and trochaic
rhythm. A system, however we write it down on paper, is

really one long sequence, an even *N* pairs of trochaic
feet (measures) with the last measure cut short by one
place (catalexis) and with a set cadence-rhythm (p. 282 f.).

Menander never does this sort of thing; and Terence
only does it at the beginnings of lively scenes following
spoken verse and leading to recitative by the line (e.g.
155 ff., 288 ff., 517 ff.); that is, in the same contexts
that Plautus might have written polymetric song (C).
Thus while keeping to iambic and trochaic metres, Terence
still really conforms to the traditional tripartite
structure of older Roman Comedy.

Attention is drawn in the Apparatus criticus and the
Notes to the translation to *where* switches of metre
happen, and they are important for the reader of the
translation as *the* articulations of Terence's play; 'acts'
and 'scenes' as defined by later Roman grammarians and
as conceived originally by Menander are irrelevant, and
only partly agree with Terence's structure anyway.
(cf. p. 10, p. 41).

2. *Proportions.* Simply counting lines in different metres,
we find that the distribution in *Brothers* is as follows:

ia^6 (S)	tr^7	ia^8	ia^7	other
58.1%	19.3	18.9	0.5	3.2%

In his five other plays:

53.1%	22.9	13.1	7.6	3.2%

And in Plautus' 20 plays (with wide variations):

37.6%	40.6	1.9	6.1	13.8%

Since, however, ia^6 (iambic senarii) are lines only about
three-quarters as long as each of the recitative metres,
the proportions of *Brothers* on the one hand spoken and on
the other 'chanted' (whatever that means) are about even
(51%::49% by volume), and even less of Plautus was simply
'spoken' than the figure 37.6% suggests.

For the abbreviations tr^7, ia^8, ia^7 see p. 281.

3. *Character and presentation by metre.* Taking that into
account, we find that the proportions of each role divided
between speech and recitative are as follows:

	S	R(C)	Total
DEMEA	18	10	28%
MICIO	18	5	23
SYRUS	6	8	14
AESCHINUS	2	8	10
SANNIO	2	5	7
HEGIO	4	1	5
GETA	1	4	5
CTESIPHO	0	4.5	4.5
SOSTRATA	0	2.5	2.5
CANTHARA	0	1	1
	51	49	100

Between them, Demea and Micio have just over half the script,
and of that, a good deal more than half is spoken; Syrus
is the most versatile, as befits his role. On the other
hand, of the young men and the women, only Aeschinus ever
speaks rather than chants; in Menander, we should expect
only about a sixth of the play (a couple of scenes, say)
not to have been in iambic trimeters, the equivalent of the
spoken *senarii*.

There independently appears to be a high correlation
between those parts of the play where Terence is departing
from the substance of his model and those parts which are
in recitative. Of these, only two in trochaic septenarii
(540–91, 679–706) appear from analysis to be 'translation'
in the stricter sense, and these may well preserve Menander's
choice of metre. But none of the scenes in iambic octonarii
(the measure specially favoured by Terence in this play)
seem on examination to be like that: change of form here
seems to go with change of substance.

We have deliberately avoided definition so far of the
nature of 'iambic' and 'trochaic' rhythm except by referring
to a 'simple pattern of alternation'. In the various brands
of English verse which we call iambic and trochaic, that
alternation is of stressed and unstressed verse-places,
'weak-strong' iambic and 'strong-weak' trochaic; by and
large, word-accents fall in strong places, and by agreeing
with the intrinsic verse-beat, directly express the rhythm.
But this was not the 'strength' of strong and 'weakness'
of weak places in Terence or Plautus: see Appendix IV A
and C.

Appendix IV: Rhythm in Terence's Iambic and Trochaic Verse

A. *Phonetic considerations and conventions*

There are good working conventions for reading Classical Latin (Allen 1965). But unfortunately the features of the language most relevant to the making of Latin verse and to our reading it with easy appreciation of 'what counts' in the scansion are the least well recorded in ordinary spelling - syllabification, syllabic quantity, natural accentuation, elision.

Some of the clear-cut rules of scansion correspond to clear-cut distinctions of speech, but others categorize this way or that certain features of speech which did not lend themselves to black or white distinction.

Later on Catullus and others set about tidying this up so that the rules which apply in Plautus and Terence are not quite the same or as simple as they are in Virgil or Ovid or Seneca.

It is not assumed here that the reader knows about 'longs' and 'shorts' in Latin poetry, but it would be usual and helpful to the reader to come to Terence's verse with *some* grasp of scansion in Virgil and Ovid, since it is technically easier, e.g. Halporn *et al.* (1980).

On the other hand, there is a sense in which even the reader who knows little or nothing about any of that can get some perception of rhythm in Terence. He can take the *DOTS UNDER THE LINES* in the text as marking 'the beat' and leave it at that. That is not what the dots actually mark, and that perception of rhythm will be halting, partial, and distorted. But any awareness is better than none; and late Roman readers will already have been doing much the same, see p. 279.

1. <u>SYLLABIFICATION</u>. The principle is that within a word, syllables will by preference be open, not closed by a consonant, 'word' here meaning a group of syllables under one main word-accent, and including any 'satellites' - forms which cannot *end* a coherent utterance by themselves (prepositions and conjunctions mainly) or cannot *start* one, e.g. *-que, -ne, quidem, quoque, igitur*. Thus e.g.

e-ti-na-gen-dó:-qui-dem + pé-ri-it

not

ét + ín + ag-énd-o: + quíd-em + pér-i-it

There are also forms which differ in meaning or nuance according to their status as independent accented words or unaccented satellites – emphatic and unemphatic forms of the personal pronouns and adjectives, the verb 'to be' in its strong and weak senses, to mention only two such variables; the distinction is not always clear or certain.

Exceptions to the rule are *s* + *ptc* in uncompounded words (*ues-tis*) but not in words with prefixes or suffixes beside a stem (*a-du-le:-scens*); and *ptc*, *bdg* + *l*, *r*. These obey the rule in uncompounded words (*pa-tris* + *a-gro:s*, not normally *pat-ris* + *ag-ro:s*), but not in the attachment of prefixes or 'satellites': *ob-ru-it*, not *o-bru-it*, *ad-rem* not *a-drem*.

******IN THE TEXT* the dots under the lines mark, metrically, the switches from weak places to strong (equivalent to dividing the verse into feet, 'weak-strong' iambic, 'strong-weak' trochaic), and, phonetically, the beginnings of the syllables which begin in strong places. When the syllable begins with a vowel, the dot perforce appears under it, but refers to its *onset*.

2. SYLLABIC QUANTITY. There are long and short versions of each vowel in Latin; the long are here marked with a colon. The distinction was as important in the language as, say, that of *l* and *r* or *bdg*, *ptc*, but was not noted in ordinary spelling.

Within 'words', short syllables are open and have a short vowel. All others are long, either 'by nature' (long vowel or diphthong) or 'by position' (short vowel followed by consonants divided between that syllable and the next). It is traditional to refer to syllables as long and short, but we shall follow Allen (1973) in referring to them as heavy and light respectively.

A heavy syllable counts two time-units in verse, a light syllable, one time-unit. This is based on the opposition of long and short vowels in the structure of the language and the equation of a pair of light syllables with one heavy in speech: *rá-pi-do:s* = *lón-go:s*, *e-le-mén-tum* = *ar-mén-tum* in duration. In Terence's verse, such pairs of light syllables are rhythmically equivalent to one heavy syllable (**resolution**).

The same definition of heavy syllables applies at word-end (here marked +), but final light syllables can be open *or closed by one consonant*; the factor 'word-end' prevents the transference of the consonant to a following initial vowel.

But neither kind of final light syllable truly matches an internal one. The pairs of light syllables in *dí:-ce-re + táu-rum, dí:-ce-ret + dúrum*

quáe-re + ta-lén-ti:, quáe-ret + a-lén-ti:

are 'unbalanced', and resolution's 'exposed' or 'split' in
this way are strictly avoided except in the first foot,
and that rarely. But + *Gé-ta* +, + *ré-git* + are balanced,
and freely allowed as resolutions in any place that can
be resolved; for purely metrical restrictions see p. 281.

If the first syllable in a word or phrase is light and
the next is heavy *and* unaccented, that syllable is more or
less liable to scan light as the second element of a
resolution (*IAMBIC SHORTENING*), this being caused by a
neighbouring accent: 40 *séd éx frátre*... 73 *stúdét pár
referre*...

This is specially frequent in phrases involving *ille,
iste, ipse*: 15 *quód ísti dicunt*... 17 *quód illí maledictum*...;
for exceptionally among disyllables, these were usually
accented on the latter syllable, not the first.

If we suppose that all strong places have a verse-beat
and that Roman dramatists aimed at making natural word-accent
agree with it and express it as far as possible, we are
going to find unnecessary difficulty in iambic shortening.
For we shall find the word-accent causing the shortening
in the 'right' place very often (e.g. 17, 73), but even
more often and disturbingly in the 'wrong' (15, 40). But
see below, p. 280.

Elision before the reduced syllable is very frequent
and does not count as 'splitting' a resolution – one sign
that final vowels do not *wholly* disappear in elision (158
ég(o) ístám..., 442 *hom(o) ántíqua*...). But punctuation
may not intervene, and only rarely follows the reduced
syllable (118, 261); nor should it, because Iambic
Shortening was properly a feature of the uninterrupted
phrase. Exceptions are normally only allowed in the first
foot.

When there is no consonant between a light initial
syllable and an unaccented heavy one next to it (*méàs,
déòs*), sometimes these scan in two places of the verse
as light-heavy (three time-units), sometimes in one as
two time-units. Iambic shortening could explain this
(*méòs, déòs*) – if we assume that Latin was a language like
German with consonantal glottal stops (as in 'bo'l' for
'bottle') between vowels. But here the alternative solution
is consistently preferred: the first vowel is specially
short, such words are the next thing to heavy monosyllables,
and can scan as such (*SYNIZESIS*) or as light-heavy as
convenient.

Terence sometimes drops a -*s* after a short vowel before
a consonant at line-end to get a light syllable in line-
cadence (873 ...*desertu' sum*), following Plautus in this.
For Terence, this is a definite artifice, on a par with
his use of the obsolescent forms *siet*, etc. there for *sit*.
He keeps the -*s* to make position before a consonant with
complete freedom: any chance encounter will do and it
happens at the rate that chance predicts it should in each
foot. The implication is that the -*s* is also kept in chance
encounters in the ambiguous weak places which could be
either long or short in principle. But *magis quibus satis
nimis*, etc. are almost always two light syllables before
a consonant in Terence: that is best explained as Iambic
shortening.

For further detail of syllabic quantity in Terence see
Lindsay (1900), (1922), Laidlaw (1938).

*******IN THE TEXT* the following marks are used to indicate
syllabic quantities:

ᴗ : a single light syllable

ᴗᴗ : a pair of light syllables (resolution)

ᴗᴗ̌ : resolution involving iambic shortening

◠̌ : prosodic hiatus, see below, p. 276.

All light syllables are marked in one of the four ways
indicated: syllables unmarked are heavy (or elided).

— : a heavy syllable, only marked to prevent misreading
in particular words.

ᴗ : a heavy syllable resulting from some contraction of
internal syllables which may or may not always apply
in that word.

◠ : *brevis in longo*, a final light syllable counting two
time-units by licence, usually only at line-end and
places analogous to line-end.

3. WORD-ACCENT. Monosyllables are accented only if they
really are monosyllables and not satellites to something
else. Disyllables are accented on the first syllable
unless they too are satellites. But there are exceptions
(Townend 1950); see above (p. 273) for the most
important.

In longer words the 'rule of the penultimate' applies.
If the second last syllable is heavy it takes the accent
on the first of the pair of time-units in the syllable.
If it is light the accent goes back if possible two more
time-units, otherwise one:

a-gén-do:, a-má:re; dí:-ce-re, cóm-mo-do:s;
pró-pi-ti-o:s, mú-li-e-re rather than pro-pí-ti-o:s,
mu-lí-e-re (*cf. the doubt about the accent of e.g.
'capitalist' in English*); rá-pi-do:s.

Satellites may re-define the second last syllable of a
'word' (*a-gendó:-qui-dem*) but the theory that so does
elision (*scri:-bén-do:* but *scrí:-ben-d(o)ád-pu-lit*, etc.)
has been refuted by Soubiran (1966). Elision *never* affects
the place of word-accent.

English-speaking readers will introduce secondary accents
before the main one in long words like *àduorsários,
lìberàlitáte* and there is no harm in this; whether the
Romans did too is another matter. But (*pace* Drexler 1932,
1967) it is a mistake to give a secondary accent to the ends
of words of or ending with the cretic pattern of *dí:ce-rè:s*
or the dactylic pattern of *dí:-ce-rè*.

For the role of natural accents in Iambic shortening,
see above. A satellite can sometimes lighten a naturally
heavy syllable (*hĭcquĭdem, sĭquĭd*), cf. 'holĭday', 'tuppenny'
in English.

****** *IN THE TEXT* accents are not marked: for given the
syllabification and the quantity of the penultimate syllables,
their places are defined.

4. ELISION AND RELATED PHENOMENA. When vowels meet
between words, the phonetic factor '+' disappears; the final
vowel disappears in scansion, and the quantity of the
initial syllable is what counts. For us, this is the
trickiest aspect of all to come to terms with in reading
and performance.

Note especially that final vowels include all syllables
in -*m*, the sign at word-end of a long vowel somehow
nasalized. We should adopt the practice of rounding our
lips as if to say -*w* without actually saying it: at least
that makes elision, better called *synaloepha*, 'melding
together', feasible.

Note also that initial *h*- does not prevent elision,
but that initial *u, i* + vowel (= *w, y*) always do.

Soubiran (1966) has shown that only short final -*e* may
be supposed simply to have disappeared in elision; it does
so even before consonants sometimes (hence -*n* for -*ne*,
nemp', ill' in the text here and there). Other vowels, long
and short, were 'reduced', flowing into the second.

The result of an elision is therefore a complex syllable
beginning with or without a consonant in the one word and
ending in the next; the *beginning* of the elided syllable is

still 'there', together with the word-accent in the case of emphatic *me, te,* etc. when elided (as they frequently are); but its *end* has given way to the next word: the two words have fused together phonetically. Soubiran recommends as a purely conventional model the Italian pronunciation of vowels in contact rather than the French, and that can work reasonably well.

Terence is stricter than Plautus about hiatus. He makes it a principle that lines should scan continuously on paper as self-contained sentences spoken by one person, regardless of meaning, 'pregnant pauses' (26 *Storax...*), punctuation, or change of speaker. Hiatus is only normally allowed between lines and *any* vowels in contact between words within lines normally mean elision, at least on paper. In reciting, we should certainly substitute our own ideas of what seems convincing, and respect what seems natural pacing and tempo, letting the rhythm as affected by elision look after itself.

The vowels or diphthongs in monosyllables liable to elision sometimes have to 'disappear' like any other final vowel, and sometimes the scansion requires them to count as only 'half-elided' (so-called '*PROSODIC HIATUS*'), this in Terence normally only as the first element of a resolution. Further, we often cannot tell from scansion whether e.g. *quae agis* or *cum eo* is to be interpreted the one way or the other.

But as Soubiran has pointed out the dilemma is really of our own making. Neither expedient is a precise phonetic description, and both are convenient alternatives for dealing with what we should pronounce as a 'reduced' syllable as in other elisions. The two vocalic elements in a 'resolution' involving prosodic hiatus will be more like a diphthong than the clearly distinct pair of light that we hear in e.g. *ra-pi-do:s*; cf. on *SYNIZESIS* p. 273.

******IN THE TEXT* Hiatus is marked ⁞ ; elision is not marked as such, but visual attention is drawn to it in strong places by the placing of the dot under the start of the syllable suffering elision, not under the 'winning' initial vowel.

B. *Terence as 'English Verse'*

A glance at the schemes in section C will show that QUANTITATIVE iambic and trochaic verse is not isochronic – lines in the same metre potentially vary in absolute length; the iambic senarius can be as short as 18 or as long as 23 time-units.

This is alien to the verse we call iambic and trochaic
in English. In so far as *we* think about time-units and
lengths at all, it is obvious that regular lines in a
given metre are all the same length - isochronic - because
the governing beats intrinsic to the strong places must
be equidistant.

On the other hand there are two basic points in which
it is widely held that the verse of Plautus and Terence
really is like ours and unlike its truly quantitative
Greek ancestor and later Roman descendant (for Menander,
see Handley 1965; for Horace and Seneca, Raven 1965).

First a distinction of odd and even feet is supposed
not to matter in Plautus and Terence any more than it does
in English verse.

The only metrical unit is the foot, 'weak-strong'
iambic and 'strong-weak' trochaic, and within the line
they are all in principle alike.

But in other writers, while the places marked A in the
scheme are free to be long or short, the places marked
C have to be short; Menander occasionally allows a
resolution here, but never a heavy syllable. Such verse
is in 'measures', *pairs* of contrasting feet, and *needs*
no beat to contrast 'strong' and 'weak' as basic; a
beat in the B's, however, does help to contrast them
with D's.

Second, natural word-accents in Plautus and Terence
fall by and large in strong places; there is no such
correlation in Greek verse, but it is the very essence of
English rhythm.

But given the rules of Latin word-accent, and the
metrical stipulation that single light syllables belong
only in weak places, word-accent is *bound* to fall more
often in strong places than in weak.

English speakers are tempted to put the cart before
the horse here. The purely quantitative rule about
strong places and weak is merely negative: strong places
must not be realised by single light syllables. Further,
on the traditional understanding of it, there is no
pattern at all in the quantitative arrangement of weak
places, except at line-end. Surely there must be some
more positive rhythmical principle.

Many find this (a) in postulating an inherent beat in
each strong place and (b) in further supposing that it was
an aesthetic principle that 'Roman dramatists aimed at
agreement of ictus and accent as far as they possibly
could'.

These axioms go back to Bentley (1726) and permeate
subsequent Anglo-German accounts (Lindsay 1900, Ashmore
1908, Lindsay 1922, Fraenkel 1928, Drexler 1932, Laidlaw
1938, Harsh 1949, Raven 1965, Drexler 1967, Martin 1976,
Willcock 1976, Halporn *et al.* 1980). But the French have
never been convinced (Nougaret 1943, 1948) and the concept
of ictus is absolutely denied in the most systematic
discussion of Plautus' verse, that by Questa (1967).

There is indeed a decisive objection to supposing that
ictus played the same kind of role in Plautus and Terence
as in English verse. If weak places are *unpredictably*
long or short, then the beats too must be spaced at
unpredictable intervals; that is, they must lack the very
characteristic for which we postulated them and which is
essential to our metric.

Consciously or unconsciously, we are forcing Terence
into an isochronic mould if we listen for a beat. We are
rendering weak places all the same as each other.

But those who deny ictus fail to come up with anything
better; for they too fail to discern any overall
organisation in the way that weak places are handled, and
we are left with a metric which is subject to a *negative*
rule: that every other place will not be short: prose in
a very thin disguise.

The present editor is eccentric in believing that there
is pattern in the management of weak places in Plautus and
Terence and that though this differs from the pattern to
be found in either Menander or Horace it puts them firmly in
the main tradition of Greco-Latin iambo-trochaic quantitative
verse-writing. Word-accent is a merely secondary factor,
cf. p. 281-3.

But there is this to be said for the ictus-theory, that
it affords a simple means for us to hear *something*
rhythmical in Terence some of the time; we may, indeed we
must ignore distinctions of long and short in the weak

places, and need only bother about quantity to identify
resolutions. For though we render the line isochronic,
we still recognize that as a source of variety. Besides,
this way of reading Terence is authentic in that Romans
too will have read Terence roughly like this after a sea-
change in the Latin language which rendered accented
syllables all relatively long and unaccented syllables
relatively short, perhaps already by Donatus' time
(c. 350 A.D.); but this will have gravely distorted many
resolutions.

It was standard lore among the Roman metricians of the
Imperial period that the senarius *ter feritur*, 'has three
beats'; in the Renaissance, Antesignanus (1560) introduced
the practice of marking these with the acute accent, and
this, taken up by Bentley (1726), became virtually a
standard feature in English and German editions of the
19th c. But Bentley and the rest in fact assumed an
ictus in every place; marking every other was deemed help
enough, but some editors marked them all, and we revive
the practice here for the nonce:

57   *pudór(e) et líberálitáte líberós* (ia^6)

806   *auséúlta páucis nísi moléstumst, Démeá -* (ia^6)

'blank verse' with an extra foot;

685   *ín qua cluitáte tándem t(e) árbitráre uluerê?* (tr^7)

197   *mínime míror qu(i) ínsaní(e) occípiunt*
                                    éx iniúriá, (tr^7)

'Soldier from the war returning, spoiler of the
                                    taken town';

340   *tua fám(a) et gnátae uít(a) in dúbium uéniet;*
                                    túm si máxumé (ia^8),

'The wave is very still; the rudder loosens in our hand'.

Here the beats all chime with primary accents or what
strike our ears as plausible secondary ones; this is clear
'success', the lines are technically 'good', simply
because ictus and accent agree; weight in the weak places
does not matter. According to the Anglo-German view, a
certain amount of 'failure' is tolerable and to be expected,
as in the line-end

997   *... séd de frátre quíd fiét?::sinó,*

where ictus falls on the 'wrong' syllable in the last two
words. It is assumed that Plautus and Terence could never
have *wanted* to write lines like that; in effect, *any* line

ending with a disyllable has an intrinsically inferior
rhythm in the cadence, permitted only *faute de mieux*, for
it must involve clash in the last two feet.

But 'failure' is distressingly frequent in Plautus and
Terence if it is true that harmony of ictus and accent was
a consistent aim in their verse. We have another 'good
line' in

793   *commúnis córruptéla nóstrum líberúm!*

but the rejoinder is a dreadful 'failure':

794   *tandém reprim(e) iracúndi(am) átqu(e) ad té redí:*

and in, for instance,

40   *atque(e) éx m(e) hic nátus nón est séd éx fratr(e);
                                        ís adeo...*

the strongly contrasted words *me* and *fratre* are set quite the
'wrong' way.

The reader who listens for 'harmony' has two choices.
Either he is going to thump out all his ictuses, or
consistently respect word-accents. But if we make Aeschinus
and Demea respect the ictuses in 997, there is something
jarringly artificial in the neglect of natural accentuation
in the last words.

On the other hand, if we make them respect natural accent,
there is to our ears an even less welcome complete want of
rhythm in the cadence: 'something' rhythmical abruptly gives
way to 'nothing'; similarly 793 against 794.

But of the two ways, the latter is the preferable. For thus
we are at least aware of contrast in the texture of the
writing, though in far too sharp and abrupt a manner.
Terence was not contrasting 'something' and 'nothing'
rhythmical in 793/4, but 'something' and 'something else';
in the quantitative terms now to be considered, both lines
are closely similar variants of *A B C D A B c D A B c D*
differently articulated; word-accent is a merely secondary
expression of that difference. So far from aiming at
coincidence of ictus and accent, Plautus, and still more
Terence, were concerned to *control* the inevitable bias
of the Latin language for word-accents in strong places
by making weak places *the* ones to house specially
emphatic word-accents - as in 40. Line-ends in disyllables
are not 'failures': they lend a specially formal ring to
the cadence; it is *the* way to end a 'solemn' line, cf. p.
232 , and is by no means randomly deployed.

C. *Metrical Schemes and the Nature of the Rhythm*

Iambic:

$$\underset{\smile}{-} - \smile - \qquad \text{measure} \qquad (ia^2)$$

$$\underset{\smile}{-} - \overset{\smile}{-} - \underset{\smile}{-} - \smile - \qquad \text{quaternarius} \qquad (ia^4)$$

$$\underset{\smile}{-} - \overset{\smile}{-} - \underset{\smile}{-} - \overset{\smile}{-} - \underset{\smile}{-} - \smile - \qquad \text{senarius} \qquad (ia^6)$$

$$\underset{\smile}{-} - \overset{\smile}{-} - \underset{\smile}{-} - \overset{\smile}{-} - \underset{\smile}{-} - \overset{\smile}{-} - \underset{\smile}{-} - \smile - \qquad \text{octonarius} \qquad (ia^8)$$

$$\underset{\smile}{-} - \overset{\smile}{-} - \underset{\smile}{-} - \overset{\smile}{-} - \underset{\smile}{-} - \overset{\smile}{-} - \underset{\smile}{-} - \wedge - \qquad \text{septenarius} \qquad (ia^7)$$

A B C D A B C D A B C D A B C D

Trochaic:

$$- \overset{\smile}{-} - \underset{\smile}{-} \qquad \text{measure} \qquad (tr^2)$$

$$- \overset{\smile}{-} - \underset{\smile}{-} - \overset{\smile}{-} - \underset{\smile}{-} \qquad \text{quaternarius} \qquad (tr^4)$$

$$- \overset{\smile}{-} - \underset{\smile}{-} - \overset{\smile}{-} - \underset{\smile}{-} - \overset{\smile}{-} - \underset{\smile}{-} - \overset{\smile}{-} - - \qquad \text{octonarius} \qquad (tr^8)$$

$$- \overset{\smile}{-} - \underset{\smile}{-} - \overset{\smile}{-} - \underset{\smile}{-} - \overset{\smile}{-} - \underset{\smile}{-} - \overset{\smile}{-} - \qquad \text{septenarius} \qquad (tr^7)$$

B C D A B C D A B C D A B C D A

Rhythm It is in general handy to write *A* for a heavy syllable in A, *bb* for a resolution in *B*, *c* for a light syllable in C, and *d+* for *brevis in longo* in D, etc.

But here in the schemes *brevis in longo* (p. 274) and resolution (p. 272) are omitted as strictly prosodical features. For while frequent resolution (say six in two lines) or its sustained absence are important in varying the pace or tone of lines (see Gratwick and Lightley 1982), it does not affect the basis of the quantitative rhythm. Any place that can count two time-units may be resolved; but not the last in a line, and never more than two in succession; and it is twice as frequent in strong places (B's and D's) as in weak (A's and C's). In the following, for brevity and clarity, *A B C D* includes the cases of *aa bb cc dd*. For the phonetic restrictions, see above p. 273.

If there is an ictus inherent to the strong places in these metres (a matter of dispute) it belongs in the editor's opinion to the B's, not the D's; it declares 'This is a B, not a D', not 'This is a strong place, not a weak'. This accords with the antique doctrine that the senarius *ter feritur*, cf. p. 279; and such differentiation though not essential, is for us useful: it defines 'odd' and 'even' without involving quantitative distortion of A's and C's.

THE WEAK PLACES (A's and C's) may or must be long or short according to circumstance. But, against received opinion, their freedom is not without prejudice one way or the other and this deserves promotion to the abstract schemes as of greater importance than resolution. The usual custom is to mark the 'free' weak places as all 'indifferent' (x or ⏕). Here we note the bias of A as ⏓ and of C as ⏔.

This bias has two aspects. First, setting aside the case of ...*B c D/* in line-cadence, there is an overall bias in the other weak places of three to one in favour of long and resolved realisations against short. This is in the nature of the language: single light syllables are at a premium, their relative rarity lends them a special rhythmical status.

But second, the bias in favour of long and resolved is still greater in A's. Lines run out ...*A B c D/* ten times more often than ...*a B c D/* however word-end falls.

If word-end falls in B, then ...*A B/ c D/* is an absolute rule; ...*a B/ c D/* does not scan (Luchs' law; Luchs 1872). This *imposes* 'clash of ictus and accent'.

At line beginning, *A B*... is six times more frequent than *a B*...; but there is no objection here to *a B/* as such.

On the other hand ...*B C D*... within lines out-numbers ...*B c D*... only in the ratio of three to two. Given the basic bias *against* light syllables, this represents a definite preference for them in C-places.

When unaccented word-end falls in D, then ... *B c D/* is an absolute rule in the beginnings of senarii, and very nearly an absolute rule everywhere else. Terence must certainly have meant the rare exceptions to be noticed as unusual. They have the same character as ...*B C D/* at the end of 'limping iambics' in Catullus. This is Meyer's law reformulated; cf. Meyer (1886), *CHCL* ii. 89 f.

These and other statistical observations convince the editor that Terence (and Plautus) perceived *the* unit of iambic rhythm as ...*A B c D*... and ...*B c D A*... of trochaic. For them, ...*B c D/* had a special character of 'completeness' absent from any other sequence of three places, including ...*D a B/*, which is tolerated in early and mid-line, but not as a preparation for line-cadence.

There is no objection to ...*a B C D*... or ...*A B C D*...
as long as they are 'bridged' with what follows (no
unaccented word-ends in D). *a B/ c D/* and *a B c D/* are
rare not only because of the basic bias, but also because
A B c D is positively preferred for pure rhythmical
reasons.

These rules have numerous consequences for the
arrangement of words. Only two may be mentioned here.
Magnum factum cannot fit as *A B/ C D/,* or *C D/ A B/,* only
as *B C/ D A/* or *D A/ B C/.* But *dictatores* is able to go
as *C D A B/.* There is an asymmetry here which while
favouring word-accent in strong places, does not rule out
'clash' in *C D A B/.*

Similarly a line may start *duri senes* as *A B/ c D/* with
clash, but never *senes duri* as *a B/ C D/*; but that is
perfectly at home elsewhere as *c D/ A B/.* These *purely
quantitative* rules put regard for word-accent in Plautus
and Terence firmly in second place as a mere expression of
the way that words are being arranged in measures of four
places.

*******IN THE TEXT* the special status of word-end in D is
marked by *triple spacing.*

Line-cadence and catalexis (∧ in the schemes)

Iambic verse begins in A and aims at some cadence...*B c D/*;
that, reinforced by *brevis in longo* and/or hiatus, marks
pause by itself. But pause may be formally marked by
CATALEXIS, the omission in iambic or trochaic lines of the
eighth expected weak place; in the Latin names and
abbreviations, it is the weak places in a line that the
numbers specify, so 'septenarii' are by definition
catalectic lines. The element omitted is a C in iambic
and an A in trochaic progression.

Trochaic rhythm begins in B and needs more than just
word-end in an A to bring it to a close; it is this that
Terence exploits in constructing trochaic systems. There
is no such thing as a trochaic senarius; the 'units' are
pairs of measures (*quaternarii*), and these require *both*
catalexis *and* the cadence ...*B c D/* to impose a pause.

284

List of editions (*), books, and articles referred to

Allen, W. S. (1965). *Vox Latina*. Cambridge.
(1973). *Accent and Rhythm*. Cambridge.

*Antesignanus, P. (1560). *Terentius*. Leyden.

Arnott, W. G. (1963). 'The End of Terence's *Adelphoe*:
A Postscript', *Greece and Rome* 10: 140-4.

(1964). Review of Rieth/Gaiser (1964), *Gnomon* 37:
255-63 (important).

(1975). *Menander, Plautus, and Terence*. *Greece and
Rome* New Surveys in the Classics IX. Oxford.

(1979). *Menander* vol. 1 (*Aspis - Epitrepontes*). Loeb
Classical Library. New York and London.

*Ashmore, S. G. (1908). *The Comedies of Terence*. New
York.

Arusianus Messius: ed. Keil, H. in *GLK* t. vii. Leipzig.

Astin, A. E. (1967). *Scipio Aemilianus*. Oxford.
(1978). *Cato the Censor*. Oxford.

Baldry, H. C. (1959). 'The Republic of Zeno', *Journal of
Hellenic Studies* 79: 3-15.

Beare, W. (1964). *The Roman Stage* (3rd ed.). London.

Becker, E. (1873). 'De syntaxi interrogationum obliquarum'
in *Studien auf dem Gebiete des archaischen Lateins* ed.
W. Studemund, Bd. 1: 254. Berlin (*on 996*).

*Bentley, R. (1726). *P Terentii Afri Comoediae*. Cambridge.
(Contains the essay still basic to conventional
understanding of Old Latin dramatic metric, *De metris
Terentianis* σχεδίασμα: i-xix).

Bethe, E. (1903). *Terentius Codex Ambrosianus H 75 inf.
phototypice editus*. Leyden.

Bianco, O. (1956). 'Sul testo degli *Adelphoe*', *Annali
della scuola normale superiore di Pisa* 25: 104 (*on 687*).

Bieber, M. (1961). *The History of the Greek and Roman
Theater* (2nd ed.). (Lavish illustrations.)

Blanchard, A. (1983). *Essai sur la composition des
comédies de Ménandre*. Paris.

Bonner, S. F. (1977). *Education in Ancient Rome*. London.

Booth, A. D. (1978). 'The Appearance of the *schola grammatici*', *Hermes* 106: 117-25.

*Bothe, F. H. (1806). *P. Terenti Afri comoediae*. Berlin.

Brown, P. G. McC. (1983). 'Menander's Dramatic Technique and the Laws of Athens', *Classical Quarterly* n.s. 33: 412-20.

(1986). On Menander, Plautus, and Terence in the *Oxford History of the Classical World* ed. J. Boardman, J. Griffin, and O. Murray: 438-53.

Büchner, K. (1974). *Das Theater des Terenz*. Heidelberg.

Callier, F. (1975). 'La *libertas* et les valeurs politiques dans le théâtre de Térence (*Ad*. ii. 1)' *Association Guillaume Budé: Congrès de Rome*, v. 1: 412-23. Paris.

(1982). 'A propos des *Adelphes* de Térence: le personnage d'Hégion et la morale aristocratique', *Latomus* 41: 517-27.

Carrubba, R. W. (1968). 'The Rationale of Demea in Terence's *Adelphoe*', *Dioniso* 42: 16-26.

Casson, L. (1976). 'The Athenian Upper Class and New Comedy', *Transactions of the American Philological Association* 106: 29-59.

CGL: Corpus glossariorum latinorum ed. Goetz, G. 1888-1901. Leipzig.

Charisius: ed. Barwick, K. (1925). Leipzig.

CHCL: Cambridge History of Classical Literature vol. 1 (1985) ed. P. E. Easterling and B. M. W. Knox, vol. 2 (1983) ed. E. J. Kenney and W. V. Clausen.

Compagno, B. (1978). 'Dottrina pedagogica e relativismo nell' epilogo degli Adelphoe', *Pan* 6: 127-38.

Craig, J. D. (1929). *Ancient Editions of Terence*. Oxford.

Crook, J. A. (1967 a). 'Patria potestas', *Classical Quarterly* n.s. 17: 113-122.

(1967 b) *Law and Life of Rome*. London.

Denzler, B. (1968). *Der Monolog bei Terenz*. Zurich.

Dodds, E. R. (1959). *Plato, Gorgias*. Oxford.

Donatus: ed. Wessner, P. (1902-8), 3 vols. Leipzig.

Dorey, T. A. (1962). 'A Note on the Adelphi of Terence', *Greece and Rome* 9: 37-9.

Drexler, H. (1932/3). *Plautinische Akzentstudien.* 2 vols. Breslau. (on 4, 111, 175, 272, 527, 646, 749, 819, 826, 946.)

(1934). *Die Komposition von Terenz' Adelphen und Plautus' Rudens* (*Philologus* Suppl. 26 Heft 2): 1-40.

(1967). *Einführung in die römische Metrik.* Darmstadt.

Duckworth, G. (1952). *The Nature of Roman Comedy.* Princeton.

*Dziatzko, K. (1884). *P. Terenti Afri comoediae.* Leipzig.

*Dziatzko, K. and Kauer, R. (1903). *Ausgewählte Komödien des P. Terentius Afer, erklärt von K. Dz.,* II: Adelphoe, *2te Auflage, bearbeitet von R. K.* Leipzig.

Erasmus, D. (1508). *Adagiorum chiliades tres.* Venice.

Eugraphius: ed. Wessner, P. (1908), *Donati...commentum* t. 3. Leipzig.

Evanthius: *ibidem* t. 1.

*Faërnus, G. (1565). *P. Terenti comoediae.* Florence.

Fantham, E. (1968). 'Terence, Diphilus, and Menander: A Re-examination of Terence, Adelphoe Act II'. *Philologus* 112: 196-216.

(1971). '*Hautontimorrmmenos* and *Adelphoe.* A Study of Fatherhood in Terence and Menander', *Latomus* 30: 970-998.

*Fleckeisen, A. (1858). *P. Terenti comoediae,* 2nd ed. 1898, Leipzig.

Fraenkel, E. (1928) *Iktus und Akzent im Lateinischen Sprechvers.* Berlin.

Forehand, W. E. (1973). 'Syrus' role in Terence's *Adelphoe'*, *Classical Journal* 69: 52-6.

Gaiser, K. (1964): *see* Rieth/Gaiser (1964).

Garton, C. (1972). *Personal Aspects of the Roman Theatre.* Toronto.

(1976) Review of Büchner (1974) and Pöschl (1975), *Classical World* 70: 203-7.

GLK: Grammatici Latini ed. Keil, H. and others, 8 vols., 1855-1923. Leipzig.

Goldberg, S. M. (1980). *The Making of Menander's Comedy* London.

(1981) 'Scholarship on Terence and the fragments of Roman Comedy 1959-80', *Classical World* 75: 77-115.

Grant, J. N. (1971 a). *A Commentary on Terence's Adelphoe*. 2 vols. PhD thesis, St Andrews. Typescript.

(1971 b). 'Notes on Donatus' Commentary on Adelphoe', *Greek, Roman, and Byzantine Studies* 12: 197-209 (on 275, 323, 938f.).

(1972). 'Terence *Adelphoe* 67 and an alleged Meaning of *adiungere*', *Classical Quarterly* n.s. 22: 326-7.

(1973 a). 'The role of Canthara in Terence's *Adelphoe*', *Philologus* 117: 70-5.

(1973 b). 'γ and the Miniatures of Terence', *Classical Quarterly* n.s. 23: 88-103.

(1975 a). 'Contamination of the Mixed Mss. of Terence: A Partial Solution?', *Transactions of the American Philological Association* 105: 123-53.

(1975 b). 'The Ending of Terence's *Adelphoe* and the Menandrean Original', *American Journal of Philology* 96: 42-60.

(1976). 'Three Passages' [952-8, 348-50, 821-7] 'in Terence's *Adelphoe*', *American Journal of Philology* 97: 235-44.

(1980). 'The Beginning of Menander, Ἀδελφοί β'. *Classical Quarterly* n.s. 30: 341-55.

(1986) *Studies in the Textual Tradition of Terence*. Toronto.

Gratwick, A. S. (1984). 'Free or not so Free? Wives and Daughters in the Late Roman Republic' in *Marriage and Property* ed. Elizabeth M. Craik: 30-54. Aberdeen.

Gratwick, A. S. and Lightley, S. J. (1982). 'Light and Heavy Syllables as Dramatic Colouring in Plautus and Others', *Classical Quarterly* n.s. 32: 124-133.

Greenberg, N. A. (1980). 'Success and Failure in the *Adelphoe*', *Classical World* 73: 221-36.

Grimal, P. (1982). 'Considérations sur les Adelphes de Térence', *Comptes rendus de l'Académie des Inscriptions et Belles-Lettres*: 38-47. Paris.

Grove 6: The New Grove Dictionary of Music and Musicians ed. S. Sadie. London, 1980.

Guyet, F. (1657). Notes in J. A. Boeclerus' *P. Terenti Afri comoediae*. Strassburg.

Haffter, H. (1934). *Untersuchungen zur altlateinischen Dichtersprache (Problemata* Heft X). Berlin.

Halporn, J. *et al.* (1980). *The Meters of Greek and Latin Poetry*. Oklahoma. (1st ed. London 1965).

Handley, E. W. (1965). *The Dyskolos of Menander*. London.

Harsh, P. W. (1949). *Iambic Words and Regard for Accent in Plautus*. Stanford.

Havet, L. (1900). 'aleari', *Archiv für lateinische Lexicographie* 11: 578. (*on 33*).

Hermann, J. G. J. (1816). *Elementa doctrinae metricae*. Leipzig.

Hunter, R. L. (1985). *The New Comedy of Greece and Rome*. Cambridge.

Johnson, W. R. (1968). 'Micio and the Perils of Perfection', *California Studies in Classical Antiquity* 1: 171-86.

Jones, L. W. and Morey, C. R. (1931). *The Miniatures of the Mss. of Terence prior to the Thirteenth Century*. 2 vols. Princeton.

Kauer, R. (1901). 'Zu den Adelphen des Terenz', *Wiener Studien* 23: 87-105.

Krauss, J. (1853). 'Ueber die iambischen Tetrameter bei Terentius', *Rheinisches Museum* 8: 559 (*on 527*).

K.-Th.: Körte, A. and Thierfelder, A., *Menandri reliquiae* vol. 2. Leipzig, 1959.

Lacey, W. K. (1968). *The Family in Classical Greece*. London.
(1986). 'Patria potestas' in *The Family in Ancient Rome* ed. Beryl Rawson: 121-141. London and Sydney.

Lactantius Placidus. ed. Jahnke, R. (1898). Leipzig.

Laidlaw, W. A. (1938). *The Prosody of Terence*. Oxford.

Lefèvre, E. (1969). *Die Expositionstechnik in den Komödien des Terenz*. Darmstadt.

Leo, F. (1913). *Geschichte der römischen Literatur*, Bd. 1. Berlin.

Lindsay, W. M. (1900). *Plautus, Captivi*. Oxford.
(1922) *Early Latin Verse*. Oxford.

*Lindsay-Kauer (1926). *P. Terenti Afri comoediae.* Oxford.

Lloyd-Jones, H. (1973). 'Terentian Technique in the *Adelphi* and the *Eunuchus'*, *Classical Quarterly* n.s. 23: 279-84.

Long, A. A. (1974). *Hellenistic Philosophy.* London.

Lord, C. (1977). 'Aristotle, Menander, and the *Adelphoe* of Terence', *Transactions of the American Philological Association* 107: 183-202.

Luchs, A. (1872) 'Quaestiones metricae' in *Studien auf dem Gebiete des archaischen Lateins* ed. W. Studemund, Bd. 1: 3-75. Berlin.

Luck, G. (1964). *Ueber einige Interjektionen der lateinischen Umgangssprache*: 56. Heidelberg. (*On 488/9*).

Ludwig, W. (1968). 'The Originality of Terence and his Greek Models', *Greek, Roman, and Byzantine Studies* 9: 169-82.

MacDowell, D. (1978). *The Law in Classical Athens.* London.

McGlynn, P. (1963/7). *Lexicon Terentianum.* 2 vols. Glasgow.

Madvig, J. N. (1873). *Adversaria critica* vol. 2: 20. Copenhagen. (*On 278*).

*Marouzeau, J. (1949). *Térence,* tome III: *Hécyre - Adelphes.* Paris, Budé.

Marti, H. (1959). *Untersuchungen zur dramatischen Technik bei Plautus und Terenz.* Zurich.

(1961/3). 'Terenz 1909-1959', *Lustrum* 6: 114-238 and 8: 5-101 and 244-64.

*Martin, R. H. (1976). *Terence, Adelphoe.* Cambridge.

Meyer, W. (1886). 'Ueber die Beobachtung des Wortaccentes in der Altlateinischen Poesie', *Abhandlungen der philosophisch-philologischen Classe der königlichen Bayerischen Akademie* 17 (1): 1-121.

Mountford, J. F. (1934). *The Scholia Bembina in Terentium.* London.

*Muretus, M. A. (1555). *P. Terentii Afri comoediae.* Venice.

Nicoll, J. R. Allardyce (1963). *The World of Harlequin.* Cambridge.

Nonius Marcellus. ed. Lindsay, W. M. (1903). Leipzig.

Nougaret, L. (1943). *La métrique de Plaute et de Térence*. Paris.

(1948) *Traité de métrique latine classique*. Paris.

OCD: *Oxford Classical Dictionary*, 2nd ed. by N. G. L. Hammond and H. H. Scullard, 1970. Oxford.

OLD: *Oxford Latin Dictionary*. (1968).

Orlandini, A. (1982). 'Lo scacco di Micione (Ter. *Ad.* 924-97)', *Giornale italiano di filologia* 34: 99-112.

Otto, A. (1890). *Die Sprichwörter und sprichwörtlichen Redensarten der Römer*. Leipzig.

P. Hib.: *Hibeh Papyri* Part 1 ed. Grenfell, B. P. and Hunt, A. S., 1906. London.

P. Oxy.: *Oxyrhynchus Papyri* ed. Grenfell and Hunt and others, 1898... London.

Palmerius, J. M. (1580). *Spicilegiorum...commentarius primus*. Frankfurt-am-Main. (*On 952*).

Pfeiffer, R. (1968). *History of Classical Scholarship from the beginning to the end of the Hellenistic Age*. Oxford.

Phillimore, J. S. (1922). 'Terentiana', *Classical Quarterly* o. s. 16: 175 (*on 236*).

Pöschl, V. (1975). *Das Problem der Adelphen des Terenz (Sitzungsberichte der Heidelbergischen Akademie der Wissenschaften, Phil.-Hist. Kl.,* 1975 Heft 4. 14).

Prete, S. (1970). *Il Codice di Terenzio Vaticano latino 3226 (Studi e testi* 262). Vatican City.

Priscian: ed. Hertz, M. in *GLK* t. ii-iii (1855, 1859). Leipzig.

Questa, C. (1967) *Introduzione alla metrica di Plauto*. Bologna.

(1984) 'Lyrica Terentiana (*Ad.* 610-17)', *Numeri innumeri: ricerche sui cantica e la tradizione manoscritta di Plauto* (Ricerche di storia della lingua latina 18): 399-415. Rome.

Raasted, J. (1957). 'Zwei fragmente eines Terenz-Kodex (10-11 Jhdt)', *Classica et Mediaevalia* 18: 120-9.

Raven, D. (1965). *Latin Metre*. London.

Reeve, M. D. (1983) in *Texts and Transmissions: A Survey of the Latin Classics* ed. L. D. Reynolds, on Donatus: 153-6; on Terence: 412-20. Oxford

Rieth, O. and Gaiser, K. (1964). *Die Kunst Menanders in den Adelphen des Terenz*. Hildesheim.

Rist, J. (1972), *Epicurus: an Introduction*. Cambridge.

Rosivach, V. J. (1972) 'Terence, *Adelphi* 165-6', *Classical Review* n.s. 22: 8-9.

(1973): 'Terence *Adelphoe* 155-9', *Classical Quarterly* n.s. 23: 85-7.

(1975). 'Terence, *Adelphoe* 60-63', *Classical Philology* 70: 118-9.

Sandbach, F. H. (1966). Review of Rieth/Gaiser, *Classical Review* n.s. 16: 47-8.

(1972). *Menandri reliquiae selectae*. Oxford.

(1973). (With A. W. Gomme) *Menander: A Commentary*. Oxford.

(1975 a) 'Menander and the Three-Actor Rule' in *Le monde grec...hommages à Claire Préaux* ed. J. Bingen *et al*.: 197-204. Brussels.

(1975 b). *The Stoics*. London.

(1977). *The Comic Theatre of Greece and Rome*. London.

(1978). 'Donatus' Use of the Name Terentius at the end of Terence's *Adelphoe*', *Bulletin of the Institute of Classical Studies* 25: 123-45.

*Sargeaunt, Sir John (1912). *Terence with an English Translation*. 2 vols. Loeb Classical Library. London and New York.

Skutsch, O. (1985). *The Annals of Q. Ennius*. Oxford.

*Sloman, A. (1887, repr. 1950). *P. Terentii Adelphi with Notes and Introduction*. London.

Sonnenschein, E. A. (1925). *What is Rhythm?* Oxford.

Soubiran, J. (1966). *L'élision dans la poésie latine (Etudes et commentaires 63)*. Paris.

*Spengel, A. (1879). *Die Comödien des P. Terentius erklärt von A. S*. Bd. II: *Adelphoe*. Berlin.

Stampini, E. (1891). *Gli Adelphoe di Terenzio con Introduzione e commento*. Turin.

Sydow, C. (1878). *De fide librorum Terentianorum*. Diss.
Berlin. (*On 29*).

Thierfelder, A. (1960). 'Knemon, Demea, Micio' in *Menandrea:
Miscellanea philologica* (Univ. di Genova Pubbl. dell'
Istituto de Filologia classica 13): 107 ff. Genoa.

Townend, G. B. (1950). 'Oxytone Accentuation in Latin
Elegiacs', *American Journal of Philology* 71, 22-39;
'More Oxytones in Latin Dactylic Verse', *ibid.* 365-78.

Tränkle, H. (1972). 'Micio und Demea in den terenzischen
Adelphen', *Museum Helveticum* 29: 241-55.

*Umpfenbach, F. (1870). *P. Terenti comoediae*. Berlin.

Vischer, R. (1965). *Das einfache Leben*. Göttingen.

Walbank, F. W. (1957/1979). *A Historical Commentary on
Polybius*. 3 vols. Oxford.

Warmington, E. H. (1940). *Remains of Old Latin* vol. 1:
Ennius and Caecilius. Loeb Classical Library. London
and Cambridge Mass.

Watson, A. (1971). *Roman Private Law Around 200 B.C.*
Edinburgh.

Webster, T. B. L. (1950). *Studies in Menander*. Manchester.

(1974). *An Introduction to Menander*. Manchester.

Wessner, P. (1902-8). *Aeli Donati quod fertur commentum
Terenti*. 3 vols., Leipzig.

Willcock, M. M. (1976). Metrical appendix to *Plautus Casina*
ed. W. T. MacCary and M. M. W.: 211-32. Cambridge.

Wright, J. (1974). *Dancing in Chains: The Stylistic Unity
of the Comoedia palliata*. Rome.

I N D E X E S

1. *Index locorum* (references are to pages)

2. *Topical Index* (references in italic are to pages; in Roman to lines of the Latin text)